FAKE WARRIORS

Second Edition

Identifying, Exposing, and Punishing Those Who Falsify Their Military Service

HENRY MARK HOLZER
ERIKA HOLZER

A **Madison Press** Book
Highlands Ranch, Colorado

ISBN 978-0-9852437-8-4

Cover and interior formatting by Streetlight Graphics

This book was proudly printed in the United States of America.

www.henrymarkholzer.com
www.henrymarkholzer.blogspot.com
hank@henrymarkholzer.com

This book is available in print on Amazon and in eBook editions on Amazon as well as other online retailers.

COVER PHOTOGRAPH

"Inevitably, on Memorial Days and Veterans Days, photographers gravitate to The [Vietnam Memorial] Wall or its smaller replica, which travels around the country, for appropriate images they can send to the nation's newspapers. * * *[1]

"On Memorial Day, [May 28,] 1996, *The Dallas Morning News* ran a huge front-page color photograph of a . . . scraggly veteran dressed in a boonie hat and fatigues, weeping in anguish, his face pressed to the black plexiglass surface of The Wall's traveling replica. 'Reflecting on the Fallen,' was the headline, and the caption described [him] as a U.S. Marine veteran who fought in Vietnam. ['Marine veteran who fought in Vietnam, pays honor to a friend as he visits the Vietnam Wall Experience, a traveling replica of Washington Vietnam Veterans Memorial Wall, after Brooklyn's Memorial Day parade.']

"The Associated Press photograph appeared in numerous other papers around the country. But [a] *Morning News* reader . . . pointed out that [the man] was wearing a camouflage BDU jacket first issued in 1983, a commercially-manufactured bush hat, a full-color 3d Marine Division patch not authorized for wear after 1947 (and not worn on camouflage in any case), and a pin for the 1st Reconnaissance Battalion, part of the 1st Marine Division, not the 3d. *A search of military records revealed that* [the man] *had never served in the Marine Corps or any other branch of the service.*" (The preceding three paragraphs are from B.G. Burkett and Glenna Whitley, *Stolen Valor, How the Vietnam Generation Was Robbed of its Heroes and its History*, 586).[2]

On July 13, 1996, *The Dallas Morning News* ran a correction: "On Page 1A May 28, a Memorial Day photo showed [a man] who identified himself as a Marine veteran who fought in Vietnam. *Federal officials say that* [he] *did not serve with the Marines in Vietnam*."[3]

OTHER BOOKS BY THE AUTHORS

HENRY MARK HOLZER

The American Constitution and Ayn Rand's "Inner Contradiction"

Best Opinions of the Supreme Court of the United States (Vol. I: Race)

The Supreme Court Opinions of Clarence Thomas, 1991–2011 (Second Edition)

The Supreme Court Opinions of Clarence Thomas, 1991–2006 (First Edition)

The Keeper of the Flame

"Aid and Comfort": Jane Fonda in North Vietnam (with Erika Holzer)

Fake Warriors: Identifying, Exposing, and Punishing Those Who Falsify Their Military Service (with Erika Holzer) (First Edition)

Why Not Call It Treason? Korea, Vietnam, Afghanistan and Today

The Layman's Guide to Tax Evasion

Speaking Freely: The Case Against Speech Codes (ed.)

Sweet Land of Liberty? The Supreme Court and Individual Rights

Government's Money Monopoly: Its Origin and Scope and How to Fight It (ed.)

The Gold Clause: What it is and how to use it profitably (ed.)

ERIKA HOLZER

Ayn Rand: My Fiction-Writing Teacher

Fake Warriors: Identifying, Exposing, and Punishing Those Who Falsify Their Military Service (with Henry Mark Holzer) (First Edition)

"Aid and Comfort": Jane Fonda in North Vietnam (with Henry Mark Holzer)

Eye for an Eye (fiction)

Double Crossing (fiction)[4]

DEDICATION

To Mary Schantag and the late Chuck Schantag of P.O.W. Network, and the many others who have kept the vigil against Fake Warriors.

To Capt. Isaac Camacho (USA Ret.), Col. Joe Kittinger (USAF Ret.), Capt. John Michael McGrath (USN Ret.), and the countless other authentic warriors whose heroic deeds lesser men immorally seek to appropriate.

To the Special Operators of the United States armed forces, especially the late SEAL Adam Brown the tip of the spear who, usually in the shadows and risking violent death, confront America's deadliest enemies.

To those of the United States military who never returned to the land they were fighting for.

ACKNOWLEDGEMENTS

By the time we finished researching and writing the first edition of this book, scores of people — military and civilian alike — had been of assistance to us.

There were Phony Busters who have for years fought the good fight against Fake Warriors, and whose archives burst with case histories that were readily made available to us.

There were those who have served in the United States military in branches often invoked by Fake Warriors in their imposture: SEALs, LRRP/LRP/Rangers, Special Forces, Air Commandos, SOG operatives, Pararescuers, Force Recon, even CIA agents — and others.

There were those knowledgeable about military medals, decorations, and awards — and what it takes to earn them.

There were prisoners of war, who had been held in both South and North Vietnam.

There were authorities on American military uniforms.

There were experts in the falsification of documents.

There were mental health professionals, including a forensic psychiatrist.

There were the authors of books on Vietnam, lying, impostors, psychiatry, and related topics.

There were the valuable sources of archival and legal material made available to us by librarians and others.

When, for the first edition, we began acknowledging everyone who contributed to the research and writing of this book, it became obvious that there were too many to name individually. So we decided that rather than filling pages with a long list of names, we'd thank all of them personally. Which is what we did.

However, looking back, we realized that certain individuals should have been singled out for specific acknowledgement because of the importance of their contributions. And now there are those who have contributed to this second edition of *Fake Warriors.*

They include Mary Schantag and her late husband Chuck, founders of P.O.W. Network who have been exposing Fake Warriors for some two decades. They opened their archives to us and provided invaluable introductions. Mary is the author of Appendix A.

Former Navy Captain Mike McGrath has been another indefatigable Phony Buster who has been exposing Fake Warriors for years. To Mike goes the credit for Appendices B through G.

B. G. Burkett and Glenna Whitley, co-authors of *Stolen Valor*, first brought the Fake Warrior phenomenon to widespread public attention.

Jerry Merna's help with military medals, awards, and the like has been indispensable.

K.J. Jones, Billy Waugh, Ben Drake, Steve Robinson, Steve Sherman, Steve

Jaeger and Terry Roderick provided detailed information about the nature of their specialized branches of service.

Jackson Killion, Saint Louis School of Law class of 2013, researched earlier versions of the Stolen Valor Act, and their legislative history. In addition, he provided invaluable other Stolen Valor Act research that did not find its way into the final version of Chapter 7. Mr. Killion was also helpful in identifying military organizations that we had added to our list of those to be informed about the book's publication.

Judith Sansweet (www.proofreadnz.co.nz) and (www.santelepublishing.com) put the text through the final fires of professional proofreading as she polished the manuscript for print and digital publishing. As before, Judith was a pleasure to work with in the always delicate matter of editing an author's writing. (Deviations from the *Chicago Manual of Style* — some necessitated by the requirements of legal writing with which, for better or worse, the authors have been imbued for over a half-century — are entirely their doing, not Judith's.)

Val Edward Simone (www.morningsidepublishing.com) is not merely an e-book maven. He is also a fellow author, one who generously initiated me into the wonders of this new form of publishing.

TABLE OF CONTENTS

He who permits himself to tell a lie once, finds it much easier to do it a second and third time, till at length it becomes habitual; he tells lies without attending to it, and truths without the world's believing him. This falsehood of the tongue leads to that of the heart, and in time depraves all its good positions.

Thomas Jefferson, Letter to Peter Carr, August 19, 1785

INTRODUCTION

"Thinking of these impostors brings tears of rage to my old eyes." [5]

An Air Force 'Colonel' — in uniform, wearing wings and multiple ribbons – was observed by Captain John Michael McGrath (USN Ret.)[6] leading the 2001 Monument, Colorado, July 4th parade.

Soon after, Captain McGrath was invited to speak at the Cripple Creek, Colorado, "Salute to American Veterans," which drew some 20,000 attendees. On the program was then-United States Senator Ben Nighthorse Campbell, who led a caravan of about 100 motorcyclists from Denver into Cripple Creek, preceded by a police escort. Also in attendance at the Salute were World War II POWs, members of the Veterans of Foreign Wars, American Legion, Vietnam Veterans of America, and other veterans service organizations. There was a fly-over by Air Force fighter jets. In short, the Salute to American Veterans was a patriotic event, attended by hundreds, if not thousands, of veterans who had honorably served their country.

As the Salute speakers were getting organized on the dais, Captain McGrath and Senator Campbell were joined by 'Colonel' Connolly, who had led the earlier July 4th parade in Monument.

After declining 'Colonel' Connolly's invitation to introduce McGrath to the

Senator (McGrath and the Senator were already acquainted), McGrath instead introduced himself to Connolly. As soon as McGrath noticed that Connolly wore the POW ribbon, and knowing full well that, given his age, Connolly could not have been a Vietnam War POW — quite apart from the fact that Captain McGrath knew the identity of every Vietnam POW — he said to Connolly, "I see you have a POW medal. Were you a POW?" When Connolly answered that he was, McGrath asked where the 'Colonel' had been held, expecting Connolly's answer to be Korea." Instead, "South Vietnam," was the 'Colonel's reply.

Having had considerable experience with POW impostors for several years before the Connolly encounter, including an episode a week earlier in Denver — and having anticipated that he might encounter impostors at the "Salute to American Veterans" gathering — Captain McGrath brought with him the official Department of Defense list of Vietnam prisoners of war. "Tell me how you got captured," McGrath pressed. Connolly then related his story. He had been shot down; his gunners had been killed; he and two others had been captured. "How did you escape?" asked McGrath. "Well," Connolly replied, "I didn't actually escape. The enemy let me go."

When McGrath confronted Connolly with the official list of POWs, showing the 'Colonel' that his name wasn't on it, Connolly said the omission was a 'mistake', and said that he would call the Pentagon on Monday and straighten out the error.

The Salute ceremony began. 'Colonel' Connolly rose and addressed the assembly, his tone solemn as he described a POW/MIA ceremony held around the country to commemorate those authentic American heroes. (It was learned only later that a Junior ROTC contingent was supposed to participate in that part of the program, but that 'Colonel' Connolly had dismissed the high school students, usurping for himself their role in the program).

Seated next to Senator Campbell, Captain McGrath informed him that Connolly was not a POW — and probably not an officer, or even in the Air Force. Agreeing with McGrath that this kind of fraud was serious, the

Senator encouraged him to get to the bottom of it.

While McGrath and Campbell were talking, Connolly apparently left. But after the ceremony, McGrath spotted him in town. The 'Colonel' was leaning on his cane. Approaching him, McGrath said, "Tell me again about that capture and escape." Connolly launched into his tall tale about being captured in South Vietnam. "What were the names of the two guys you were captured and escaped with?" McGrath asked. Connolly gave McGrath the names of his two alleged gunners. Neither of them were on the official POW list.

McGrath showed his own Navy ID card, and asked Connolly to show his official Air Force ID card. Connolly said he had left it at home.

That did it. McGrath told Connolly he was a fake, a phony, a fraud — and generally dressed him down. He then gave Connolly two choices: "Take off your coat with the phony medals, apologize to the event's organizers and tell them what you did, or I'll prove you're a faker who's violating federal law." Connolly persisted in the charade.

When, on the same day, the Cripple Creek police understandably declined to do anything about Connolly, McGrath immediately contacted OSI [Office of Special Investigations] at the Air Force Academy in Colorado Springs. He left an unambiguous message that day. He left another message the next day, and was told that someone would contact him. No one ever did.

On Monday, McGrath contacted a Special Agent at Peterson Air Force Base, and the two of them soon verified that no William C. Connolly had ever served in the Air Force. The uniform, the medals, and the story that went with them were bogus — a clear violation of several federal criminal laws.[7]

Once Connolly's non-military status had been confirmed, neither Peterson nor OSI had jurisdiction. Connolly was a civilian. This was a case for the FBI.

McGrath was reassured. Despite the initial setbacks — the Cripple Creek police having no jurisdiction, and the Air Force Academy OSI having ignored him —– at least the Peterson OSI had handed over the case to two FBI Special Agents in the Colorado Springs office.

Contacting the agents, McGrath provided them with extensive information:

- He turned over photographs of Connolly in uniform;
- He related the events in Cripple Creek and how Connolly had lied to the organizers of the veterans' ceremony;
- He reported that local veterans had met Connolly and heard his lies; including the story that he had been in Special Forces, had performed covert activities, and was a Colonel;
- He informed the FBI that he had information about Connolly having lied his way into American Legion Post 38 in Security, Colorado, from which he was expelled for, among other things, repeatedly bringing his young child into the post's bar room;
- He provided considerable other information about the 'Colonel': his address, social security number, wife's name and employment and date of birth, daughter's name, his car model and license plate, and much more;
- He expressed his fear about an impostor getting so close to a United States Senator;
- He said he had proof of Connolly's bogus claim to the Air Force Academy that he was a decorated Air Force colonel;
- He said he had proof that Connolly had used the gym at Peterson Air Force base;
- He said he had proof that Connolly attended a retirement ceremony at Space Command Headquarters;
- He told the FBI he had Connolly's calling card, complete with the United States Air Force Academy's official seal, showing that Connolly was the "head Coach of the USAFA Judo Club and Team"[8];
- He offered to produce evidence that Connolly had lectured to an Air Force Academy class on the subjects of Vietnam and being a POW;
- He provided the FBI with questions for them to ask Connolly,

calculated to expose his lies;

- He expressed the hope that something could be done;
- He concluded (prophetically), in an e-mail to the FBI Special Agents, with the statement: "Please don't let this case get swept under the rug. I hope your office sees fit to refer the case to a federal attorney."

Soon after, the FBI informed Captain McGrath they knew Connolly had never served in any branch of military service, and that they would investigate and present the case to the United States Attorney's office. They told McGrath that they would visit Connolly at his home to "scare him out of his impersonation," and that probably would be the end of the matter.

Eventually, despite the evidence amassed by Captain McGrath, the FBI told him the case was going nowhere. On October 12, 2001, less than a month after McGrath had contacted them, the Bureau informed him that unless he, *himself,* could prove Connolly had derived some financial benefit from his masquerade, the Bureau would drop the matter. After all, McGrath was told, Connolly's conduct was "only a misdemeanor."

One of the FBI Agents asked McGrath this rhetorical question: "Do you want to embarrass a poor old man?"

The media was not so sympathetic. Channel 9 TV in Denver and Channel 5/30 in Colorado Springs exposed 'Colonel' Connolly in a fifteen-minute documentary. Yet, even then, with the conclusive, documented case laid out for the FBI in full public view, the Bureau did nothing.

The Connolly case, in just one relatively small American city, merely hints at what until recently as been a largely unknown national scandal. *For many years there have been, and there are now, thousands upon thousands of similar cases throughout this country. Unless something is done about the countless Fake Warriors like Connolly, this scandal will continue unabated, as it has for decades.*

Doubtless we will be asked again, as we were nearly a decade ago when we wrote the first edition, "Why bother to write a book about Fake Warriors?" Or — to paraphrase those two FBI agents from Colorado Springs — *"Why embarrass a lot of poor old men?"*

We bothered in 2003, and we're bothering again in 2012, because Fake Warriors have done great damage, and those injuries continue unabated.

We were concerned about the Fake Warrior phenomenon ten years ago, in the first edition of *Fake Warriors: Identifying, Exposing, and Punishing Those Who Falsify Their Military Service.* The problem has not only grown since then, it has grown *exponentially* because of the Afghanistan and Iraq wars, and America's special operations around the world. Today, it seems there is a Fake Warrior under every rock. Indeed, the Supreme Court's June 2012 ruling that Section 704(b) of the Stolen Valor Act of 2005 is unconstitutional will only add fuel to the Fake Warrior problem.

The costs of Fake Warrior conduct continue to mount, and anyone who thinks it is merely offensive and relatively harmless is misinformed . . . as were we, before becoming aware of the phenomenon.

During the research and writing of our prior nonfiction collaboration, *"Aid and Comfort": Jane Fonda in North Vietnam*[9] — which proves that Fonda's 1972 propaganda trip to Hanoi could have supported an indictment for, and a conviction of, treason — we were privileged to meet many patriotic Americans. Most of them were Vietnam veterans. Some had been Vietnam prisoners of war. They made us aware, for the first time, of the Fake Warrior phenomenon that they, and others, have been courageously (and frustratingly) battling for years.[10]

Thus, our exposure of Fonda's treason was the trigger that led to the book we completed in 2003, the first edition of *Fake Warriors*.
In the early 2000s, the existence of so many military impostors was a shocking revelation to us — as it has been to those members of the American public who are aware of the phenomenon. Once we began to investigate that phenomenon, we found the idea of writing a book on the subject irresistible — and, once again, our Fonda book was a strong motivating force. We had

learned too much about the pain and suffering endured, not only by the Vietnam War POWs, but by other troops who served in that theater. Our empathy with these veterans was considerable.

But empathy aside, the more we learned from our research about Fake Warriors, the more outraged we became about the wrongs being perpetrated by military imposters. As Americans and as lawyers, throughout our personal and professional lives, we have sustained a deeply ingrained sense of justice,[11] and in writing a book about the Fake Warrior phenomenon there was an opportunity to help correct a grievous wrong.

The consequences of those wrongs are incalculable. Innocents — widows, wives, and children in particular — experience shame and disillusionment when a Fake Warrior husband or father is exposed. Laws criminalizing Fake Warrior behavior continue to be unenforced, undermining the rule of law. National security is compromised. Huge sums of money are squandered in the payment of false claims to military impostors. Readers of nonfiction books about the military are misled by authors whose credentials are fake and experiences invented. The legitimate accomplishments of veterans who honorably served America are hijacked. Worse, real accomplishments are increasingly shadowed by suspicion among people who conscientiously try to distinguish between the real and the fake. The well has been poisoned by the proliferation of Fake Warriors.[12]

These and many other harmful consequences of the words and conduct of Fake Warriors are intolerable. For the last forty years, Fake Warriors too numerous to count — politicians, lawyers, authors, actors, and others — have gotten away with their masquerades. Indeed, many have prospered — often at the expense of those who have fought in Vietnam, Afghanistan, Iraq, and elsewhere around the world.[13]

We have discovered, to our dismay, that the problem is so extensive it can't even be dented through the efforts of the handful of individuals who have, for years, grappled with the thankless task of exposing impostors.

We've concluded that the Fake Warrior phenomenon can be dealt with most effectively through a broad-based effort designed to increase public awareness both of the problem, and of how, over time, it can be alleviated and ultimately largely resolved. A widely disseminated book is the best way to accomplish this goal. It is our hope that by arming large numbers of Americans with facts and analysis, as well as by identifying the potent legal resources available to them, these citizens will join wholeheartedly in the lonely battle which, until now, has been waged by the dedicated few. That's why nearly ten years ago the a first edition of *Fake Warriors* was published, and why now the authors have written the second edition.

In anticipation of two possible misconceptions regarding the second edition of *Fake Warriors*, we have two important disclaimers.

Lest anyone confuse our book with a couple of others that have examined the subject of military impostors only in passing — their principal theses being devoted to broader topics[14] — this book is devoted *entirely* to the Fake Warrior phenomenon.

A second caveat: As in the first edition of *Fake Warriors,* we don't focus on *individuals*. Rather, we have deliberately chosen to address the *phenomenon* of military imposture.[15] The few exceptions, where we name names, are included only to illustrate a specific point. We have adhered to this principle even when dealing with some of the more notorious Fake Warrior cases — people who are the grist of the Internet mill. In spite of these disclaimers, we expect to be queried about why, for example, we haven't chastised historian X for inflating his military rank, or exposed author Y for never having served in Vietnam, or haven't criticized Senator Z for lying about his Silver Star. Suffice to say, we have a different purpose. We strongly believe that to get bogged down in a fruitless, finger-pointing exercise of naming names would only undermine what we seek to accomplish with this book: to provide an overview of a shameful phenomenon in order to better deal — *in principle* — with the issue of military imposture.

Accordingly, Chapter 1 — "Why are there Fake Warriors?" — answers the most frequently asked question about military imposters: *Why* do they lie? The chapter explains their psychological and other motives. We draw on the law developed in a World War II treason case to explain the crucial distinction between a Fake Warrior's legally irrelevant *motive* and the legally essential *intent* that is necessary to sustain a criminal conviction. The chapter also examines specific motives and addresses the related issue of Fake Warriors' alleged contrition.

Chapters 2 and 3 identify the scope of the Fake Warrior problem, and posit the book's subject: The American population now contains countless military impostors including those whose behavior is not only immoral, but often illegal and fraught with harmful and sometimes even dangerous consequences. Specifically, Chapter 2 — "Who are the Fake Warriors?" — lays bare the largely unknown fact that the Fake Warrior phenomenon is real, it is pernicious, it is widespread, and that impostors come from every imaginable strata of our contemporary society. Chapter 3 — "What harm do Fake Warriors cause?" — shows that Fake Warrior imposture is not a minor social peccadillo, but victimizes vast numbers of Americans, and produces considerable harm.

The next three chapters address the book's theme: Fake Warriors must be identified, exposed, and punished.

Chapter 4 — "How do Fake Warriors Get Away With It?" — reveals the devices typically used by Fake Warriors and exposes the social and institutional enablers whose indifference, and sometimes connivance, makes it possible for the impostors to carry on masquerades that, too often, go unpunished.

Chapter 5 — "How can Fake Warriors be Identified and Exposed?" — demonstrates how to identify Fake Warriors, reveals certain distinct patterns which can be ascertained from their statements and conduct, provides the major categories into which most Fake Warrior fabrications fall, and explains how one goes about exposing them.

Chapter 6 — "How Can Fake Warriors Be Punished?" — discusses the constitutional distinction between *pure speech* and speech accompanied by action — a distinction central to the legal fight against Fake Warriors. The chapter describes the many legal and social tools available to combat military imposture. For example, an impostor's lies can violate federal and state criminal fraud, perjury, and other laws. He may also violate federal statutes criminalizing misuse of the military uniform and decorations, and federal statutes criminalizing false statements to federal officials. We also set forth the respective roles of police and prosecutors, how it is possible to induce prosecutors to bring charges against Fake Warriors, how private attorneys are in a unique position to make a major contribution in identifying, exposing, and punishing impostors, how the legislative and executive branches of our government — state *and* federal — can be utilized effectively and, last but not least, how individual initiative can help turn the tide.

Chapter 7 is devoted entirely to the Stolen Valor Act: its genesis, journey through Congress, prosecutions brought pursuant to it, and an introduction to the Supreme Court's decision as to Section 704(b)'s constitutionality.

Chapter 8 presents the entire opinion of the Supreme Court of the United States on the constitutionality of the Stolen Valor Act's core provision, with commentary by the authors.

Chapter 9 offers the draft of a proposed federal statute which cures the flaws present in the now-unconstitutional Section 704(b) of the Stolen Valor Act. Conceived and prepared Professor Henry Mark Holzer several years ago, the federal Fake Warrior Act cures the deficiencies found in the Stolen Valor Act by the Supreme Court of the United States in the *Alvarez* case. It also avoids the constitutional and other problems present in the recently introduced Heck-Brown bill, the Stolen Valor Act of 2011.

We conclude with dramatic case histories of impostors who have confessed to their imposture, and with a plea to patriotic Americans — veterans and non-veterans alike. We urge our fellow citizens to recognize that the Fake Warrior phenomenon is a national disgrace which harms our nation and many Americans in cruel and insidious ways. Once that recognition exists, the next logical step will be action by an informed and aroused citizenry.

This was the explicit goal of *Fake Warriors'* first edition. It remains the goal of the second.

Perhaps the most important weapons in the identification, exposure, and punishment of Fake Warriors is being able to obtain military records and quickly to ascertain if a suspected imposter is speaking the truth about what he claims. This book provides seven tools to make that task easier.[16]

Appendix A explains the official documentation needed to obtain the military records of someone suspected of being a Fake Warrior.

Appendix B is the official list of every American *civilian and military* prisoner of war who *escaped* captivity during the Vietnam War.

Appendix C is the official list of every American *civilian* (and certain selected *foreign national*) prisoners of war who *escaped* during, who was *released* during, or who was *repatriated* at the conclusion of, the Vietnam War.

Appendix D is the combined list of all *military* prisoners of war who *escaped* during, who were *released* during, or who were *repatriated* at the conclusion of the Vietnam War.

Appendix E is the Official list of Vietnam War United States Prisoners of War who died in captivity.

Appendix F is the official list of Vietnam War Medal of Honor recipients. Like the foregoing lists, the Medal of Honor lists are ironclad. If someone's name is not found in Appendices E or F, he was not awarded the Medal of Honor for service in Vietnam, or anywhere else, during that war or thereafter.

Appendix G is the official list of Medal of Honor recipients from the end of the Vietnam War to today.

Fake Warriors can be identified. They can be exposed. They can be punished.

To do so, is to respect all those who have served our country honorably.

CHAPTER 1

WHY ARE THERE FAKE WARRIORS?

". . . he faced the firing squad; erect and motionless, proud and disdainful, Walter Mitty the Undefeated, inscrutable to the last." [17]

In James Thurber's short story *The Secret Life of Walter Mitty*, by the time Mitty faced a firing squad, 'Commander' Mitty's fearlessness had driven an eight-engine Navy hydroplane into a hurricane, 'surgeon' Mitty's operating room skills had saved the life of a millionaire banker, 'marksman' Mitty's expert court testimony had bested an arrogant District Attorney, and 'Captain' Mitty's heroism had braved the skies over France during World War I.

In the movie version of Thurber's story, which starred the late comedian Danny Kaye, Mitty's exploits were even more daring. Both story and film dramatized these larger-than-life exploits as harmless figments of Walter Mitty's imagination — his 'secret life.'

But *why* Walter Mitty lapsed into his absurdist, but ultimately benign, reveries is never made explicit in story or film. It's left to implication: Mitty, a milquetoast of a man, leads a humdrum, henpecked life.

Why Fake Warriors indulge in *their* particular, far from harmless, fantasies can be considerably more complex than what motivated Walter Mitty's daydreaming.

It is a serious mistake to generalize about why people falsify their military service, to claim credit for deeds never done and awards never received. That the reasons are varied and encompass a wide range of human psychology is demonstrated by Chapter 2's representative list of Fake Warriors who have come from every strata of our society.

When Fake Warriors include historians and college professors, lawyers and judges, police chiefs and process servers, newsmen and soccer coaches, ministers and movie stars, murderers and best-selling authors, U.S. Senators and presidential candidates, it is a foregone conclusion that the motives for engaging in such deplorable conduct must be wide-ranging.

The basic dictionary definition of an impostor is "a person who deceives or cheats others, especially by pretending to be someone or something that he is not."[18] One authority, Charles Ford, MD, enlarges on the definition:

A much more pathological and pervasive form of lying and deceit is that which occurs with impostors. . . . [[19]] These individuals may assume various roles . . . and live ongoing lies. It has been proposed that these individuals act out their imposture in an attempt to achieve a sense of identity and confidence. . . . In a similar vein, [another writer] suggested that impostors strive to eliminate friction between an exaggerated ego ideal (the grandiose self) and the devalued, inferior, guilt-ridden part of their egos (their sense of self). [That writer] also stated that these impostors behave as if their ego ideals were identical to their sense of self, and they expect everyone else to acknowledge this to be the case. In other words, acceptance of the deceit by others soothes the impostor and reduces the internal conflicts. Thus, the impostor attempts to fool himself or herself that his or her life is not a lie.[20]

While Dr. Ford's observations apply to some Fake Warriors, they barely scratch the surface. Everyone has encountered people who lie and masquerade for all sorts of non-Freudian reasons. Some obvious examples:

- To obtain money and tangible property.
- To hide criminal or other wrongful behavior.
- To avoid punishment for wrongs or crimes committed.
- To get attention.
- To relieve loneliness.
- To achieve notoriety.
- To obtain public office.
- To embellish an otherwise undistinguished or under-distinguished
- academic, military, or personnel record.
- To manipulate people and/or achieve power over them.
- To indulge in the cheap thrill of putting something over on the gullible or unsuspecting.
- To experience excitement.
- To compensate for a variety of things: an ordinary life, rejection
- by society, social inferiority, lack of respect, personal or business failures, a feeling of being unattractive, an escape from one's own identity.
- To be a big shot.
- To polish one's professional image, or further one's career at the expense of others more deserving.
- To defuse the envy one feels for accomplished people.
- To fuel ambition.
- To feed an "ego" that suffers from low or pseudo self-esteem.
- To take wishful thinking and Walter Mittyish fantasies to an
- extreme.

- To feed the needs of enablers, spouses among them, who thrive on tall tales at the expense of the truth.
- To feel glamorous, smart, cool.
- To impress the opposite sex by creating a macho or sexy persona.
- To see oneself as larger-than-life — a man's man.
- To benefit from purported association with prominent people, or to hobnob with them.[21]

Although it is not the goal of this book to delve deeply into the underlying psychiatric or psychological motivations that cause Fake Warrior conduct, one observation is highly instructive. A former US Army Ranger, now a Veterans Administration psychiatrist who has treated many Fake Warriors, believes that, at root, a majority of military impostors are motivated by a profound sense of inadequacy, and their lack of self-esteem is usually exacerbated by extreme substance abuse. This psychiatrist told us that many of the patients he has seen at the VA know, at bottom, they are impostors, but lose that awareness as they become delusional.

We asked the psychiatrist about what, in his considerable experience, might motivate relatives of Fake Warriors to play along with their loved ones' imposture. His answer supported our thesis, developed in Chapter 4, that many people cross the line from being mere bystanders to becoming active enablers of Fake Warriors. Spouses, children, and other relatives, he told us, often derive a sense of pseudo self-esteem by having an alleged war hero in the family. In effect, the psychiatrist said, enablers are protecting a false sense of *their own identity*.[22]

Why, as we'll see, would a Pulitzer-prize-winning professor lie about service in Vietnam? Clearly, the man was driven by a need to play a "glamorous" role — to have participated, as it were — in the Vietnam War history that he taught.

A counterinsurgency author displayed a more "practical" need: His imposture provided him with credentials for the fiction he wrote. Equally "practical" was the lawyer out to impress former Marines who were in a position to appoint him to the bench. The macho movie star, on the other hand, even though he was an established actor and highly skilled at his craft, may have sought to polish his image as a tough guy either for practical career-enhancement reasons, or because his self-esteem was shaky — or both. The convict's motive was more obvious: He was looking for an angle that would shorten his prison term. The ROTC instructor falls into the category of sexual predator of unsuspecting high school girls. The police chief clearly could benefit in his job from the "take charge" image that his imposture afforded him — as could the Congressman out to impress people with his alleged war record. The director of a veterans' memorial may have been driven by a host of different needs: big shotism, inferiority complex, Walter Mittyish fantasies, even guilt at *not* having served his country. The list is even longer, as we'll soon see.

Or, as Fake Warrior Richard Davis[23] said in a revealing moment of candor: "[*I had*] *to find a reason to validate my being on this earth.*"[24]

Given the wide variety of needs and motives — some of which many otherwise decent people might fall prey to — one could be tempted to feel sorry for a Fake Warrior, especially a man who repents and appears to be genuinely contrite. Richard Davis possessed all the earmarks of a lonely man who thrived on the acceptance and comradeship of the veteran community:

> [At the Veterans of Foreign Wars] I was enjoying the camaraderie of the other vets I had met there. I was at a very low point in my life, very low self-esteem. I was drinking a lot. I had no friends. . . . I found a new set of friends at the VFW. I was accepted by the majority at face value. . . ."[25]

And, as Davis discovered, lies can metamorphose into a kind of narcotic — a need that feeds upon itself until it becomes virtually insatiable:

> I did this [lied about being a pararescue medic] to appear as

> though [he] and I had something in common; i.e., being in the military and holding rather elite (in my mind) positions. He being a chopper pilot, me being a medic. He was impressed as he held combat medics in very high esteem. I felt rather elevated in his eyes. Once I got my feet wet, I decided to jump in. The more I added to my war chest, the more attention [I received] and [the more I was held] in high esteem by the veterans. I felt very important. Brave. A real hero. Sad, but true.[26]

More than sad. Pitiable. But it needs to be said that where Fake Warriors are concerned, undue sympathy is misguided. It can undermine one's effectiveness in fighting imposture. Readers should remind themselves why they're reading this book. Innocent people are being hurt by Fake Warriors. Tangible harm is being done. A rank injustice is being perpetrated on our *genuine* war heroes by the needy, the greedy, the irresponsible, and the insecure.

We have discussed the subject of motive for two reasons: to shed light on what spawns the Fake Warrior mentality, and to provide a necessary preface to an important legal principle. *Motive, though explanatory, is not a legal defense to either civil or criminal Fake Warrior behavior.*

But while motive is irrelevant to both guilt and punishment, *intent is an indispensable element.*

In our book, *"Aid and Comfort": Jane Fonda in North Vietnam,*[27] we spelled out in detail the crucial legal distinction between motive and intent in order to underscore the fact that, when it came to the charge of treason, Fonda's insecurities and obsessive cause-seeking in no way diminished her legal culpability. In support of our argument —that, based on her broadcasts and other conduct in war-time North Vietnam, Jane Fonda was indictable and convictable for treason — we relied on the following legal precedent from the case of *United States* v. *Chandler*:

> The *Chandler* case is as good place as any to address, and dispose of, the issue we raised in the Introduction of this book: *motive.*

> In that chapter and the following one, we established that Jane Fonda was, in her own eyes, a person of little or no worth, lacking, by her own admission, self-esteem and a sense of her own identity. Her personal identity crisis drove her to seek what might be called pseudo self-esteem through the approval of others and by attaching herself to a series of causes. One need only recall: Fonda's upbringing; her drifting from one meaningless activity to another; her expatriate days with [French movie director Roger] Vadim and his clique of pseudo-intellectual French Marxist friends and associates; her militant New Left escapades with Indians, feminists, farm workers, and the Black Panthers; and her hitching her star to Tom Hayden and his pro-Communist, anti-American, 'revolutionary' movement. We noted that, in large measure, Fonda's own pro-Communist, anti-American sentiments were motivated by that lack of identity.
>
> We are not here addressing her 'intent' — to injure the United States and help the North Vietnamese — nor the 'means' she employed to achieve that end: traveling to Hanoi, making pro-Communist, anti-American broadcasts, and engaging in related conduct. We are focusing . . . exclusively on Fonda's 'motive'. In [defendant] Chandler's case, it was anti-Semitism. In Fonda's, it appears to have been that driving need to 'find herself'. In the context of a treason prosecution, what, then, is the relevance of *motive*?

Chandler appealed his conviction, in part, on the ground that the trial judge erred in his charge to the jury concerning *intent* and *motive* by making the following distinction between the two: Glendon—The next two paragraphs are a blocked quote within the blocked quote.

> In the law of treason, like the law of lesser crimes, *every person is assumed to intend the natural consequences that he himself knows will result from his acts.* And, in this case, if you find the defendant Chandler committed a voluntary act or acts which actually gave aid and comfort to the enemy and at that time and in his

> circumstances he knew, or with his knowledge had reason to know that the natural consequence of his act would be that aid and comfort would result to the enemy in the conduct of its war against the United States, *you would be warranted in finding from the commission of the acts themselves that he intended to give aid and comfort to Germany,* that he intended to adhere to the enemy, that he intended to strike at his own country and betray it and the fact that his motive might not have been to aid the enemy is no defense. In other words a person cannot do an act which he knows will give aid and comfort to the enemy and then attempt to disclaim criminal intent and knowledge by saying that one's motive was not to aid the enemy.
>
> Motive cannot negative an intent to betray, if you find the defendant had such an intent. *Where a person has an intent to bring about a result which the law seeks to prevent, his motive is immaterial.*[28]

Was the trial judge correct in drawing this important distinction between motive and intent in a treason prosecution — a distinction that would allow a prosecutor to negate whatever psychological and/or other problems may have accounted for Fonda's actions?

Said the United States Court of Appeals for the First Circuit regarding Douglas Chandler: "We think the above charge stated the law with sufficient accuracy. The argument is made that treason is a crime dependent upon the actor's motives; that the jury should have been told that the defendant could not be found to have had an 'intent to betray' if they believed that he acted from patriotic motives upon the sincere conviction that what he did was for the best interests of the United States. Appellant is surely wrong in that contention."[29]

It could be no other way. Said the federal appeals court:

> [I]n the first place, consider the subtle task which would be imposed upon the jury by an inquiry of that kind. [Chandler] had

> become . . . "fanatically anti-Semitic." What part did this factor play in his motivation? * * * Did Chandler carefully inquire into the supposed facts upon which his intense views and opinions were based? In weighing the evidence, did he make a conscious effort to discount the distorting influence of his prejudices, before arriving at his conclusions? *Whether Chandler was "sincere" in what he did, whether he had the heart of a patriot, is a matter that may be sifted out at the last Great Judgment Seat; but the law of treason is concerned with matters more immediate.*
>
> Furthermore, if [Chandler's] argument in this connection were sound, it would of course be applicable whatever might be the character of the overt acts of aid and comfort to the enemy. Suppose Chandler had obtained advance information of the Anglo-American plans for the invasion of North Africa and had passed the information on to the enemy. Would a treason prosecution fail if he could convince the jury that, in his fanatical and perhaps misguided way, he sincerely believed his country was on the wrong side of the war; that he sincerely believed his country's ultimate good would be served by an early withdrawal from the war; that he sincerely believed that the best, perhaps the only, way to accomplish this good end was to bring it about that the first major military operation of the United States should be a resounding fiasco, thereby stimulating such a revulsion among the American people that the perfidious administration would be forced to negotiate a peace? It is hardly necessary to state the answer to that question.[30]

The court concluded:

> When war breaks out, a citizen's obligation of allegiance puts definite limits upon his freedom to act on his private judgment. *If he trafficks* [sic] *with enemy agents, knowing them to be such, and being aware of their hostile mission intentionally gives them aid in steps essential to the execution of that mission, he has adhered to the enemies of his country, giving them aid and comfort, within*

> *our definition of treason. He is guilty of treason, whatever his motive.*[31]

Putting aside, then, the question of *why* Fake Warriors lie about their military service, let's look at who the imposters are.

CHAPTER 2

WHO ARE THE FAKE WARRIORS?

"Trouthe is the hyeste thing that men may kepe." [32]

The Connolly case discussed in the Introduction is merely one example of this book's subject: that the phenomenon of Fake Warriors is real, pernicious, and widespread; and of our theme that impostors must be identified, exposed, and punished.[33] Indeed, impostors who lied about military service in Vietnam have permeated America's culture for at least forty years, joined in recent years by phonies lying about their roles in Afghanistan, Iraq, and elsewhere in the world. Their lies have included everything from the mundane to the exotic — even to the delusional.[34] And, sadly, most Fake Warriors have not been identified or, if known, have never been exposed, let alone punished.

Sad, too, is that Fake Warriors come from every imaginable strata of society. A *Pulitzer Prize-winning college history professor* claimed he had been a platoon leader in Vietnam with the fabled "Screaming Eagles" — the 101st Airborne.[35]

Another *PhD professor of history,* author of several books on counterinsurgency, lecturer at four of the service academies (twice "Lecturer of the Year"), claimed he had been a covert operative.[36]

A *leading historian of the Vietnam War* — author of several books on the conflict, lecturer at war colleges, adjunct fellow at a prestigious think tank, and consultant to the Department of Defense — claimed, among other things, that he had engaged in special operations.[37]

An *adjunct history professor* at a community college claimed he had been a SEAL and Special Operations officer.[38]

A *major league sports team manager* claimed he had been on search-and-destroy missions in Vietnam.[39]

A *newspaper publisher* claimed he had been a jet fighter pilot in Vietnam.[40] Another *newspaper publisher* claimed he had been a wounded Special Forces sergeant, and then a POW.[41]

A *consultant to the Fox News Channel* on the war in Afghanistan claimed he had been a lieutenant colonel in Special Forces and received the Silver Star for bravery.[42]

A *judge* claimed he had won two (!) Medals of Honor.[43] Another *judge*, more modest but equally deceptive, claimed only one.[44]

A *Marine judge advocate* (a lawyer) claimed he had dodged shrapnel, helped evacuate Saigon when it fell, and was awarded various medals for his feat — including some obscure French decoration.[45]

A *civilian lawyer* claimed he had been a POW (two years after American troops had left Vietnam), and been awarded the Medal of Honor.[46]

A *candidate for a County Commissioners court* claimed he had been a SEAL and took part in classified operations.[47]

A *police chief* claimed he had been a Vietnam POW.[48] *Another police officer* claimed he had been a SEAL.[49]

A *police constable* claimed he had been awarded the Medal of Honor, the Silver Star, the Bronze Star, and had parachuted into Cambodia — where he rescued a Lt. General and carried him on a stretcher through hostile country for nine miles.[50]

A *Captain of the South Carolina Highway Patrol* claimed he had been in Special Forces, had been captured, and had escaped.[51]

A *process server for a large metropolitan court system* claimed he had been a "Special Forces Ranger" and a POW.[52]

A *senior ROTC instructor* in a large school district, holding the retired rank of major, claimed he had been a Ranger and a member of Special Forces, and had been awarded a Combat Infantryman Badge, a Purple Heart, and various decorations for valor.[53]

A *murderer* claimed he had endured horrendous combat experiences as a Marine in Vietnam (and, as a result, had his life sentence commuted.)[54]

Another *murderer* claimed to be the most decorated Texan since World War II's Audie Murphy.[55]

A *bodyguard* for Hollywood mega-stars claimed he had been a SEAL, wounded in a horrendous firefight.[56]

A *fireman* claimed to have been tortured as a POW, after which he'd escaped and had a friend die in his arms.[57]

A *minister, later an army chaplain,* claimed he had been a Green Beret, Ranger, medic, explosives expert, and master paratrooper.[58]

Another *minister* claimed he had been a three-tour SEAL, and had been shot down and wounded while flying off an aircraft carrier.[59]

A *Wall Street corporate takeover expert* claimed he had engaged in "black operations" for the CIA, had been wounded, and had cut the throats of his enemies.[60]

Another *investment house executive* claimed he had flown fixed-wing and helicopter aircraft for the CIA, that he spoke an Iranian dialect, and that he'd worked for the CIA in Iran.[61]

Yet another *financial wheeler-dealer* claimed to have flown jet fighters and had been awarded the Medal of Honor.[62]

A *non-commissioned officer running air police security for the Delaware Air National Guard* claimed he had been a wounded Green Beret.[63]

An *employee of the B-1 Bomber Systems Program* at an air force base — later an applicant for an important position with the Senate Select Committee on POW-MIA Affairs — claimed that on a covert mission over Laos, he took over the plane's controls when the pilot was hit, sliced off the head of two Viet Cong with the aircraft's wings, crash-landed, was captured, tortured, escaped, and bravely returned to kill nine of his captors.[64]

A *national veterans' organization's executive secretary* claimed he had been a pilot and an officer, and had been wounded in Vietnam. Another *leader of the same organization* claimed he had flown forty-seven combat missions in Viet Nam.[65]

A *post commander* of one of America's premier veterans' organizations, named an "All American," claimed to be a sniper and a trained expert in underwater demolition and survival. His alleged expertise was used in secret work throughout Indochina and Thailand, which included the training of tribesmen; of course, he had been wounded.[66]

Yet another *post commander, chairman of the New York State Veterans' Legislative Coalition*, claimed he had lost both of his hands while on a secret mission.[67]

A *state commander of a national veterans' organization* claimed not only to have been a Marine POW, but to have escaped as well.[68]

Another state commander claimed he had been a POW after his entire squad had been captured, tortured, skinned, and executed.[69]

An *executive director* of a Vietnam Veterans' Resource and Service Center claimed he had been a guerilla and had fought in countless firefights.[70]

A *co-founder of a national veterans' organization* claimed he had been captured by North Vietnamese troops, but then abandoned by his captors.[71]

A *founder of a state chapter of a national veterans' organization* claimed that, as an army nurse, she had to cope with insects crawling from wounds and "rivers of blood."[72]

A *founder of two chapters of a POW organization*[73] — vice commander of one of them — claimed he had been a POW.[74]

A *director of a veterans' memorial* claimed he had served in Special Forces, had been wounded, and had worked for the CIA.[75]

A *Disabled Veterans' Outreach Program Coordinator* claimed he had been a POW.[76]

The *manager of an armored car company* claimed she had been captured, and had escaped by shooting an enemy soldier in the face with a .45.[77]

A *member of a city arts commission* claimed he had been a POW, director of Special Operations, a test pilot, and had served on the Joint Chiefs of Staff.[78]

A *United States customs inspector* claimed he had been a SEAL.[79]

The *founder of a state epileptic foundation* claimed that, as a CBS sound engineer, he was captured by the Viet Cong, tortured, and "traded" back to

US forces.[80]

A *prominent movie actor*, who specializes in macho roles, claimed he had been a Marine wounded in combat.[81]

A *computer security chief* claimed he had been a SEAL, before becoming a POW.[82]

A *county Revenue and Finance commissioner* claimed he had been an officer, served as a Green Beret, and received a Purple Heart and other combat medals.[83]

A *saloonkeeper and commander of a veterans' color guard* claimed to have been an expert in jungle warfare and special weaponry, and had been awarded the Medal of Honor, five (!) Purple Hearts for Vietnam service, and various other decorations for valor.[84]

A *race car driver* claimed he had been a POW.[85]

The *president of an elite airborne division association* claimed he had been awarded thirty-one decorations, and had been wounded five times.[86]

A *Department of Public Works superintendent/veterans counselor/veterans affairs activist* claimed he had worked with the CIA and performed top-secret missions — including assassinations — throughout Indochina.[87]

A *state health counselor* claimed she had been a captain in the Nurse Corps, and had been wounded by shrapnel.[88]

An *OSHA inspector* claimed he had been in Special Forces.[89]

A *high school principal* claimed he had been a Green Beret, had performed covert missions in Cambodia, and had once crawled out from under a pile of dead bodies.[90]

A *legitimately heroic chopper pilot* — actually wounded twice — falsely claimed he had been captured, mistreated, allowed to escape, and shot at by American troops.[91]

Marine sergeant who, in fact, had fought in Korea, claimed he'd been on forty clandestine missions into North Vietnam, while wearing a wooden leg, and was twice wounded.[92]

A *best-selling author* claimed he had once been an assassin.[93]

A *renowned martial arts master* claimed he had been a POW both in Korea and in Vietnam.[94]

A *retired banker*, accused of molesting his girlfriend's young son, claimed he had been a Green Beret.[95]

An *employee of a security officer training school* claimed he had been a SEAL, had been tortured by the Viet Cong, and was a POW for seventeen months.[96]

A *children's soccer coach* claimed he had been a POW in both Korea and Vietnam.[97]

A *general contractor* claimed to have been a brigadier general who had fought as a Ranger with Special Forces, been wounded, and had received the Medal of Honor.[98]

A *businessman in the oil industry* claimed he had been awarded the Medal of Honor.[99]

A *Grand Marshal of a Memorial Day* parade claimed that, as a two-tour Green Beret, he had received a battlefield promotion to major, and had trained Montagnard tribesmen.[100]

A local *commander of no less than three national veterans' organizations*, who was often in charge of Memorial and Veterans Day ceremonies, claimed he had been a SEAL, had engaged in secret operations, and had been wounded eleven times.[101]

A *candidate for the presidency of the United States* — an ardently religious man — claimed he had endured heavy combat.[102]

A *United States Senator,* running for the Democrat Party presidential nomination, claimed he had flown fighter jets and photo-reconnaissance missions.[103]

A *Congressman* claimed he had served with Army Special Forces.[104]

A *Connecticut state representative* claimed he had fought in Vietnam.[105]

Another *state representative running for governor* in an adjoining New England state claimed he had been a Green Beret.[106]

A Texas *city councilman* claimed he had been a Naval officer in Vietnam, and had flown jets.[107]

A *Mafioso* — later to join the government witness protection program as an informer against the mob — claimed to have been a Green Beret, and to have been wounded in a fierce firefight.[108]

A *first vice president of an NAACP chapter* claimed to have been a retired Lt. Colonel who had run covert helicopter missions and been twice wounded.[109]

A director of a Youth Challenge Program claimed he had been a SEAL, and had been awarded Purple Hearts and the Navy Cross.[110]

A *principal speechwriter for the New York State Assembly Speaker — at one time a press secretary for a presidential candidate* — claimed to have been the most highly decorated veteran in the State of New York.[111]

A *psychiatric social worker,* in the act of raping a female patient in a hotel room, claimed to have been a government assassin.[112]

A *private investigator* claimed to have been a retired colonel and veteran of special operations.[113] Another *private eye* claimed to have been a wounded Green Beret who had engaged in assassination — and had trained cannibals to fight for the United States.[114]

A *retired Air Force Senior Master Sergeant employed as Superintendent of Information Management at an Air Force Base* claimed he had been a POW, but escaped.[115]

And, believe it or not, *a legitimate hero of the Landing Zone X-ray battle in the Ia Drang Valley* (the subject of a book and movie entitled *We Were Soldiers Once . . . and Young*), *who actually lost a leg in that engagement and was awarded the Silver Star*, claimed to have been awarded the Medal of Honor.[116]

This list could go on and on. But while it would continue to convey the *extent* of the Fake Warrior problem, it would not, by itself, disclose the *harmful consequences* of Fake Warrior conduct. This can be understood only through a sampling of actual cases which dramatically illustrate the damage that has been done to countless innocent people.[117]

CHAPTER 3

WHAT HARM DO FAKE WARRIORS CAUSE?

"Believe me, Captain, bar talk bullshit goes in one ear and out the other with most of us retired sailors. The burn in our hearts is the flouting of the Navy Cross on civilian rags when many a shipmate never came home, their valor never acknowledged." [118]

While it is tempting for some people to toss off as nothing more than 'harmless boasting' the tall tales told by Fake Warriors, the fact is their words and deeds have seriously harmful consequences to real people in the real world.

Fake Warriors who falsely claim they committed atrocities in Vietnam sully the reputations of all who served honorably there.[119]

Fake Warriors who abuse girlfriends, wives, even children, often falsely attribute their vicious conduct to combat caused trauma — and obtain undeserved leniency.[120]

Fake Warriors can access materials to which they would otherwise not be entitled,[121] and enter places where they do not belong.[122]

Fake Warriors can obtain extra credit for civil service positions.[123]

Fake Warriors steal huge sums from the Department of Veterans Affairs.[124]

Fake Warriors, especially when they are exposed, denigrate the accomplishments and suffering of the nation's real heroes.[125]

If a military lawyer is discovered to have been a Fake Warrior, criminal convictions can be jeopardized and even reversed.[126]

A Fake Warrior's spouse and other family members can become so invested in their loved one's imposture that they lose all sense of judgment and often suffer severe instability and mental anguish.[127]

A Fake Warrior who succeeds in his imposture can cause great embarrassment to well intentioned, but sloppy, public figures who don't bother to check the phony's story.[128]

These are a sampling of the harmful consequences visited upon individuals and institutions in our society by the lies of Fake Warriors. Although it's not possible here even to catalogue, let alone describe in detail, all the damage done, the following cases illustrate the adverse impact of Fake Warrior lies.

We begin with a seemingly benign example.

A Vietnam veteran and some friends attended a Texas auto show and struck up a conversation with a salesman about Japanese cars. The salesman noticed that the vet was wearing a baseball cap with his unit designation embroidered on it, and the following verbatim conversation ensued:

> Salesman: I was in Vietnam.
>
> Vet: Me, too. Where were you?
>
> Salesman: Up near the DMZ [Demilitarized Zone], but most of my

time in North Vietnam.

Vet: North Vietnam? What did you do?

Salesman: Black ops, if I told you, I'd have to kill you [jokingly].

Vet: Nothing's black ops anymore. There is nothing you can't talk about. So what did you do?

Salesman: I was told I couldn't say anything about it, but I led a five-man execution squad.

Vet: Are you sure about that? There are people out there just looking for people who claim to have been in Vietnam black ops. One of them is a Navy Captain[[129]] . . . but if I pass your phone number on to him, he's liable to give you a call.

Salesman: Well, he can do that whenever he likes.

Vet: What was your unit?

Salesman: It was a special unit.

Vet: Yeah, but you had to belong to a unit, what was it?

Salesman: It was the . . . of the 75th Artillery.

Vet: Seventy-fifth Artillery, what?

Salesman: Just the seventy-fifth; I was in the . . . of the 75th Artillery in Germany. "Vee" Corps.
Vet: "Vee" Corps in Germany, but when you were in Vietnam on the DMZ, you were in "One" Corps?

Salesman: No, I think it was "Three" Corps.

<u>*Vet*</u>: No, "Three" Corps was down around Saigon, "One" corps was in the DMZ area.

<u>*Salesman*</u>: Yeah, that was I was in "One" Corps.

<u>*Vet*</u>: Look, it wasn't called "One" Corps; it was called "Eye" Corps. You'd better stop telling that story because people are wise to people who make up stories about Vietnam.[130]

We can imagine to how many would-be car buyers this salesman told the same story, or some variant, to enhance his chances of selling them a vehicle. While the *blowhard* category of Fake Warriors doesn't rank high on our list of impostors, still, we can extrapolate from the car salesman to countless other impostors who fabricate their military history as part of a sales pitch.

Lying to consumers may be a slick and sleazy affair, but lying to the courts has far more serious consequences. Consider the following case of a convicted drug dealer.

In connection with his pre-sentence report, the dealer — convicted of *five* felony counts of selling crack cocaine and heroin to an undercover agent — suckered his probation officer into believing that the dealer had been a POW in Vietnam. Picking up the thread, the dealer's defense attorney waxed eloquent to the court about his client's inhumane treatment in a Vietnam prisoner of war camp. Before his client escaped, the lawyer told the court, "guards broke [the dealer's] jaw, urinated on his food, and terrorized him during his three months and 18 days as a hostage." That, according to the dealer, together with depression and the death of his parents, led him to use drugs, and using drugs led to selling them.

Although the drug dealer was staring at the prospect of fifty-plus years in prison, the prosecution — presumably disarmed by the dealer's POW imposture — asked for only ten. The defense countered seeking probation and drug treatment. The gullible judge, noting the dealer's alleged heroism in Vietnam, mitigated the dealer's sentence to only four years.

Not an uncommon scenario: the commission of a crime, mitigation sought because of a completely fabricated story of heroism during the Vietnam War, followed by a lenient sentence.

In this case, however, on the day after the dealer had been sentenced, the prosecutor received a telephone call asserting that the alleged ex-POW was a fraud. The sentencing proceeding was reopened.

So far so good.

Even better, the drug dealer's lawyer withdrew from the case, telling the judge, with admirable candor, that he wished he could say what was on his mind, but that the attorney-client privilege prevented him from doing so.[131]

The drug dealer, no fool he, caved in and confessed. Not only had he not been a POW, but he had never even served in the military.

The judge was not happy, and said so, chastising the defendant for perpetrating "a fraud on the court." The drug dealer's light sentence had stemmed from his alleged terrible experiences in Vietnam, which were "a very substantial factor" in the judge's consideration. "The sentence would have been very different," had he known the truth, said the judge. The defendant had foolishly gambled by concocting a tissue of lies.

Despite the fraud that the defendant had perpetrated on the court and confessed to, the District Attorney did not ask for an increase in the drug dealer's original sentence of four years. The judge, magnanimous to the end, ignored the upper limits of his sentencing discretion, and settled on a mild increase by kicking up the four years to seven with eight years' probation thrown in.[132]

While this Fake Warrior was at least exposed and his conduct punished, one cannot help but wonder how many other criminal sentences have been ameliorated by sympathetic judges because of moving, albeit false, stories of military heroism.

It's bad enough when a judge allows himself to be misled by a Fake Warrior, but consider the irony of a sitting judge who is, himself, an impostor.

Many states require that lawyers seeking a judgeship must first apply to a judicial selection screening committee, whose job it is to pass on the applicant's qualifications. From a list of those recommended, the appointing authority — the governor or mayor, for example — makes a selection.[133]

In California, a former prosecutor applied to such a committee. The man's credentials were impressive: a diploma from a prestigious law school and a master's degree in psychology; member of a highly respected law firm; service with the Marines in Vietnam, where he was wounded; un-removable shrapnel still in his groin; covert work for the CIA.

No wonder the governor's judicial appointments aide, also an ex-Marine (as was the governor), was impressed. Indeed, among the many applicants for the judgeship whom the aide had interviewed, he later remembered the former prosecutor because of his "unusual war experiences." Not surprising, then, that the veteran-hero was appointed to the State of California bench.

Sloppy vetting, however. How much effort would it have taken to run a background check before appointing someone to the bench in California? It turned out that except for the law degree[134] and having been a prosecutor for a while, the lawyer-applicant's background was a pack of lies.[135]

Eventually, the truth surfaced and the State Commission on Judicial Performance charged the judge with "providing false information regarding his background and qualifications." Resolving not to go down without a fight, the unrepentant judge hired a former member of the watchdog State Commission to represent him. "What we have here," asserted the judge's glib lawyer, "is a series of non-intentional misrepresentations. Some of these things he made some mistakes on, sure, but we think we can explain them."[136]

But not well enough: The Commission found the judge guilty of willful misconduct and conduct prejudicial to the administration of justice. Faced with the choice of prosecution or resignation, the judge resigned from the bench. Were professional disciplinary proceedings commenced? No. The former judge went into private law practice — perhaps representing Fake Warriors.[137]

Despite the fact that American troops were gone from Vietnam in 1973 — nearly forty years ago — one has to question how many lawyers from that era, when applying for judgeships, successfully embellished, or even invented, their military records.[138]

There is a double fraud at work in these kinds of cases. When a Fake Warrior, seeking judicial office, claims a military record to which he is not entitled, and then benefits from the lie, he steals more than a judgeship. An important position crucial to our democratic system that would have gone to a legitimate candidate has been usurped and wasted.

Outrageous? Absolutely. But not quite as outrageous as stealing a person's identity.

Veterans' benefits, administered and paid by the Department of Veterans Affairs, are often inadequate to meet the needs of those who served our country. Nonetheless, for whatever they're worth, they are doggedly sought. A few years ago, the Inspector General of the VA sent a man to prison for 24 months, had him put on probation for another 36 months, and obtained a restitution order for $40,000. The defendant, not a veteran, had assumed a dead man's identity — his twin brother's — and with it VA benefit payments intended for the deceased. Here's what happened:

For more than five years, continuing to use his [dead] brother's identity, [the impostor] devised several schemes to defraud the VA. Following his brother's death, [the impostor] endorsed and cashed his brother's VA benefit checks. [He] also admitted that he filed numerous false, fictitious, and fraudulent documents in order to obtain a home mortgage guaranteed by the VA. [He] provided bogus income information and made false certifications regarding his intentions to occupy the property as his primary residence when, in fact, family members occupied the property while [he] lived elsewhere. . . . The property ultimately went into default, which could result in a potential loss of over $37,000 to the VA.[139]

The VA isn't the only victim of Fake Warrior theft. Even veterans organizations have not been immune.

For years, an officer of a South Carolina VFW post had claimed that he'd been a POW in Vietnam for six months. When he spoke at a 2001Veterans Day event at a local high school, his bio repeated the bogus POW claim. The post's commander and senior vice commander began investigating. Ascertaining that the officer had been lying, they also learned that his name was on P.O.W. Network's "phony" list of impostor POWs.

In his defense, the VFWofficer made a typical excuse: His records were being kept secret by the government. "I was taken captive," he said. "I want to live a quiet life. I'm not talking to anyone anymore." Indeed. Soon after, this impostor resigned the post position he had held for some seven years. The officer blamed Agent Orange. "I'm in very poor health and I needed to get away," he said.

The post's senior vice commander was only too aware of the harm that had been done: "The bad thing about it is the embarrassment to all veterans. . . . He would make speeches to schools and things like that and make those claims. That makes us look bad when it's proven otherwise. I felt it was shameful to our post, so something had to be done about it." Yet, shameful or not, the vice commander did not take an uncompromising stand against this proven impostor, but rather allowed him to remain a VFW member. He had, after all, served overseas.

It was a decision the post leadership would soon regret.

In mid-January 2002, the former VFW officer was arrested and charged with stealing from the post. According to a detective, "Three or four members of [the post] obtained an American Express card in the name of the VFW and then proceeded to make charges that were not used for the post. The other members of the post did not have knowledge of this." Purchases totaling more than $10,000 were for such personal items as book club orders, restaurant bills, gasoline, cigarettes, music, AOL online services, out-of-state motels and spas, animal feed, U-Haul rental, and merchandise from Eddie Bauer and Barnes & Noble. "We found out by accident that the credit card existed," the post commander said. "One of the other members opened a bill and found the [credit card] statement. * * * The VFW does not have vehicles to buy gas for. We don't have pets. The VFW never sold cigarettes. Nobody approved those purchases. Nobody even knew about them." The impostor — by then a criminal defendant — understandably had no comment.[140]

While common thievery is an especially low blow when delivered to one's fellow veterans, consider the chutzpah of trying to scam the very people whose business it is to expose impostors! Several years ago, someone attempted to swindle money out of P.O.W. Network. The late Phony Buster Chuck Schantag received this email: "[I'm a] former Army vet with 82nd [A]irborne, 1st 75th [R]angers, [S]pecial [F]orces, and 101st airborne, participant in Panamanian conflict and [D]esert [S]torm. After returning from [V]ietnam almost 2 years ago, I returned with questions yet unanswered, and with doubt. I am trying to find sponsors for a 2d trip to Vietnam, to include Laos this time, is there a remote possibility that this [P.O.W.] network can *help me bring one of our own's back home*."[141]

Translation: The alleged vet-warrior had been back in Vietnam looking for MIAs, and was now soliciting money to return to Indochina to, so he implied, bring back a missing-in-action American. The obscenity of this scam is self-evident, and elicited the following (too-polite, in our view) response from Chuck Schantag: "Special Forces and Rangers???? Care to Explain??" In reply, this Fake Warrior merely stood on his pedigree, ignored Chuck's pointed questions, and continued to push his mission. "I believe that with what I learned almost two years ago [it] will help me do a better job when I return."[142]

Unlike the alleged Army vet who took on Chuck Schantag, the kind of man who cons lonely women is very much in touch with reality. His motivation? Simple greed.

> [A truck driver] told stories of sitting in a tree with his buddy underneath him. "Charlie" [a Viet Cong] saw his buddy and shot him out of the tree, but the truck driver was so still "Charlie" didn't see him and he survived. He claims he was a POW for 10 days, then it was 6 weeks, then it was 10 weeks. He said his job was to find the individual that his commanding officer gave him a photo of and "take him out," he says he was a SEAL and the name of his "group" was the "Flying tigers" and they were the most decorated "squadron" in the Vietnam war. He . . . says he did four "tours" in Vietnam, he says that he won a Congressional Medal of Honor but that his experiences in Vietnam were so horrific that he sent it back to the President (hence the reason no one has ever seen it).

If these absurd boasts had been confined to bar rooms, where the truck driver could cadge drinks from the gullible or chat up other patrons, little harm would have been done. But an ex-girlfriend was not so lucky:

> He dazzled her with his stories and she totally bought into it. I use the term 'bought' because she co-signed a loan for him so he could buy a truck (18 wheels). He got the truck, began making lots of money, and then just dumped her. She was devastated! A year later, when he was in need of cash, he spent two months deceiving her into believing that he had a change of heart and truly loved her. She bailed him out again and, of course, he bailed on her. She must now sell her home. Yes, it is her own fault, but to claim to be a SEAL and then to exploit someone's obvious loneliness is pathetic!![143]

This case is but one of scores we've found where unscrupulous men have taken advantage of a woman's loneliness.[144] (We have found no cases where the roles were reversed.)[145]

Much more vulnerable than women are the children who have been victimized by Fake Warriors.

In August of 1999, a high school in the Fort Worth Independent School

District was assigned a retired army major as the new Senior Instructor for ROTC. He appeared to be well qualified: five years previous experience in Junior ROTC, a Ranger/Special Forces veteran with Vietnam service, and individual and unit awards for valor, a Combat Infantryman Badge, and a Purple Heart. The major cut a formidable figure, especially with the impressionable young girls at that Texas high school.

Together with the major, there were two senior non-commissioned officers teaching the high school's ROTC courses. Almost immediately, one of the NCOs, a Special Forces veteran with years of Vietnam service, suspected something wasn't ringing true. When the NCO tried to engage the major in conversation about their supposedly shared experiences, the major was vague and wouldn't pursue the subject. Worse, his behavior with the students was flagrantly inappropriate — touching young girls, contriving to be alone with them, driving them home after school. Even after the two NCOs exchanged heated words with the major, he denied any wrongdoing and continued his inappropriate behavior.

The NCOs persisted. They raised the subject of the major's medals, suspecting he was wearing unauthorized decorations. This resulted in more obfuscating by the major. In disgust, one of the NCOs called the school where the major had previously taught ROTC. An NCO there confirmed the caller's worst suspicions: All the major's medals, and what they purported to represent, were phony.[146]

> At this point, the major was three months into the school year. Deciding to take action, the NCOs informed the Director of Army Instruction about what had been learned concerning the major's previous teaching assignment. An investigation was conducted including allegations of sexual misconduct, and the major was fired. Although his certification from the Army was revoked and he could no longer teach ROTC anywhere, no one knows what he may have gotten away with at that Texas high school, or elsewhere, coming on as a war hero to the naive female students.[147]

While children are at risk from sexual predators who masquerade as war heroes, they are also vulnerable psychologically. "I am 15," wrote a boy inquiring about his father. "I heard you [a Phony Buster] helped this guy find the truth about [a Fake Warrior] and I would like to do the same for my dad except that I would not like it published on the Internet. I am e-mailing to ask if you can find out about my dads [*sic*] army service. I suspect that he might have served in Vietnam 72-75 with the 5th SFG, but since he always changes the subject I was wondering if you could find out the TRUTH for me."

Using methods described in Chapter 5, the Phony Buster checked the father's records and had the sad task of enlightening the son: "Have the record from St. Louis. One page. * * * He did NOT serve in Vietnam. He was National Guard Feb 1 74 until he transferred to the Air Force March 75. Retired 1996."[148]

Who knows what psychological damage this brave teenager endured when he learned the truth he was seeking — and whether the impact was transient or long-lasting?

At least this boy had the option of confronting his father and, perhaps, together, the two of them could come to terms with the painful situation. But more often, it's much too late to undo the psychological damage done to a Fake Warrior's family.[149]

The sister of a suicide wrote this letter to a Phony Buster:

> My brother . . . was a Vietnam Vet; a few days after the Pentagon and World Trade Buildings were bombed [he] disappeared. Oct.7, 2001 his son found his body. He died from a self-inflicted gunshot to his heart.
>
> Prior to his death he told his wife and two children that he was "feeling the effects of Agent Orange," that he was going to leave and be gone for about two months, he stated that he was sick and had to get better. All I can say is that he did "leave."

Since his funeral I have been told stories that [my brother] had been a POW, but was freed by American troops. The stories being told are that [he] crossed trained with the Navy Seals and was a sniper. The Seals would get [him] in the locations and leave him until his mission was accomplished and then the Seals would get him out of the area.

On one occasion [my brother] along with the Navy Seals were captured while running a mission. I don't know how long he was actually a POW but I was told that he was kept in a bamboo cage only large enough to stay in a squat position and through the day the VC would run through the jungle with them in the cages. It was a big deal when they come to a village; they would drag them through the streets, naked, with wire wrapped around their necks, they were stuck with sharpened bamboo, urinated on . . . and at night the enemy would turn the pigs out of there pens and dump my brother along with the other men down in the pig pens for the night. The next day it would start all over again.

One day they were in their cages being carried through the jungle and all of the sudden the VC dropped their cages and took off running. The American troops were coming in. At first the Troops didn't see [my brother] or the others and ran past them. One of the Seals lost his composure and started eating through his cage (thick bamboo?) blood was pouring from his face from the splintering bamboo, but once he got out of the cage, he stood straight, gathered his composure, and freed the others from their cages.

I don't know if what I told you is true, [my brother is] not here and I can't ask him, and I am sure that if the story is true a lot has been left out of the actual events that had occurred. Could you help me find out if this story is true or a made up hero's tale? [My brother] was loved by a lot of people (over 400 at his funeral) so I can easily see how stories could be embellished to keep his memory alive.

> As for me I am searching for answers because I loved my brother very much and I can't lay him to rest until I know what really did happen to him. It was traumatic enough for him to take his life years later and that is enough for me to want the true answers and not made up hero's tales. * * *
>
> [My brother] was with the Navy Seals on a Recon mission. The Seals captured a man and they (seals) were skinning a man alive to get information from him. [My brother] snapped and shot the man they were torturing to put him out of his agony. Things didn't go to well for [my brother] with the Seals after he shot the man. Again I don't know if it's another "hero's" tale or if it actually happen[ed], however I can't really say that would be a "heroes tale," but rather a nightmare from Hell.
>
> If you don't want to help me I understand, but I saw how important it is to you to discredit frauds and that you would have the means to discover truth from fiction. Here is the information that I have gathered from his discharge papers and deployment book.

The suicide's sister then provided the Phony Buster with her brother's name, branch, rank, and other information relating to his military service.

The response she received should have been devastating:

> This is the kind of e-mail that [disturbs] me most. Having to tell a loved one that their family member was not who he says he was. I am truly sorry but no [one with your brother's name] was ever captured or was a POW for any period of time in Southeast Asia. You can check it out yourself at (www.pownetwork.org). Their data is a result of over ten years of research. They have never been proven wrong.
>
> You can check out the Seal claim by contacting (www.authentiseal.org).[150] Here again I suspect that [your late brother] never worked with or had anything to do with seals in RVN. I work very

> closely with both of these sites and I can assure you that nobody worked with seal ops that wasn't a Seal. I applaud your desire to get the truth. Many people don't want to hear it. I'm just sorry that I had to be the one to tell you.

The deceased's sister's reaction to the truth about her brother and his lies is a classic example of rationalizing — perhaps the only way she could cope with the newfound knowledge of her beloved brother's elaborate deception. Twice she had pressed the Phony Buster on the question of whether this was just "another hero's tale" or if the exploits had "actually happened." But when she received the answer, she veered away from the whole subject, expressing only relief that her late brother had never been subjected to the grisly torture he'd described to family and friends in such detail (torture that accurately described what many *genuine* POWs endured.) Thanking the Phony Buster, the Fake Warrior's sister wrote:

> I am very happy to hear this news. I know that Vietnam was not a good place for anyone so just knowing that my brother was not a part of something so horrific gives me peace of mind. I just can't fathom that anyone would want a loved one remembered that way. Again Thank you.[151]

Fake Warriors can be so self-absorbed that they never make real to themselves the pain and disillusionment they are capable of wreaking upon loyal and loving family members. And families are especially vulnerable immediately after a Fake Warrior has died. A funeral is a time for mourning and a time for paying tribute. The obituary in the local newspaper properly commemorates the accomplishments of the deceased, providing his grieving family with something to cling to. But what if a glowing obituary falls apart under scrutiny? What if a Fake Warrior's 'accomplishments' are publicly challenged at the very time his loved ones are trying to cope with their loss? Here's an obituary:

> Ronald Peters[152] . . . died . . . at his home after a long battle with complications from military-related injuries and illness. * * * He was a 20-year veteran of the Army. He retired as sergeant major

> in 1970. He was a member of the Army's Special Forces unit and a first inductee Green Beret. He served in combat in both the Korean Conflict and the Vietnam War.
>
> His military achievements included a Congressional Medal of Honor "for bravery in the face of insurmountable danger; for single-handedly being responsible for the rescue of an entire platoon and innocent South Vietnamese civilians from certain demise."
>
> He was also awarded three medals of commendation "for bravery and actions above and beyond the call of duty," seven Purple Hearts (two in Korea and five in Vietnam), six Oak Leaf Clusters and four Bronze Stars. He was an expert in jungle warfare and special weaponry.
>
> He was responsible for the training of the South Vietnamese soldiers under his command. * * * He was a member of the . . . Disabled American Veterans Color Guard, serving as its commander for many years through the 1970s and 1980s. He was also a member of the Vietnam Veterans of America . . . and the Veterans of Foreign Wars. * * *[153]

Doubtless this obituary was written by a family member based on tales the deceased had regaled his family with over the years, and accepted at face value

by the local newspaper,. Unfortunately, the major element of the tale is palpably untrue. *The deceased was not a Medal of Honor recipient.* Much of the rest of the obituary's glorification of the man's military exploits is equally false.[154]

The obituary triggered at least two letters-to-the-editor from Phony Busters:

> [The deceased] did not have a Medal of Honor. There is a good chance that he didn't have most of the other stuff that is attributed to him, also. Check the book, STOLEN VALOR, and see if he's listed

> as an MOH recipient. He's not. I work exposing fake SEALs, mostly, but the database for MOH is as airtight as ours and this guy is [not] on it. Too bad we couldn't have gotten to him before he assumed room temperature. We'll find out what else he lied about. Don't want that stuff on his gravestone.[155]

The other letter-to-the-editor was from a Vietnam veteran who had actually served in Special Forces:

> I regret to inform you that there is no listing for [the deceased] being presented a Medal of Honor during Vietnam. There is no entry for [the deceased] for World War II or Korea either. Since he is not a recipient of the Medal of Honor that casts doubt on the claim of his having been Special Forces also.
>
> The person who wrote the obit also said: "and a first inductee Green Beret." I have no idea what is meant by this. * * * You cannot be inducted into Special Forces; you have to be a volunteer. First for the Army, then for Airborne School, and then for Special Forces. The Medal of Honor is an easy thing to check when someone claims to have been awarded one. You can check at this URL: (http://www.army.mil/cmh-pg/moh1.htm) and the book *Stolen Valor* has a complete list of those who have been awarded the Medal of Honor from the Vietnam War. It should be standard practice for someone in the media to check this out before going to press.[156]

Amen! Imagine the acute embarrassment of the deceased's family if either of these letters had been printed and the bereaved had learned about their "hero's" lies?

Now, imagine a conscientious relative of a deceased Fake Warrior, stuck with the unenviable task of wading through a bureaucratic maze in a quest to uncover the truth:

> When our cousin died . . . funeral arrangements had already been

made by people outside the family. We tried to tell the personal representative and [the funeral home] that our cousin had not been in the military, but no one would listen to the family. They went ahead and had a full military funeral. We were told that he had served as a sniper in the Special Forces during the Vietnam War. They said his work was so top secret that his files were sealed along with his purple heart and they could never be touched. They said the family would never have known about it because he went on such secret missions.

The family was incredulous. His mother was so upset and confused, she didn't know what was happening. We all knew that he hadn't been in the service, but how were we going to prove it. We made a time line of his life. We asked for his DD 214 discharge. They promised to send it, but never did. We talked to the funeral home and [they asked] "why are you so concerned, just drop it."

They said arrangements were made by the VA, so they gave us the Veterans commissioner's number. The commissioner said he didn't have anything to do with it, that why did it matter because it is better to give a military funeral to someone that wasn't in the service than to leave someone out that was in. We didn't agree with that. We called the [state] Military Honors Program to see what the procedure was on military funerals and if they verified if a person was in the military or not. They said they had a form with his claim number on it, so it had to be so. They called back later and said they ran the number and a black screen came up so that meant it was top secret. We then . . . went to various links and learned a lot. Through the Freedom of Information Act, Form 180, we requested information. While waiting for the reply, we contacted [the VFW. They were] very helpful in suggesting what to do to get answers. We received a letter back from the National Personnel Records Center. They had conducted extensive searches of every record source and alternate records and could not come up with any data that our cousin had served in the military. They even checked with the FBI but there was nothing.

I had given them a number that the personal representative had said was his service number. The Records Center said it was a VA file number and to contact them to obtain information from that file. I called the Regional VA office. When they put his name or social security in the computer, nothing would come up. When I gave them the file number, the screen said our cousin's name and San Bruno, CA, October 1961. I called San Bruno, CA. It is a National Cemetery. They don't have files there. I called the VA back and talked to another representative. She wanted to know why I was so concerned about this. She said "drop it, he is dead and gone, so just let it go." She said no one was hurt having a military funeral. I told her I was sorry she didn't understand but we were going to keep searching. I talked to [the VFW] again and [they] said the VA office is required to have the discharge papers on file. I called the [state] Regional VA Office. . . . At last I reached someone who was very helpful. She searched and cross-searched. She even checked with the social security to see if he had ever collected any benefits, but there was nothing. She said she could honestly say he was never in the service and there isn't even a hair of evidence that would make her think otherwise. I told her now that we know for sure he was not in the military that we, the family, [cannot] accept the military marker that the [local] people had requested.

The crisis our country is in now we believe stronger than ever that by honoring those that do not deserve it, we dishonor those who do. I called the Memorial Program Service in Washington, DC and explained the situation. She said the screen did not match the application. She did some extensive searching and said he was not in the military that the marker needed to be returned.

We now know that our cousin must have been a military phony. The tales
he must have told his friends, co-workers and students. Why they wouldn't listen to the family, we'll never know. I don't know what they had to gain, but they would make up stories to go along

> with his. To put closure to this, we had to keep searching until we knew the truth. There were times when the fire would almost go out, but then there would be a flicker of hope. If it hadn't been for [the help from the Phony Buster], we wouldn't have known where to turn, as we kept trying to find someone to listen to our cause. Thank you very much and keep up the good work.[157]

This kind of confusion and embarrassment is all too common. It is easy to understand how gullible family members can be taken in.

But shouldn't the press be held to a higher standard of accountability when they publish someone's alleged military exploits?

> There's only one way to handle this: I am profoundly sorry. The last story published under my byline represented a failure on my part to practice journalism the way I learned it. The story . . . related [a local man's] agonizing experiences in the Marines as a prisoner of war in NorthVietnam [for about two months] until he escaped . . . with a fellow POW. . . who was killed while fleeing.[158]

Why did this reporter take the impostor's letter at face value? Why did the reporter only speak to the so-called hero over the telephone? Why didn't he personally interview the man? Why didn't he independently verify through official sources the impostor's wildly improbable story? Why was he so gullible as to believe that Post Traumatic Stress Disorder had erased the impostor's memory for details? Why, in short, was an experienced journalist taken in by a Fake Warrior?

The answer is as revealing as it is worrisome:

> First, it was easier than having to work hard or to give up the story.I was moved by his saga of deprivation, escape and psychiatric damage. I was inspired by his tale of laborious, if imperfect, recovery. I was flattered by the notion that after 31 years of self-imposed silence, he would have selected me as a person who would read and hear his story and empathize with him. I was

> rendered sleepless by the recurring thought that my older son, spring-break-vacationing this week in Cancun, Mexico, is a year older than [the impostor] was when he endured what he said he endured and suffered what he said he suffered.

But there was more. The reporter, in a disarmingly candid expression of honest introspection, owned up that *"as a non-veteran, and probably guilt-ridden for it, I am a sucker for Vietnam veteran stories."*[159] His apology was satisfactory as far as it went, but it was wholly inadequate as a recognition of the harm his story may have caused.[160]

In contrast, one journalist's *mea culpa* expressly — and honestly — identified the damage caused by her having swallowed and reported a Fake Warrior's story:

> I had insulted the memory and honor of thousands of man and women who did in fact serve in Vietnam and thousands of others who died in the conflict. The magnitude of my error hit me and it hit me hard. I accept full responsibility for . . . the pain it has caused both the veterans and their families, the local community and the family of [the impostor].[161]

Because in all these examples people were hurt, and because pain and injury are unique to each individual, it is not possible to characterize any one story as being 'worse' than any other. But were that possible, the following story must rank near the top. We recount it here in detail.

A Phony Buster received a letter from a woman in the midst of planning her wedding and holding pre-nuptial receptions:

> My name is Jerri.[[162]] I am about to marry a man that might have made up his entire history. I'm getting too many questions about his past.
>
> He told me he was the man who walked off the plane upon returning, kissed the ground. I think that was Life Magazine. He

> was a POW twice in Vietnam. The last time he was one of the last POWs to return. He said he was Navy. Some of the decorations don't match Navy. He said he was part of a group that was part of some kind of shared Navy/Marine division.
>
> I don't know if this make any sense, this is just what I was told. He has a box full of medals and a long list of stories. What I do know is that his name is [John Doe][[163]]. * * * He was in the Navy, that much I do know.
>
> * * * Was he ever a POW, let alone twice? I'm about to marry this man. He's going to move in with me. I shouldn't have these questions, and I'm sorry I do, but if I don't get answers I can't do this. I'm 26, he's 53. there is a possibility that he made it up to "impress" me I suppose, but I have to know one way or the other.

Because the Vietnam POW list is readily available, the Phony Buster immediately responded to Jerri's desperate query, informing her that John Doe had never been a prisoner of war.

Within hours Jerri emailed back, her desperation so intense it's almost palpable:

> There is no mistake? The man I've been involved with made up his Vietnam experience? Made all of it up? No doubt he was never a POW? I believed in him. I am set to marry this man. He made up all the stories he told me? He was never a POW, ever, in Vietnam, not ever? What am I going to do? What do I say to him? I don't know what to say or do.
>
> I wanted you to say it was all true. I was just being overly cautious. I wanted to believe him. I love him. I wanted to believe him. I wanted to so much. What do I do? There can't be a mistake? I've been in love with a man who doesn't exist then? Nothing he told me about Vietnam and what happened after in his life is true? I believed it all. My family took him as their own. Even with the

> age difference, my loved ones, the ones that matter most to me, accepted this man. What do I do now? I'm sorry I just don't know what to say now. I wanted you to tell me I had a wonderful man and he was listed and not to worry. Can't be any mistakes, are you sure he isn't listed?

It was no mistake, as she soon found out for herself.

> I begged him for the truth tonight and he stuck by the story. * * * Lies. All lies and he was never a POW, ever. * * * He told his daughter all the lies too. None of it was true apparently. How he was injured, the scars, the damage done to his knees . . . . all lies. * * * I'm crushed. I can't even tell you how disappointed I am. I can't get beyond being numb right now.
>
> He has until midnight tonight to tell me the truth, if he doesn't I'm going to turn him and his box of fake medals in to anyone who keeps track of these kinds of things. The truth deserves to be told, even if he refuses to do it. He had me believing it all. I feel so stupid. I'm so ashamed I believed him.
>
> I can't tell my family the truth. I can't face them with that. I just will cut ties and he can tell his family what he likes. I'm just crushed. He wasn't the man he said he was. My whole future was changed by a couple of emails. I don't know where to turn now. He spent hours in bed telling me this story and that story and what happened to him, and where this scar was from and that one. Even a St. Christopher's medal that I have worn since he gave it to me. Even the story behind it is a lie if he was never captured. * * * You have no idea the stories he told me. He used them to get me to meet him, and used them to get me into a relationship, and eventually into bed. You have no idea what length this man lied to me.

Jerri was a brave woman whose integrity would not allow her to walk down the aisle with a man she knew to be a complete fraud. But what sets her apart from most people who have been betrayed in this fashion by a loved one is her decision to go public. Because she cared about righting a terrible wrong, because she was driven by a sense of justice, she sought the Phony Buster's advice about how to prevent her impostor boy friend from conning anyone else.

Jerri understood in principle why what had been done to her was so reprehensible:

> The man . . . used the pain of others for his personal gain. Night after night I would listen to him, for hours each day, about his life, about his past. All of it was made up. Much more than just POW status, but that hurts more than anything else. *People died for what he struts around carrying. Men suffered their last moments of life for what he can tell stories about. That is the worst wrong I can think of. . . .*[164]

In her last e-mail Jerri confided to the Phony Buster, adding one more piece of deeply personal information:

> "*I'm pregnant*. I won't allow my son to grow up with a man who has no honor. . . . I can raise this child on my own."[165]

For this woman's sake, for the sake of so many other victims of this egregious form of deceit, Fake Warriors must be stopped.[166]

CHAPTER 4

HOW DO FAKE WARRIORS GET AWAY WITH IT?

"I found my old DD-214 and doctored it up. . . ." [167]

Introduction

So far we've seen the many reasons Fake Warriors engage in their imposture;[168] that the Fake Warrior phenomenon is real, pernicious, and widespread, and that the impostors come from every imaginable strata of contemporary society.[169] We have also seen that their conduct is not a minor social peccadillo, but rather victimizes countless Americans and produces considerable harm.[170]

How does their imposture begin? What sustains the charade? How do Fake Warriors get away with it?

The story of one long-time impostor, now repentant, is typical. It is both revealing, and serves as an introduction to answering the questions above.

> Over the Christmas holiday, I was up in [a Northwestern] state. .

> . . While spending an outing . . . I was approached by a man . . . having seen my Korea veteran cap, he just wanted to "thank me for serving my country." His next routine was to tell me that he too was Air Force, and that he had been a PJ (Rescue Medic) [Air Force pararescuer] and had been a POW in Vietnam for a couple of years. He was very pushy about "proving himself," and showed me the POW license plate on his car . . . and a card saying he was in a "Purple Heart" group. I never saw a man more interested in telling his story, and when I left he had to give me a big hug and introduce me to his wife. From the time I left, I had the feeling this guy wasn't what he said he was. He was trying too hard to tell us things we had no need to know."

This Korean veteran's instincts were good, and when he returned home, he found the impostor's name on P.O.W. Network's website.[171]

Let's call the impostor Richard Davis.[172] The product of an abusive home, Davis was only eleven when he was separated from his mother, step-father, and four sisters, and landed in a state-run juvenile facility. Paroled at age fifteen, young Davis hit the road and hitchhiked around the country.

Two years later, a joy riding charge bought him six months in jail, after which he enlisted in the Air Force and went through basic training. After a short time, his enlistment was found to have been fraudulent. Nor was Davis a high school graduate. He had even lied about the joy riding jail term. Receiving an honorable discharge in the mid-Sixties "for the good of the service," Davis married (twice), began working, did drugs and too much alcohol, had a professional license revoked, had a run-in with the law, and then left the city where he was living and moved to a southern state.

As Davis recounts it:

> I found employment selling cars. One of my co-workers had been a chopper pilot in Viet Nam. He invited me to have a few drinks with him at the local VFW. Prior to this, I had told him I had been in the Air Force. I told him I had been a medic.[[173]] I never said or

implied that I had been to Viet Nam. He assumed I was a Nam vet and asked me to join the VFW.

After going to the club a few times, I was asked by the Commander if I would join as there was a membership drive going on. I told him I had never served overseas or in combat and he said "you wouldn't be the only member that never saw action." I filled out the paperwork and became a member. I was enjoying the camaraderie of the other vets I had met there. * * * I was accepted by the majority at face value and that made it very easy for me to lie about my military record. Never went into much detail with anyone when talking about my made-up military experience. I would just usually listen to the other vets talk. I would on occasion interject some story about food or a funny story or situation that I had heard someone else recount. I never made myself out to be a suffering hero. When asked about my experience as a POW, I would say "it's in the past and it's better left there."

There are two significant points in Davis's account of how he began his imposture. One was the VFW membership drive, which suggests that those responsible for approving applicants were not as scrupulous as they should have been in evaluating Davis's credentials. (We will revisit such institutional shortcomings later in this chapter.) Second, included in the application paperwork that Davis submitted during the post's membership drive, there was no copy of his DD-214 — the official "Armed Forces of the United States Report of Transfer or Discharge." The post didn't require one! If it had, and if Davis's actual DD-214 had been given even the most superficial scrutiny, this official government document would have immediately revealed Davis' imposture. At the very least, the DD-214 would have revealed that he had not been a medic and had never served in Vietnam — let alone that he had been a POW.

Within a year, Davis had moved to a neighboring southern state:

At which time I had given myself a Purple Heart and a Bronze Star. . . . I transferred my membership to [a local] VFW. I was told I would

> have to produce a DD-214 in order to renew my membership the following year. I found my old DD-214 and doctored it up[174] to show that I had served in Viet Nam as well as being awarded two Purple Hearts, the Bronze star and the Airman's Medal!![175] I was really accepted by the guys then. I even started going to the local vet center for group counseling. I never expounded on my "valor" in Vietnam and it was assumed by many that I just didn't want to talk about my experiences. I did listen closely to other vet's stories and picked up many euphemisms used by GIs in Vietnam. I was not only accepted, but even honored by many as having been a true hero.
>
> I had heard that former POWs got free license tags.[176] I found an old letter I had received from the Department of the Air Force, and used the letterhead to write a brief description of my captivity by the North Vietnamese. In essence, it stated that I was a P.J[177] and was attempting to rescue a downed pilot. I submitted the letter as proof to the [state] Department of Motor Vehicles, and received my POW tags.
>
> I was really on a roll then. I used the same letter to become a life member of American Ex-POWs.[178] I was a life member of the Purple Heart society and the Disabled American Veterans. * * * . . . after both sons had gone into the Air Force,[179] I remarried . . . and continued my charade of being a war hero. [We moved to another southern state], where I applied for POW tags and got them. My present wife was employed by the VA in research.
>
> [After another move], I again applied and received POW [automobile license] tags.[180]

There are several significant developments in the story of Davis's ongoing imposture. Although the second VFW post Davis joined, unlike the first, did require a copy of his DD-214, the post apparently didn't bother to scrutinize that document (even though, as we'll see later in this chapter and the next, most falsified DD-214s are easily detected).

Three different state motor vehicle departments didn't do any better. Like the VFW post, they couldn't, or didn't bother to, verify Davis' claim to POW automobile license plates. Why not, when there are readily and publicly available lists of every POW who either escaped, was released early, or was repatriated from Vietnam?[181]

Given all the people to whom Davis submitted his forged Air Force letter (and there were quite a few), why didn't anyone bother to check the letter's authenticity?[182]

It's noteworthy that, according to Davis, no one at either VFW post was ever suspicious of him. As a result, throughout his imposture, Davis admittedly "never felt at risk." You have to be feeling pretty secure to organize three separate chapters of the Military Order of the Purple Heart![183] Davis topped off this feat by using one of the VFWs as a meeting place.

And although a Fake Warrior himself, Davis was by this time so wrapped up in his role-playing that when some braggadocio type showed up at the VFW and falsely claimed to have been a Navy SEAL, Davis, in a fit of righteous anger (not to mention, supreme hypocrisy) denounced him.[184]

How is this possible? How does an impostor who served only a few months in the military — or, for that matter, someone who served longer, or not at all — get away with such an elaborate and sustained charade? Davis's case was an extensive imposture: member of an elite unit, awarded medals for heroism, decorated for war wounds, having been a POW. How do these Fake Warriors fool so many savvy people — authentic veterans, officers, and members of veterans organizations, governmental bodies like the VA, and motor vehicle departments? Where does a Fake Warrior get the hubris to organize and lead *three* chapters of legitimate Purple Heart recipients, or to expose another Fake Warrior? How does an impostor summon the nerve to forge a letter that purports to be from the Air Force, and that attests to his lies?

The answer to these specific questions — and to the more fundamental question raised in this chapter — "How do Fake Warriors get away with it?" — is simple enough. They have help. Let's examine three important — indeed indispensable — ways in which they obtain it.

Props and Falsified Documents

We've seen how Richard Davis purchased Purple Heart and Bronze Star medals at a gun show. Unfortunately, gun shows, flea markets, garage sales, mail-order catalogues, and, sad to say, classified ads in certain military magazines, all facilitate Fake Warrior fraud by carelessly or indifferently providing impostors with convincing props: military awards, decorations and the like to which they are not entitled[185] To make matters worse, the Twenty-first Century has given us the Internet. For a few dollars,[186] a Fake Warrior can adorn himself with an actual Distinguished Service Cross, a Navy Cross, an Air Force Cross, a Silver Star, a Bronze Star, a Purple Heart — or any other medal that strikes his fancy, in whatever quantity he desires.

Even our nation's most hard-earned highest decoration, the Medal of Honor, has been for sale.[187]

Given that the conscienceless purveyors of these unearned medals have no shame, and probably haven't broken any laws, still, they should be condemned by citizens who deplore Fake Warriors who seek to mimic the achievements of our authentic veterans.

Another handy prop is some kind of military automobile license plate. Once again, Richard Davis's experience is a classic example of the ease with which a Fake Warrior can obtain, say, a POW — or even a Medal of Honor — license plate. In Davis' case, 'all' he did was forge a letter; but a forged DD-214 document would have served him just as well. It's too easy to obtain military plates. Virtually every state in America offers some version,[188] whether it pertains to veterans, the combat-wounded (Purple Heart), Disabled American Veteran, or — the two most popular — a POW or Medal of Honor plate.

Every one of these license plates carries with it an explicit aura of honor (and often, other benefits as well).[189]

It is depressing to contemplate the inescapable fact that many thousands of impostors throughout America are driving around with license plates they have no legal or moral right to affix to a doghouse, let alone a car. Who's providing the props that help the Fake Warrior stage his show? It's the bureaucrats: from top brass administrators on down to clerks who issue the plates without first developing, and then implementing, a reliable system of verification.

Richard Davis may have resorted to props, but the essential building block upon which his imposture rested was a falsified DD-214 document:[190]

> I found my old DD-214 and doctored it up. [Not hard to do; Fake Warriors too numerous to count have done the same.] On the DD-214 I cut white strips of paper and pasted them over parts needed to falsify.[[191]] I typed in the needed fillers. I then photo copied.[192]

While our next chapter, "How Can Fake Warriors be Identified and Exposed?" explains in detail how to spot a doctored DD-214 by examining several key information blocks on that document, in Davis's case the blocks he had to doctor on his legitimate DD-214 for his purposes were Numbers 11c (Reason and authority), 22 (Total active service, and foreign or sea service), 23a (Military Occupational Specialty: MOS) and — most important for the game Davis was playing — 24 (Decorations, medals, badges, commendations, citations, and campaign ribbons awarded or authorized).

Why Number 11c? Because the original entry would have shown that Davis had been discharged, not after completing his enlistment obligation, but rather, "for the good of the service." Number 22, if left unchanged, would have revealed that Davis had served only a few months, not years. Number 23a would *not* have shown an Air Rescue or Para-Jumper Air Force Specialty Code. Number 24 certainly would not have credited him with receiving a Purple Heart and a Bronze Star.

Related to this problem of doctored DD-214s is the phenomenon of falsified resumes, sometimes referred to as "CVs." If, for whatever reason (fear of prosecution, for example), a Fake Warrior — unlike Davis — is unwilling to actually falsify his DD-214, he will often opt to create a phony CV.

To illustrate how this deception works, here's a typical case.[193] The impostor's authentic DD-214 reveals that he was an enlisted (Block 19) military policeman (Block 25), who had never served in Vietnam (Block 30), and had never been wounded or received any medals for valor (Block 24). These facts are confirmed by the official report from the National Archives and Records Administration that reflects the Fake Warrior's actual military service. Yet, our impostor's employment resume falsely self-describes him as follows: "United States Army — Vietnam Vet. Fifth Special Forces Group, 101st Airborne Rangers, Honorably Discharged as First Lieutenant, Received military decorations for valor, bravery, and conduct, including: 2 Bronze Stars, the Distinguished Service Cross, 3 Purple Hearts."

Forged DD-214s and falsified resumes are only two of the props that impostors use to make their imposture work.

Fake Warrior POWs further *their* imposture with phony ID from — of all places — the VA. A Fake Warrior in Denver — who was 'outed' by Mike McGrath — had posed as a former POW and Army Special Forces master sergeant, and was the proud possessor of an identification card from the VA with the letters POW stamped on it.[194] Some clerk at the VA had simply accepted the impostor's word that he was a former POW. Either that or the clerk had been duped by false documentation. However it happened, the VA should take the heat for not having in place adequate verification procedures.[195]

Institutional/Official Indifference and Connivance

We have seen how Davis, a quintessential impostor, had the hubris to organize no less than three chapters of the Military Order of the Purple Heart. Was it hard to pull this off? Not at all.

> I contacted national MOPH and they sent a charter package[s].

> That, with seven Purple Heart recipients, I had a new MOPH chapter. I was never concerned about being found out."[196]

The complicity of private and official organizations in the Fake Warrior's imposture can only be described as a scandal within a scandal.[197] Given the scope of the Fake Warrior phenomenon, which is scandalous enough, the spectacle of veterans' organizations aiding and abetting imposture is nothing short of outrageous.

A case in point:

> This braggart strolls into the [VFW] bar wearing every medal/award the Navy ever issued, from the Navy Cross down. He had his name engraved on a brass plaque and hung on the wall as a Vietnam POW. When questioned about his "background," he says he was CIA and his medal and POW status were secret. What's worse, he's a big spender, always buying rounds of beer for whoever listens, so no one questions him. I've questioned the Post Commander about this guy, and asked him to check the books. Nothing is being done, it's like he's untouchable. I was even informed that your [P.O.W. Network] list is inconclusive, so "he could be telling the truth." This was said to placate me, I'm sure.[198]

Unfortunately, this kind of indifference, often complicity, by local VFW leadership is more typical than not. Among Phony Busters, it is well known that many VFW posts are either unconcerned about Fake Warriors in their midst, or worse, complicit in their imposture. Lest anyone think this indictment is too harsh, consider that lists of returned Vietnam POWs are, and have always been, easily accessible.[199] It is a post commander's obligation to regularly consult such lists. Blowhard "big spenders" like the one mentioned above are commonplace, and should arouse instant suspicion on the part of a conscientious post commander. Phony Busters have informed state, and even national, VFW leaders of the identities of impostors in their ranks, and still nothing was done.[200]

Here's an example of an unsatisfactory response: A Phony Buster informed a state VFW headquarters about an impostor. As soon as she had publicized her information, angry e-mails began to pour into headquarters. The VFW's head-in-the-sand response? It shut down its e-mail and thus avoided having to deal with the complaints.[201]

While some local VFW posts have been vigilant in exposing and expelling Fake Warriors, an astounding number of others have not. The worst travesty, by far, is that the national organization shows little, if any, inclination to weed out impostors in its midst, despite a public posture that pays lip service to identifying and exposing Fake Warriors.

Take the case of the commander of American Legion, VFW, and AMVETS posts in the Pacific Northwest. The man claimed to have been a SEAL, and accordingly he led parades, wore "the Navy Cross, two silver stars, two Bronze Star Medals, and rows of other Vietnam combat decorations." His claims ranged from having been shot eleven times to, at one time, having a "half pound of shrapnel and bullets" removed from his body. The commander turned out to be an impostor and, according to Burkett and Whitley, *the American Legion post nonetheless allowed this Fake Warrior to retain his membership.* "We don't care whether our members tell war stories or not," the authors of *Stolen Valor* quoted one legionnaire as saying.[202]

A major part of the problem of impostors in veterans' organizations, generally, is two-fold. As with the Vietnam Veterans of America, membership application data is self-generated. In addition, it is not independently verified. Even in those organizations where an applicant's DD-214 is required, the applicant himself submits the document, which is usually taken at face value.[203]

Once again, the case of Richard Davis proves the shortsightedness of that process — or more precisely, the lack of process.

A survey several years ago[204] showed that there were twenty-two Vietnam POWs on the membership rolls of the Vietnam Veterans of America — *of which only nine were bona fide.* When confronted with this mind-blowing revelation, the national organization did nothing to purge the thirteen impostors, even though the official list of Vietnam POWs was readily available.[205]

In the face of such transparent dereliction of duty, a national organization such as the Vietnam Veterans of America is fair game for speculation as to its motives.

Let's consider one possibility. Putting aside the supposedly righteous attitude — "Let he who is without sin cast the first stone" — what may be happening is a modern version of the fox guarding the chicken coop. There are so many impostors of one kind or another in these organizations that often an officer to whom a complaint is made may be a Fake Warrior himself.[206] Burkett and Whitley report that in the case of the Pacific Northwest three-organization commander referred to above, "A local marine said he met [the impostor] in Vietnam in 1966, when the SEAL 'swam into my post.' When a reporter questioned [the commander-impostor's] story about being shot eleven times and being awarded numerous Purple Hearts, another vet, *also an impostor*, actually defended him . . . ."[207]

At a VFW post in Nevada, one member disputed the POW claim of another, asserting in turn that *he* was the real POW. No proof was produced of the latter claimant ever having been a POW, either — and he, too, turned out to be an impostor! To compound this multiple masquerade, an officer at the same post — an alleged recipient of the Medal of Honor — expressed a willingness to "uncover" the impostors there. This was before he, himself, was uncovered as an impostor.[208]

The sought-to-be-placated VFW member quoted above was able to obtain the POW license plate number of the "big spender." A Phony Buster thereafter informed the state's Department of Motor Vehicles. No action was taken.

In sum, numerous complaints by Phony Busters and others — veterans and non-veterans alike — to the FBI, the Office of Special Investigations, the Office of Naval Intelligence, the Criminal Investigation Division, United States Attorneys, and other investigative and prosecutorial authorities, have been shrugged off. While the Department of Veterans Affairs has sometimes prosecuted cases of Fake Warrior *financial* fraud,[209] its Office of the Inspector General, for the most part, has been indifferent to reported incidents of false claims. Over and over again, Phony Buster calls to the VA "hotline" have received either a cold reception, or none at all.[210] Exposure of a Fake Warrior, even when it occurs, is seldom penalized. Punishment, when it is rarely meted out, is of the slap-on-the-wrist variety, so the opportunity for meaningful deterrence is lost. And no matter how egregious their lies and impostures, Fake Warriors are either not removed by their organization, or, if expelled, they are often later reinstated.

Enablers

To *enable*, in common usage, is to "provide with means, opportunity, power, or authority (to *do* something)."[211] A thesaurus provides these synonyms, among others: assister, abettor, collaborator, ally, facilitator, right-hand man (or woman).

An enabler of a Fake Warrior is someone who either strongly suspects, knows for a fact, or ignores obvious signs, that the person in question is an impostor. Faced with the choice of exposing that person, making excuses, or blithely pursuing one's own agenda, the enabler invariably covers up for the Fake Warrior. The roster of enablers is long: lovers, spouses, children, parents, siblings, employers, prosecutors, reporters, even authentic veterans.

Chapter 3's auto-buying Korean vet strongly suspected the salesman was an impostor, but didn't call him on it. A prosecutor allowed a lying judge to resign, but didn't indict him. The lonely woman who allowed herself to be conned — not once, but twice — didn't turn in the lothario truck driver. The family of a deceased saloonkeeper indulged his fantasies — and possibly theirs — for years. Mike Wallace indulged his bleeding heart and, without doing his homework, facilitated an incarcerated murderer's release from prison. At least one of Richard Davis's wives admitted she had misgivings about her husband's improbably heroic stories, but she never pressed him for the truth. Law enforcement agencies — state and federal — have been inexcusably indifferent. Veterans' organizations make not accusations, but excuses.

A Fake Warrior's stepdaughter exemplifies the rationalizations that enablers invariably fall back on:

> Even if my stepfather were to admit to me tomorrow that he had lied about this [being a POW] a million times, it would not change my love for him. I would not think any less of him as a man or as a soldier; * * * When I was three and my father passed away, my stepfather took me in and gave me unconditional love — and I will give him the same.[212]

This attitude conveys a not uncommon *refusal to judge.* What does such passivity *necessarily* entail? In a word, collaboration. No matter what the reason, no matter how much it may be rooted in loyalty, an enabler is a willing party to fraud.

While the stepdaughter may have some excuse for her ill-conceived "unconditional love" for a Fake Warrior, what follows has to qualify as an especially egregious example of enabling — two, as a matter of fact:

> Your [P.O.W. Network] web site is a breath of fresh air. I ran across it when searching for information about Vietnam veteran wannabes. We lost my Brother-in-law last September 24th due to circulation problems in both his legs (which were amputated — one above the knee and one below the knee). He was a member of the local ... VFW .... He even served one year as the Post Commander ....
>
> Since *I am an in-country Vietnam veteran* (I served on a light cargo ship that delivered ammunition and supplies along the rivers of the Mekong Delta in 1970-1971) . . . I began to be suspicious of his stories about his ship, USS Lexington (CV-16), having been in Vietnam during his service in the US Navy from 1961 to 1965. From their web site I gather the Lexington was in Pensacola, Florida, since December 1963 to stay until it became a training ship in Corpus Christi, Texas, a few years later.

I don't believe he was a Vietnam veteran at all. There is a slim chance that since his ship was in Japan for a short time, he may have been in the "theatre" of Vietnam, but since they had no connection with the Vietnam conflict he wouldn't have earned a Vietnam Service Medal (which is required to join the VFW?).

In the last few years of his life, he was claiming to have been a Navy SEAL in Vietnam. Of course he told everyone that he couldn't say much about it because the missions were "top secret."

At his funeral this past September, the Post Commander made a speech about how [the deceased] had served in perhaps the most difficult and dangerous branch of the service — the Navy SEALs! Then a couple of uniformed men marched up to his casket and attached a sticker to it making him an honorary member of some Special Forces group!

Now that he is dead and buried, I thought the farce was over and done with.

Not so!

My wife and I visited his grave this past weekend (her Father is buried in the same cemetery) and on the military grave marker attached to the back of his gravestone is the word VIETNAM and on the bottom it says NAVY SEAL!

I believe what happened is his widow sent in a copy of his DD214 to have the marker made and the marker was made according to what the DD214 said. Obviously it had been altered!

Shortly after his death, she told another brother-in-law and her mother-in-law that [the deceased] had never been a Navy SEAL. Because of his health and his position in the local VFW *she didn't want to make waves.*

> I am extremely offended that the grave marker is wrong! Don't the people at the VA verify the information they put on the marker? They only ask for a "copy" of the DD214 not even a "certified copy". How can I get this corrected? This little white lie has now compromised the integrity of the very graveyard where his Father (also my wife's Father) is buried! Am I to resign to the fact that possibly all other military markers are fake? Are the American flags flying next to the graves of those who served their country put there without verification that the deceased actually served?
>
> Here's the information about my Brother-in-law [name, social security number, date of birth] . . . . As a VFW member yourself (I have never joined a veteran's organization), can you forward this information to the proper authorities? *As the Brother-in-law, I am in a very sensitive position and cannot openly pursue the remedy to this situation.*[213]

What's wrong with this picture?

Plenty. The 'in-country' Vietnam veteran brother-in-law had a moral responsibility to blow the whistle on his relative as soon as he learned of the imposture. Although he admits the SEAL story was a "farce," and claims he was "extremely offended" by his relative's charade, he minimizes the imposture by characterizing it as "this little white lie." *Much worse is his having passed the buck to P.O.W. Network*, instead of taking it upon himself to expose his Fake Warrior brother-in-law. ("As the Brother-in-law, I am in a very sensitive position . . . .") His apparent outrage at now having to be skeptical about a cemetery's military markers is hypocritical because, like other people who shirk their responsibility to the truth, this man, who knew better, opted out.

As to the widow who admitted her husband had been a fake, but "didn't want to make waves," she apparently had no qualms about sending in a forged DD-214 in order to obtain a military marker for her Fake Warrior husband's grave.

The previous chapters underscore how essential it is that these Fake Warriors be identified, so they can be exposed and punished.

How to identify them is the subject of the next chapter.

CHAPTER 5

HOW CAN FAKE WARRIORS BE IDENTIFIED AND EXPOSED?

"Please tell me how I can find out if the story I'm being told is true. I desperately need to know if my fiancé . . .is what he claims to be." [214]

IDENTIFYING FAKE WARRIORS

Introduction

We've seen that Fake Warriors who actually served in the military come from every branch, every specialty and every rank. Those who have not, come from every civilian profession, trade, and occupation. We've also seen that there are at least four recurring themes in the lies of an impostor:

- Membership in elite units that engaged in covert operations;
- Inability to provide records that allegedly were destroyed or remain classified;
- Capture by the enemy and subsequent escape; and

- Award of medals for valor and other meritorious service.

Ironically, the same tapestry of lies Fake Warriors typically weave can, simultaneously, entrap them and lead to their being eventually identified, ultimately exposed and, hopefully, punished.

Let's begin with facts *common to everyone who ever served in the United States military.*

Everyone possessed a serial number. During the Korean War Era, Army serial numbers were prefixed with RA for regular army, ER for enlisted reservists, US for draftees, NG for National Guard, and O for officers. In July 1969, both the Army and the Air Force switched to social security numbers. The Navy and Marine Corps followed suit in July 1972. Since every *legitimate* veteran has had a serial number of one kind or another, anyone claiming to be a veteran who cannot produce one is *ipso facto* an impostor.[215]

Another fast, virtually foolproof way to ascertain whether someone served in the United States military since Vietnam — and to obtain other relevant information — is through a Freedom of Information Act (FOIA) request. Most people are unaware that *the records of all discharged Vietnam War military personnel who have no current service obligations are archived at the National Personnel Records Center*, Military Records, 9700 Page Avenue, St. Louis, MO 63132-5100. (See Appendix A for information about, and how to use, Form 180 to obtain a suspected Fake Warrior's military records — if any exist.)

While waiting for the records from the National Personnel Records Center, here are some basic questions to ask a suspected impostor:[216]

- What is his full name, date of birth, and social security number — verified by his driver license or other legal document?
- When and where did he enter the service?
- When and where did he receive basic training?

- What advanced training did he receive, where, and for how long?
- What military occupational specialty (MOS) did he receive?
- What other MOSs did he have during his military service?
- Where was he stationed, when, and for how long?
- Who was his commanding officer?
- What duty did he perform, where, and for how long?
- What was his rank, and when was he promoted?
- When and where was he discharged, and at what rank?
- What medals, decorations, and/or other awards did he receive?
- Who awarded them, when, and where?
- What documentation of all aspects of his service does he possess?
- Who can verify any or all of his answers?[217]

A person who never served in the United States military will be unable to satisfactorily answer most, if not all, of the above questions. An impostor who *has* been in the service won't fare much better. The farther you get down the list of questions, the more an impostor will resort to fuzzy answers, if he answers at all.

Many impostors believe the old saw about the best defense being a good offense — so anticipate belligerence. Another thinly disguised refuge for an imposter to hide behind is the old 'I-was-a-spook' veil. If you run up against this, it's almost certain that you're dealing with a Fake Warrior.

Don't feel insecure about asking these questions because you're a layperson who hasn't served. Even though you may lack military knowledge or experience and have difficulty evaluating some of the answers, you can count on a certain percentage of those answers being inconsistent, or at variance with common knowledge and common sense.[218]

Someone who claims he was drafted for three years, when most people know or can easily ascertain that during the Korea and Vietnam eras draftees served only two years, is a transparent liar even to the uninitiated.

When a suspected impostor sounds off about more esoteric activities allegedly carried out in a highly specialized branch of the service, a lay person can get at the truth through asking the right questions that can be answered with easily ascertainable facts.

The following sections provide questions designed to unmask Fake Warrior POWs, SEALs, LRRPs/LRPs/Rangers, Special Forces members, SOG operatives, Force Recon Marines, Air Commandos, Pararescuemen, CIA agents, snipers, Medal of Honor awardees and recipients of the Army Distinguished Service Cross, Navy Cross and Air Force Cross.

Prisoner of War

Since a favorite claim of impostors is that they were prisoners of war in Vietnam, it helps to know exactly how "prisoner of war" is defined under United States law. Title 10 of the United States Code, Section 1128 provides:

> [A] prisoner-of-war medal [shall be issued] to any person who, while serving in any capacity with the armed forces, was taken prisoner and held captive — (1) while engaged in an action against an enemy of the United States; [or] (2) while engaged in military operations involving conflict with an opposing foreign force . . . .[219]

A further POW definition, applicable to benefit claims arising out of the Vietnam War, provides:

> [T]he term "prisoner of war" means any regularly appointed, enrolled, enlisted, or inducted member of the Armed Forces of

> the United States who was held as a prisoner of war for any period of time during the Vietnam conflict by any force hostile to the United States . . . .[220]

During the Vietnam War, for example, captured Americans who returned to United States control fell into three distinct categories:

1. Those captured who later escaped, successfully returning to United States control.[221]

- Those captured who did not escape, but who were released and returned to United States control prior to 1973.[222]

- Those captured who did not escape, and who were repatriated to United States control in 1973 as part of Operation Homecoming.[223]

These three categories are important to understand in ascertaining whether an alleged prisoner of war is an impostor. They're good preparation for the next step: asking questions that pertain directly to his alleged special status.

Before we get to those questions, first ask yourself this: Why is a false claim to POW status especially odious? Then take a moment to make real what legitimate Vietnam War POWs were forced to endure. As Mike McGrath, former POW and ex-president of NAM-POW, has explained it:

> The way we lived in the hell-holes of the Vietnamese prisons is so unimaginable to the average American that words alone are not sufficient to convey the experience. When we returned to the United States, we used the words *shackles, stocks, manacles* and *irons;* yet many Americans could not, or would not, picture what the words meant. * * *
>
> In trying to review my life as a POW, I notice that my drawings are too *soft*; I was unable to portray the actual *hardness* of the conditions we lived under — the dimly lit rooms and

> claustrophobia-inducing cells; the lack of adequate food which, combined with filth, caused disease and indescribable discomfort.
>
> It is difficult to sketch a vitamin and protein deficiency that results in beri-beri; and no picture can convey the impact of constant plagues of lice, heat rash, biting bed bugs, mosquitoes, cockroaches, and rats. Add to this the hostility and brutality of the guards, who had been taught from childhood to hate Americans, and the sum total is an unbelievable existence for hundreds of American fighting men who somehow survived the ordeal."[224]

Captain McGrath, not surprisingly, has been in the forefront of efforts to identify, expose, and punish Fake Warriors who claim to have been prisoners of war. He wrote this in 2002:

> From time to time we receive requests to confirm details of a story told by some person who claims to have been a prisoner of war (POW) during the conflict in Southeast Asia. False POW stories are not uncommon. *Armed with the following information, most persons should be able to determine whether a POW story is true or false.* * * * The Defense Prisoner of War and Missing Personnel Office (DPMO) is the custodian of the official list of Americans who were prisoners of war . . . during the conflict in Southeast Asia. * * * If a person who claims to have been a POW, but is not listed, believes the DPMO's list is incomplete, you might wish to invite the claimant to answer [certain]questions . . . so you can substantiate his claim to having been a POW and help him gain official DOD recognition of his POW status. *Our experience consistently shows that pretenders will give fuzzy, incomplete, and dishonest answers.* * * * Phony POW claimants will refuse to give details that can be verified. They will equivocate and feign anger that you don't believe them. They will claim CIA affiliation and claim that their mission is still classified; therefore, they are unable to give you details. That's stuff for James Bond movies, not for the truth. * * *

* * *

[The] Defense Prisoner of War and Missing Personnel Office's (DPMO) web page is at: (www.dtic.mil/dpmo/) * * * Anyone who wishes to contact DPMO to confirm that a person is or is not listed in the PMSEA should contact the DPMO Personnel Affairs Officer: Mr. Larry Greer
OASD International Security Affairs, Defense POW/Missing Personnel Affairs, 2400 Defense Pentagon, Washington, DC 20301-2400. Telephone (703) 602-2102 X169. Email: (greerl@osd.pentagon.mil).[225]

Now that Mr. Greer has retired, the fastest ways to identify an impostor are either to contact Major Carie Parker (carie.parker@osd.pentagon.mil; (703) 699-1169), or by consulting Appendix B (Official list of U.S. civilian and military prisoners of war who escaped captivity during the Vietnam War), Appendix C (Official list of all U.S. civilian and selected foreign national prisoners of war who escaped during, who were released during, and who were repatriated at the conclusion of the Vietnam War, and Appendix D (Combined list of all military prisoners of war who escaped during, who were released during, and who were repatriated at the conclusion of, the Vietnam War) for the name of every American who was a legitimate POW in Southeast Asia. American *military* prisoners numbered 662 — including escapees and non-escapees. (Appendix D provides their names, status, capture dates, places of capture, and release dates.)

As for some of the more transparent POW dodges Fake Warriors resort to, Mike McGrath has written:

> Persons who falsely claim to be former POWs typically try to avoid providing specific details about their claimed captivity by hiding behind claims that they were captured while on a mission that is still classified.
> The 'I can't compromise classified information,' ploy is phony. There are no classified missions or details. The war has been over for [many] years. CIA cover stories always fall apart when examined. We are free to talk about any mission or experience that happened. 'The fire at St. Louis [records center] destroyed my records' ploy is not valid, either. *The fire destroyed records of many Korean War veterans and some WW II veterans, but not the*

> *records of Vietnam War veterans.* Many phony POW claimants say they have Post-Traumatic Stress Disorder (PTSD) and they use this as an excuse as to why they can't remember the details to the questions you are asking. Don't believe them. It is a common ruse. A real PTSD diagnosis is rare. Ask to see his VA medical record which documents his claim to PTSD. While you are at it, ask to see his VA medical identity card. POWs have the following statement stamped on the front, directly under the ID photo: *Service Connected POW.* This statement applies to all POWS from WW II, Korea, Vietnam, and other conflicts. If it's not there, he is not considered a POW. Some phonies have claimed to have been negotiated out of prison by Dr. Henry Kissinger who they claim paid a ransom in gold [!]. Another common feature of false POW stories is a claim to have been freed in a dramatic rescue by US Navy Seals, Army Rangers, Special Forces, or other elite units.[226]

When an alleged POW is suspected of using the "I'm-not-on-the-list-for-a-good-reason" dodge, the first question to ask is whether he wants the mistake corrected and his POW status officially recognized. What legitimate POW wouldn't? If your suspected impostor declines, the reason is obvious.[227]

If your man continues to insist he was a POW, and if you feel the need for even more proof — especially if you want to be one-hundred-percent sure of your facts before you publicly expose him — press him about whether he's a Category 2 (early release) or Category 3 (Operation Homecoming repatriate), and if he answers in the affirmative to *either,* ask him the following questions:

- What was his unit when he was captured?
- Where was it located?
- What duties was he performing?
- Who was his commanding officer?
- Who were members of his unit?
- Who else was on the mission?

- Was he flying an aircraft when captured?
- What aircraft was he flying when captured?
- What base or carrier did he fly from?
- When, where, and under what circumstances was he captured?
- Who was captured with him?
- When, where, and under what circumstances was he incarcerated?
- Who was incarcerated with him?
- When, where, and under what circumstances was he freed?
- Who was freed with him?
- When, how, and from where did he leave North or South Vietnam?
- What were the circumstances of his departure?
- What was his first stop?
- What occurred at that place?
- What was his next stop?
- What occurred at that place?
- What were other stops?
- What occurred at those places?
- When, where, and under what circumstances was he debriefed?
- Who debriefed him?
- When, where, and under what circumstances was he treated medically in follow-up programs for POWs?
- What medal was he awarded for his POW status?
- When, where, by whom, and under what circumstances was

it awarded?

- What is the description of those decorations?
- What documentation of his POW status, release, and awards does he have?
- What documentation does he possess of POW-related retirement or disability?[228]

If you're dealing with a Category 1 claimant who insists he was captured and then escaped, ask him the same questions you would have asked a Category 2 or Category 3 claimant. Then add these:

- When, where, and under what circumstances did he escape, and who escaped with him?
- When, where, and under what circumstances did he return to United States control?

Needless to say, when the alleged POW either won't answer or begs off with such lame excuses as "I forgot," or "it's still classified," this should confirm your suspicion that you have a Fake Warrior on your hands.[229]

<u>SEAL</u>

Among America's unconventional warfare operatives in the Vietnam War, as today, were the Navy SEALs. Their activities included gathering intelligence from sources and locations that were, at best, extremely problematic; conducting raids and ambushes against enemy regular and irregular forces; attempting prisoner of war rescues; "liberating" indigenous people who might provide United States forces with valuable intelligence; and sometimes, although rarely, "terminating with extreme prejudice" individuals whose activities were inimical to American interests.

Given the recent publicity about SEALs — killing Somali pirates at sea, liquidating Osama bin Laden, starring in the recent movie *Act of Valor*, and the public's ongoing exposure to war films and television documentaries about war heroes, with all the attendant glamour attached to heroic exploits — it's no wonder that masquerading as a SEAL is near the top of Fake Warrior impostures. In 2002, former Navy SEAL Steve Robinson authored a book about SEAL imposters entitled *No Guts, No Glory — Unmasking Navy SEAL Impostors.*[230] It documents scores of stories of imposter SEALs, some of whom have the temerity to claim they were drafted into that elite force.

Rubbish!

What many impostors don't know, however, is that *at no time, including the Vietnam War period and since, was any man*[231] *forced to become a SEAL.* The program has always been completely voluntary. All SEALs were in the program because they chose to be, and could withdraw at any time after completing the active duty service requirements of their training contracts.[232]

We asked former Vietnam SEAL Larry Bailey what qualities were sought in a prospective SEAL. Bailey's reply:

> Well, we basically look[ed] for the indefinable quality we refer to as "fire in the gut." That's another way of saying that you've got to want to be a SEAL more than anything in the world – more than ANYTHING, at least at the time you're in training.[233]

SEAL training — which is so specialized that it's difficult to lie about — is comprehensive, lengthy, and rigorous. Currently, it takes two and a half years of training before a man is fully credentialed as a SEAL and ready for his first deployment. Moreover, the timing of certain courses, as well as geographical considerations, create pitfalls for any impostor claiming to have been a SEAL. During the early Vietnam War era, for example, anyone with SEAL aspirations first had to graduate from Underwater Demolition Team/Replacement training (UDT/R).

The Basic Underwater Demolition/SEAL (BUD/S) course consists of three phases. The First Phase, physical training, culminates in 'Hell Week'. The Second Phase consists of dive training, including open, semi-solid, and closed circuit SCUBA training. Third Phase is land warfare training.

Until early 1971, there were BUD/S Training locations on both the East and West Coasts. On the East Coast, BUD/S Training was at Little Creek, Virginia, and SCUBA Training at Key West, Florida, at the Underwater Swimmers School. The last phase of training *prior* to the SCUBA phase took place at Roosevelt Roads Naval Station in Puerto Rico. On the West Coast, UDT/R, later BUD/S, Training was conducted at Coronado, California. Portions of the land warfare phase were conducted on San Clemente Island — one of the Channel Islands off Long Beach, California. Parachute training for *both coasts* was at Fort Benning, Georgia.[234] After BUD/S Training, the men who were assigned to *either* SEAL Team One (West Coast) or SEAL Team Two (East Coast) went through extensive additional and specialized training with their respective teams.[235]

While participating in that supplemental SEAL training, a six-month probationary period began during which candidates had to qualify in additional skills before they could become a full-fledged SEAL. This probationary period culminated in a Peer Review wherein senior SEAL NCOs and Officers evaluated each man's suitability — mentally and physically — for SEAL duties. An evaluation of unsuitability would result in a man being 'washed out' and sent back to the regular Navy fleet to resume his regular non-SEAL Navy duties. This creates a potential problem in identifying a Fake Warrior who claims to have been a SEAL. Phony Busters like Steve Waterman sometime run across men who did in fact graduate from BUD/S, but who, for one reason or another, never became SEALs. This initial BUD/S training, however, provides an impostor with authentic knowledge about *some* SEAL training, which understandably, can mislead people. According to Waterman, these Fake Warriors are the most difficult to identify.[236]

Difficult, but not impossible.

Here are some important questions that should be put to anyone claiming to have been a SEAL:[237]

- Who was his swim buddy?

- Where did he train and what was his class number?
- How many classmates trained with him?
- How many classmates can he name?
- Where and when did he graduate?
- How many classmates graduated with him?
- When, where, and under what circumstances was he authorized to wear the Trident insignia?
- What SEAL Teams did he serve with, where, and for how long?
- Who were the commanding officers of each of his teams?
- How many team members can he name?
- What activities did he perform in each team, where, and for how long?
- What decorations was he awarded for his SEAL service?
- When, where, by whom, and under what circumstances were they awarded?
- What is the description of those decorations?
- What documentation does he possess to support those decorations?

Just as with an impostor POW, when an alleged SEAL fails or refuses to answer these questions — either because he 'forgot', or the answers are still 'classified', or for any other equally transparent reason — you'll know your suspicions about his being a Fake Warrior are justified.[238]

Apart from the above Q & A, an indirect yet certain way to determine if someone who claims to have been a SEAL is telling the truth is to visit one of the many Internet 'watchdog' websites that specialize in dealing with military imposters.[239]

There are a number of such websites online, and they have a very delicate task to perform.[240] Almost all are staffed by unpaid volunteers (and staff turnover is a regular occurrence). Most of the websites offer their services at no cost, and without supporting income they're subject to the financial stress experienced by all volunteer organizations).[241]

However, there is an important caveat concerning the identification of a real SEAL by name — a very ticklish point for all unofficial SEAL verifiers. Steve Robinson, for example, never volunteers names, but if he receives an inquiry which includes a name and the details offered by someone who has claimed to be a SEAL, he immediately checks the SEAL Database. If that man's name does *not* appear, Robinson sends a formal response letter which (1) states that the man's name is not listed, (2) contains caveats related to the possibility of the man in question having obtained a legal name change, and (3) restates his unofficial status and urges the inquirer to contact the NSWC directly in order to obtain an official statement from the Navy.

If the man's name *is* listed in the SEAL Database, and he is shown as successfully graduating from training *within the last decade*, then Robinson presumes that the man may still be serving in harm's way. Not wishing to violate operational or personal security, he sends a response that (1) emphatically states his unofficial status, (2) cautiously notes there may be a possible match in the historical SEAL database for the name they've provided, but that an official statement from the NSWC is required, and (3) specifically directs the inquirer to contact the NSWC Public Affairs Office to obtain it.

On the other hand, if the man's name is listed in the SEAL database and he graduated from training *more than a decade in the past*, Robinson is comfortable offering a simple response to that effect, but that any further information regarding his service will have to come directly from the SEAL himself.

One military watchdog website — that dealt exclusively with exposing SEAL imposters until it closed up shop in late 2005 — was the AUTHENTISEAL organization, staffed entirely by former Navy SEALs. Their website contained a verification request questionnaire. Just how efficacious it can be to use such a form was demonstrated in a criminal case involving a man who claimed to have been a Vietnam SEAL and a POW. According to him, the defendant shot at him. A California lawyer — whose client was facing a charge of attempted murder — took it upon himself to test the credibility of the alleged victim by filling out the AUTHENTISEAL questionnaire:

> Subject: [Name supplied].
> Claims: POW in Saigon 1962-65
> Comments: [Subject's social security number and birth date provided]. Subject claims that he was in one of 11 two man teams incursion into Vietnam and was captured 1962 and placed into "Saigon Hilton" and was liberated by 101st Airborne in 1965, month unknown. Subject claims that he was POW for 2½ years. Subject claims that the NVA contact was a double agent. Subject has right forearm tattoo "Born to Raise Hell" as standard for all SEAL Team members. This was in interview today. He has claimed that my client shot at him. My client is charged with attempted murder. I am photographing subject tomorrow. Our next court date is July 17, 2002 at Tuolumme Criminal Superior Court, Sonora, CA.
> Interest: My client is facing 15 years in prison for false claim by Sub[ject].
> City: Sonora
> State: CA
> Date of claim: June 8, 2002
> Age: 59
> Date of service: 1962-1965
> Height: 6'2"
> Weight: 237
> Hair: Gray
> Eyes: Blue
> Relation: subject of investigation
> Source phone: XXX-XXX-XXXX
> Best time to call: 7 days- 8:00AM-8:00PM PST
> Anonymous: no

> Picture: yes

The AUTHENTISEAL website was set up in such a way that if the answer to the questionnaire uses the terms *prisoner* or *POW*, a copy of that answer is automatically sent to P.O.W. Network. That's what happened in this case. Almost immediately, the defendant's lawyer received two responses.

Mary Schantag of P.O.W. Network wrote:

> Would suggest that you attempt to get a copy of [subject's] military record as soon as possible. *He has committed perjury if the statements were made under oath.* You can usually use an FOIA to get records within 30 days. Police may be able to get them sooner.
>
> As for his POW statements: The HILTON was in HANOI [not Saigon]. There were NO, repeat NO liberations of ANY POWs in a planned rescue.
>
> He is not noted on dozens of data bases noting Prisoners of War, those missing, declared AWOL [absent without official leave], held hostage, detained, or killed and their bodies NOT recovered. The Pentagon can further confirm OUR statements for you. Just call Larry Greer, 703602-2102 ext 169. The court must be made aware of his lies.[242]

Within thirty minutes of Mary Schantag's e-mail to the lawyer, a former member of SEAL Team ONE in 1971–1973 also responded with his own forceful e-mail.[243]

> Thanks for checking with us — we greatly appreciate your interest in upholding the honor of the US Navy SEAL Teams, and your search for the TRUTH.
>
> If the name you provided was spelled accurately, we do NOT have a listing in our database for anyone [with the subject's name]. In

fact we do not have ANYONE with that last name, or anything even close in spelling or pronunciation, in our entire database of nearly 10,000 names!

Unless he has undertaken a legal name change since his claimed service with the SEAL Teams, I can state conclusively that [subject] has NEVER completed SEAL training, and he is not now, nor was he ever a Navy SEAL.

[Subject's] claims regarding SEAL Team actions in Vietnam are completely fictional and bear absolutely no similarity to the actual operating procedures and tactics used by the US Navy SEALs during the Vietnam conflict. The only "two man teams" ever fielded by the SEALs in that conflict were serving as advisors for the Provincial Reconnaissance Units (PRU), and for the American-trained Vietnamese SEALs, the LDNN.

There have never (NEVER!) been any SEALs caught, captured, detained, or held as POWs . . . EVER!

* * *

I checked the list of American POWs surviving the Vietnam conflict and [Subject] is NOT listed among them! A copy of this message, with your original report attached, is being forwarded to the POW Network. I am certain they will not only confirm the information I have given you, but will request such additional information as will permit them to positively identify [subject] for the purpose of publicly exposing his fraudulent POW claims.

It is quite common for those making fraudulent SEAL claims — especially claims involving extraordinary combat heroics — to cite a "secret" training class or "secret mission" as an explanation for the lack of military documentation to back up their stories. Not being satisfied with SEAL claims alone, these individuals quite often make additional claims of special skills (sniper, courier, etc.), special status (POW), or of participation in covert operations, for

> the CIA or other "shadowy" agencies, in order to re-emphasize the "ultra-secret" nature of the work they claim to have done and the "extremely classified" and "inaccessible" nature of their military records. Of course, the overall intention is to convey to the listener that the person making the statements is not only an "incredibly extraordinary and deadly warrior," but also one of the very rare persons the government has decided is to be trusted with the most sensitive, top secret information it has . . . all in an effort to make the story teller appear "better" than those who hear his stories.
>
> I would caution you that despite anything the man might have said, there are NO secret SEALs. Before any classified operations may be undertaken, a man must first successfully complete the totally unclassified BUD/S Training program. There have been and will continue to be secret missions, but there are NO secret SEALs . . . we know them all, and [Subject] isn't one of us.
>
> If we can be of further assistance to you in your investigation, please do not hesitate to contact us.
>
> If you wish to respond to this e-mail message, please use the REPLY TO ALL button at the top of your e-mail screen display. By doing so, you will ensure that all of the SEAL Authenticator Team members, including myself, will receive a copy of your message. Thank you again for your assistance in upholding the honor of the US Navy SEAL Teams.[244]

Needless to say, the credibility of the impostor witness was completely destroyed. Which proves the efficacy of having websites and other anti-phony resources available, knowing the history of the SEALs and their predecessors — and especially, taking advantage of what the resources have to offer.[245]

This case underscores two important points. First, an impostor's lies, far from being harmless 'bar talk', can do tremendous harm to an innocent person.

Given the tendency of people in authority to take a Fake Warrior's claims as gospel, this falsely accused defendant may well have gone to prison for attempted murder. Lucky for him, his diligent defense lawyer had the foresight to seek verification of the SEAL/POW claims. Second, for would-be Phony Busters, the case is a confidence-builder. Yes, it can be that easy to identify and expose a Fake Warrior who claims to have been a SEAL.

It is fitting to conclude this section about SEALS by pointing to one of the most egregious cases we've ever seen, a Fake Warrior whose tattoos, uniforms, medals, and other paraphernalia made him look like he had just been sent over from central casting. Nothing we could include in this text provides the full impact of the phony world this imposter created. Please see (www.youtube.com/watch?v=XqHfyXoXI_A) and (www.pownetwork.org/horv/horv_900.htm) for dramatic evidence of just how far Fake Warriors will go to support their imposture. These sites are worth more than ten thousand words.

LRRP/LRP/Ranger[246]

While it's often difficult to identify Fake Warriors claiming to have been LRRP/LRPs and/or members of the Army Rangers because of the complicated histories of those units, it can be done.

This discussion of LRRP/LRP and Rangers begins with the Korean War.

> Korean combat experience demonstrated that Rangers were extremely valuable for performing close-in patrols and raids to gain intelligence and secure prisoners; setting up ambushes; establishing observation and listening posts; accompanying and protecting mechanized patrols; seizing and occupying prominent terrain features to deny enemy use; sending out flank patrols to maintain contact with nearly friendly elements; and combating guerilla activities in rear areas."[247]

Indeed, "[t]wo months after the North Koreans invaded South Korea, Army

Chief of Staff General J. Lawton Collins [had] ordered the reestablishment of Ranger units with one company to be assigned to each infantry division. In a memorandum dated August 29, 1950, Collins outlined the mission of the Ranger companies: "to infiltrate through enemy lines and attack command posts, artillery, tank parks, and key communication centers or facilities. General Collins also directed that the Rangers be formed and trained at Fort Benning, Georgia . . . . * * * Since airborne qualification was a requirement, most of the Ranger candidates [volunteers] came from . . . Airborne Divisions."[248]

For various reasons not germane here, within a year of their creation, the Ranger companies started to disband, and a few months later they were gone as separate units. [249]

Between the Korean and Vietnam Wars, Ranger graduates of Fort Benning would rejoin their regular units. During that period, two airborne long range reconnaissance patrol companies were formed under the aegis of the European Command.[250] The Department of the Army defined their task as "overt operations by highly trained infantry units, to any depth into enemy-held areas, for the purpose of reconnaissance, raids, and general disruption of enemy operations."[251]

However, it was during the Vietnam War that the LRRP/LRPs would come into their own.

Before examining that subject, a slight digression. The crescent-shaped Ranger tab contains that word in orange-gold lettering on a black background, bordered in orange-gold.[252] This distinction between Ft. Benning Ranger School graduates and non-graduates requires that different questions be asked of those claiming to have been "Rangers" in Vietnam. Keeping in mind that the word "tabbed" designates *only* someone who graduated from Ranger School at Fort Benning, this is the information you should seek from an alleged Ttbbed Ranger:

- Where did he train and what was his class number?
- How many classmates trained with him?

- How many classmates can he name?
- Who was his Ranger buddy?
- Where and when did he graduate?
- How many classmates graduated with him?
- Does he have his Certificate of Graduation?
- When, where, and under what circumstances was he authorized to
- wear the Ranger tab?
- What Ranger teams did he serve with, where, and for how long?
- Who were the commanding officers of each of his teams?
- How many team members can he name?
- What activities did he perform in each team, where, and for how long?
- What decoration was he awarded for his Ranger service?
- When, where, by whom, and under what circumstances was it awarded?
- What is the description of those decorations?
- What documentation does he have supporting those decorations?

During the Vietnam War, however, in addition to the tabbed Rangers there was yet another kind of Ranger. In mid-1964, soon after William C. Westmoreland became commanding general of MACV,[253] he realized that, given the nature of the conflict, *long range reconnaissance* was indispensable. "Although the need was apparent, the normal assets did not exist. Conventional US infantry divisions were not yet in Vietnam, so Westmoreland turned to the Special Forces to organize the first long range *reconnaissance* patrols (LRRPs) in Vietnam.[[254]] Special Forces had been 'in country' since 1957, training the Vietnamese Army [ARVN] and organizing paramilitary units of tribesmen such as the Montagnards."[255]

Although the Special Forces had done their own job, "when the first regular US troop units arrived in Vietnam in 1965, no official LRRP (reconnaissance) organizations existed in any brigade, division, or corps. Except for the embryonic Special Forces . . . teams and individual graduates of the Ranger School, soldiers experienced in LRRP (reconnaissance) operations were nonexistent."[256]

This explanation brings us to an important point regarding the identification of Fake Warriors claiming to have been LRRP/LRPs in Vietnam. *Prior to 1965, there was no official LRRP/LRP—let alone, Ranger—unit anywhere in Vietnam.*[257]

What happened next was predictable. More and more United States troops arrived in Vietnam. Their commanders, faced with a war the likes of which they'd never before experienced, quickly recognized the need for extended reconnaissance.

Accordingly, in mid-1966, General Westmoreland officially recognized the newly-created LRRP/LRP units and ordered the creation of still others. Later that year, he tasked the 5th Special Forces Group to set up a school for Long Range Reconnaissance Patrols — named Recondo — staffed by Project DELTA veterans.[258] So anyone claiming he attended LRRP school in Vietnam *prior* to September 1966 is not telling the truth.

Late in 1967, the word "reconnaissance" was dropped from some LRRP unit designations in recognition [of the fact] that those units' actual activities, while including recon, were more often raids and ambushes.[259]

What followed was the formal organization of most LRRP and LRP companies and detachments at division and brigade levels.[260] According to Lanning: "By 1969 LRRPs shared a common organization and mission but were still identified as separate companies and detachments with no numerical sequence, relation, or historical lineage."[261] This problem was rectified early in the year, *and that date is perhaps the most significant one in dealing with LRRP/LRPs/Rangers from the Vietnam War.*

In January 1969, the Army ordered that as of February 1, 1969 all LRRP/LRP units worldwide would be redesignated as letter companies of the 75th Infantry Regiment, and two new companies would be formed: 'A' Company at Fort Benning, Georgia, and B Company at Fort Carson, Colorado.[262] Two months later, the Army's Field Manual designation of the new companies was "Long Range Reconnaissance *Ranger* Company."[263] In other words, as of February 1, 1969, for the first time in Vietnam, LRRPs and LRPs were recognized as separate units.[264]

Thus, a question arises about the first three months of 1969. Someone who suspects that he has a phony on his hands should establish, upfront, *when* the claimant arrived in Vietnam for the tour during which he claims he was a LRRP/LRP or Ranger.[265]

If it was *before* February 1, 1969, he would have been assigned to a regular unit, *not* one with a Ranger designation, and certainly not to the 75th Infantry.

If he arrived *after* February 1, 1969, in order for him to have been a Ranger in name, *he had to have been assigned to the 75th Infantry.*

Anyone who was untabbed and claims to have been a named Ranger *prior* to February 1, 1969, is not telling the truth.

Likewise, anyone unabbed who claims to have been a Ranger *after* that date, but in a unit other than the 75th Infantry, is not telling the truth.

This is the easy part. As one of the authors' LRRP/LPR/Rangers expert explained: "Many Vietnam Era LRP/LRRP/Rangers have no idea of the convoluted history and lineage we have and you could mistakenly attack their credentials." We're aware of that problem, and so the following questions are aimed at testing the veracity of someone claiming to have been a LRRP/LRP/Ranger *and/or* an untabbed Ranger in Vietnam are:

- What do the initials LRRP and LRP stand for?
- Was he a LRRP or a LRP?
- Was he assigned or did he volunteer?
- At what organizational level did his unit operate?
- For what other unit or units did his unit operate?
- What was his MOS?
- Was there a unit motto, and if so what was it?
- What unit or units did he serve in?
- Did he ever operate outside of South Vietnam and, if so, where?
- What were his unit's missions?
- What was his unit's organization?
- How many men were in his team?
- What were the teams called?
- Who were his commanding officers?
- Who were his team leaders?
- Who were his team members?
- What was his rank?
- How soon before an insertion did he learn about the mission?
- What planning did he do for a mission?
- How did he dress for a mission?
- What was the M-60 machine gun called?
- What equipment did he use for a mission?
- How was he inserted?

- How many team members were usually inserted?
- What was the meaning of "SALUTE"?
- How was he extracted?
- How long was his tour?
- What is the meaning of a "stay behind"?
- What is the meaning of an "IAD"?
- What were the customary methods of extraction?
- What is a McGuire Rig?
- What reports had to be made upon completion of a mission?
- What questions were asked at a debriefing?
- With what other elements did he coordinate?
- What is meant by "RRF"?
- What is meant by the "five S's" regarding enemy prisoners of war?
- How are enemy KIAs to be handled?
- How many paragraphs are there in the Ranger Creed?

Just as in the case of Fake Warriors claiming to have been POWs or SEALs, if the alleged LRRP/LRP/Ranger fails or refuses to answer correctly at least some of these basic questions — for whatever reasons — chances are your suspicions have substance, and the claimant is a Fake Warrior.[266]

Apart from outing a Fake Warrior by asking some of these questions, other ways are through (www.ranger.org) and (www.75thrra.com).

Special Forces

The fascinating and inspiring history of the United States Army Special Forces, while well beyond the scope of this book, makes identifying, exposing, and punishing Fake Warriors who claim to have been members of that elite group in Vietnam and in the decades since all the more gratifying.[267]

Since Special Forces were ubiquitous in-country during most of the Vietnam War and in large- and small-scale conflicts since, it is often more difficult to unmask this group of Fake Warriors than to out other phonies.

But if one understands, even in a general way, what Special Forces units did in Southeast Asia (especially in Vietnam), and what they've done since then, it becomes easier to distinguish between the real and the fake.

As early as the mid-fifties, a Special Forces team spent six months training the Royal Thai Rangers in Thailand. Special Forces remained in that country in one role or another (e.g. counterinsurgency training) for nearly two decades.[268]

Beginning in late 1959, Special Forces trained various elements of the Laotian Army, gathered intelligence, and organized members of the Meo tribe into a guerrilla force. In 1961, Special Forces did the same with the Kha tribes. When, in 1962, Laos was *neutralized*, Special Forces officially left the country.

As to Vietnam, Charles M. Simpson III has succinctly summed up the SF role there:

> The first Special Forces missions to Vietnam were not too different from those conducted in so many other parts of the world in the 1950s, before counterinsurgency became both a popular word and an assigned mission for SF. All over Asia, mobile training teams had helped friendly nations develop their own special forces, and it was not surprising to find the tiny 14th Special Forces Detachment committed to such a role in Vietnam.
>
> After 1954 and the Geneva Accords, US aid became direct

> and started its long upward trend. The early MAAG [Military Advice & Assistance Group] in Vietnam was not concerned with insurgency or revolution and busied itself with repeating a recent success. American advice and money went toward building a conventional army to repel a Korean-style invasion from the north. The SF mission fell in line with this concept and helped to build an offensive guerrilla warfare capacity, the Vietnamese Special Forces.[[269]]
>
> *   *   *
>
> As time went on and the pattern of the war and the US involvement changed, Special Forces in Vietnam were to find themselves in a number of different roles and missions. Far eclipsing all the other SF activities in both size and scope was the so-called Civilian Irregular Defense Group (CIDG) program. In the conduct of that unique program over a period of nine years, Special Forces became involved in every conceivable aspect of counterinsurgency: military, economic, psychological, and political. The saga of the CIDG program involved thousands of US Special Forces soldiers and hundreds of thousands of Vietnamese civilians, millions of dollars, and approximately 100 camps spread from the Demilitarized Zone to the Gulf of Siam.
>
> It is the story of countless small skirmishes and some big, bloody battles, of carving isolated camps out of the jungle or trying to prop them up out of the delta floods. It is a story of teaching Vietnamese how to shoot, or build, or farm, or care for the sick, or run agent operations, and of dealing with the religious and ethnic minorities of Vietnam – the Montagnards, the Cambodians, the Hoa Hoa, and the Cao Dai. * * * Finally in 1970, as planned since 1966, the program was Vietnamized and the Americans later withdrew and returned to Fort Bragg.[270]

It is a truism that no one can be qualified to engage in such activities without lengthy, comprehensive, and rigorous training. And therein reside many of the questions which can help identify a Fake Warrior who claims to have been Special Forces during the Vietnam War — or since then:

- How did he enter the Army?
- What training did he receive after basic training?
- What are the details concerning his airborne training?
- What was the name of the Special Forces school he attended?
- Where was it located?
- When did he attend?
- At what locales did he do what specialized training?
- What was his class number?
- How many classmates trained with him?
- How many classmates can he name?
- When did he graduate?
- How many classmates graduated with him?
- When, where, and under what circumstances was he authorized to wear a Special Forces insignia?
- What Special Forces teams did he serve with, where, and for how long?
- What do the initials CIDG stand for?
- Who were the Commanding Officers of each of his teams?
- Who were the team leaders of each of his teams?
- What special skills did each team member possess?
- How many team members can he name?
- What activities did he perform in each team, where, and for how long?
- What decorations did he receive for his Special Forces service?
- When, where, by whom, and under what circumstances was

it awarded?

- What is the description of that decoration?
- What documentation does he possess to support that decoration?
- What was the LLDB?

Apart from outing a Fake Warrior by asking many of these questions, another way to ascertain whether someone claiming to have been a member of Special Forces is lying is by accessing the Special Forces Association website (www.sfahq.org) and its e-mail contact (sfahq@sfhq.org).[271] Once an inquiry is made, there will be someone who is well qualified to try to debunk the claims of a Fake Warrior — and usually he'll succeed.

Additional information about Special Forces in Vietnam, Laos, and Cambodia can be obtained at (www.specialforcesbooks.com).

SOG (Studies and Observation Group)

In early 1964, the Central Intelligence Agency's clandestine programs in Vietnam were shifted to a top-secret guerrilla force with the initials "MACV-SOG": "M" (Military) "A" (Assistance) "C" (Command) – "V" (Vietnam) "S" (Studies) [and] "O" (Observation)[272] "G" (Group).

The force consisted of volunteer Army Special Forces, Navy SEALs, Air Force Air Commandos, and others, and was accountable to the Pentagon's Joint Chiefs of Staff. SOG operated clandestinely in North Vietnam, the Vietnam Demilitarized Zone, Laos, and Cambodia. Its missions included:

- Performing reconnaissance in general, and of the Ho Chi Minh trail in particular;
- Recruiting non-Vietnamese indigenous fighters (e.g., Nungs, Montagnards);
- Extracting downed American pilots;

- Inserting agents into hostile territory, including North Vietnam;[273]
- Destroying enemy food supplies;
- Attempting POW rescues;
- Ambushing enemy troops;
- Assessing bomb damage;
- Directing air strikes (which was a top priority);
- Planting mines, sensors, and listening devices;
- Kidnapping enemy soldiers;
- And more.[274]

Because of the highly secret nature and operations of MACV-SOG — and to some laymen, the romance attached to its exploits[275] — it's a perfect vehicle for Fake Warrior lies and impostures.[276] As with impostor claims about working for the CIA, the SOG impostors maintain they did such super-secret work in Vietnam (which they did!) that they can't breathe a word of it. This, of course, shifts the burden onto the Phony Buster, who is put in the untenable position of trying to prove a negative.

Someone trying to out a SOG Fake Warrior must shift the burden of proof back where it belongs — onto the suspected impostor who allegedly worked with MACV-SOG.

- What does the acronym "MACV-SOG" stand for?
- What branch of service was he in?
- What unit was he in before going to SOG?
- What caused his transfer to SOG?
- What was his SOG unit designation?
- Where was he based?

- Where did he operate?
- What types of missions did he perform?
- Who served with him in SOG?
- Were they all Americans?
- If not, who were they?
- How long did he serve in SOG?
- What other forces did he serve with?
- Who were his immediate commanding officers?
- Who were his team leaders?
- What kind of uniforms and equipment did he use?
- To whom was his unit accountable?
- What special skills did he possess?

Considerable information about those who served with Special Forces throughout Southeast Asia can be obtained at (www.specialforcesbooks.com).

Force Recon

Another component of United States special operations — and like Pararescue, less well known than other higher profile elements like the SEALs — is Marine Force Reconnaissance (Force Recon).

Prior to D-Day in World War II's Pacific Theater, United States Marines were tasked with reconnoitering Japanese-held islands, especially their beaches, in preparation for amphibious landings.

Launched from submarines, with Navy Combat Demolition Units

(predecessors to the SEALs), their job "consisted of scouting the littoral areas, or beachhead, to inland; to test the soil permeability of a possible beach landing, or to clear any obstacles that may hinder an amphibious assault, and to observe any sign of enemy activity. The Navy UDT was tasked to provide the same, but from off the coastline to the littoral, or adjacent beach areas."[277]

During the Korean War, Force Recon Marines made deep reconnaissance missions into North Korea, sought out Communist guerillas, directed air and artillery strikes, and destroyed enemy tunnels and bridges.

In Vietnam, so-called "Key Hole patrols were designed purely around reconnaissance and surveillance" from behind enemy lines, usually lightly equipped and armed with defensive weapons. Evasive techniques were employed to break contact from the enemy should the need arise, because avoiding contact was paramount.[278] Force Recon did battle damage assessment, placed remote sensors, established landing and drop zones, and attempted to verify sightings of friendly prisoners of war.

After the Vietnam War, Force Recon saw action in the Persian Gulf and Afghanistan. In the latter's Helmand Province, they

> conducted a battalion-sized helicopter insert into the area of Trek Nawa, operating for 32 days straight, away from friendly lines, during that period there was contact with Taliban forces for 28 of those days using tactics and offensive action that stunned the local enemy forces. Following the missions in Trek Nawa and surrounding areas, The [battalion] deployed two companies to the Upper Saingin River Valley, again during the intense fighting in the area the Taliban gave 1st Recon the nickname "Black Diamonds" for the diamond shaped Norotos night vision goggles mounts on their helmets. Additionally, sensitive reporting on Taliban radio ICOM traffic recorded a Taliban member referring to the Marines of the Force Recon platoon, and Bravo Company operating in the area, as "the Sons of Satan" for their fierce fighting ability. The statement was close to "We will not fight them, they

are not normal Marines, they run at us when we shoot at them... if we fight them, we die... they are worse than the sons of Satan."[279]

It is not merely wrong for a Fake Warrior to appropriate the courageous achievements of Force Recon Marines, as with all impostures it is *immoral*. For this reason, Force Recon phonies, like all the others, must be identified, exposed, and punished.

If there is a suspicion that someone claiming to have been a member of Force Recon is a Fake Warrior, these questions should tell the tale.

- What specialized training did he receive, at what schools, when and where?
- Where was the pre-Force Recon school where he got his MOS?
- What was his MOS?
- Is it necessary to have a Recon MOS before a Marine can be assigned to Force Recon?
- How long must one serve in Battalion Recon before being allowed into Force Recon?
- Where was he stationed in Force Recon?
- What kind of missions did he perform?
- How long was his tour, or tours, of duty?
- What is the name of the school attended before Army Jump School?
- What is the name of the school attended before Navy SCUBA School?
- Where was Jump School?
- Where was SCUBA School?
- How long was Force Recon School?
- How long was SCUBA school?

- Where and when did he graduate from Force Recon School?
- Where and when did he graduate from SCUBA School?
- Where and when did he graduate from Jump School?
- What were his instructors' names and ranks at these schools?
- Who was the OIC for his Force Recon team?
- What special awards did he earn because he was Force Recon?

Air Commando

In response to President Kennedy's decision to create a 'special operations' capability within the United States military, in 1961 the Air Force created a squadron code-named Jungle Jim whose job would be "to provide planes and crews to go anywhere in the world they were needed to provide close air support for American and allied forces fighting behind enemy lines and to help friendly developing nations deal with guerilla uprisings."[280] This would include covert movement of personnel and supplies, handling of sensitive cargo, airborne psychological warfare loudspeaker broadcasts and leaflet drops, and other unconventional air-related tasks.[281]

Later that year, one of the squadron's two detachments left for Vietnam.

As the Air Commando role in Vietnam grew — support of ground forces, defoliation, psychological warfare, re-supply, guerrilla drops — the squadron's strength increased about ten-fold in an eighteen-month period.[282] Not only pilots were Air Commandos, as a former Air Commando put it, "All these units had mechanics . . . armorers, fuelers, supply clerks, cooks, admin, accountants, intell, docs, weathermen, and everyone else who made the planes go. They were all Air Commandos."[283]

But a Fake Warrior claiming to have been an Air Commando — either in Vietnam, in Laos "secret war' (where the Air Commandos played a large role), or since the early 1970s in places such as Afghanistan and Iraq — isn't going to claim he was a cook or a weatherman. There's much more glamour in playing the role of an ex-pilot engaged in defoliation or guerrilla drops.

Here are some telling questions to ask an alleged Air Commando:

- How did he become an Air Commando?
- Was he always designated an Air Commando?
- If the designation changed, when did it change?
- Where did he train?
- What tasks did he train for?
- How long was the training?
- What was his AFSC?
- What was the washout or dropout rate?
- What was his Wing designation?
- What was his squadron designation?
- What type of aircraft was he associated with?
- What types of missions was he associated with?
- Who were the people he worked with, especially ground troops?
- Where was he based?
- What were his areas of operations?
- How long was he an Air Commando?
- Did he work with any other branch's special operations personnel?
- If so, who were they and what missions did they perform?
- Where did those missions take place?
- What was the Air Commando motto?[284]

Another way of tripping up an alleged Air Commando is to test his knowledge of what other personnel besides pilots served in the Air Commandos. Chances are the impostor won't even know about the mechanics, armorers, and "everyone else who made the planes go."

Apart from this Q & A,285 the fastest and most certain way to verify someone's claim is through the Air Commando website (www.specialoperations.net), and its e-mail contact (aircommando1@earthlink.net). The Air Commandos are a very active association, and among its many members chances are good that someone will be able to debunk the claims of a Fake Warrior.

Pararescue

By now, thanks to books and movies, most Americans know the various organizations that constituted our nation's military special operators during the Vietnam War era and on into the present: SEALs, Special Forces, Air Commandos, LRRPs, Rangers, Force Recon, SOG and others. Some of them continued to exist after the war, and are operational now in Afghanistan, Iraq, and elsewhere in the world.

Although less well known, another group in the pantheon of special operators is the Pararescuemen.

After World War II, the Army Air Force (before it became a separate branch of the United States military) established the Air Rescue Service in 1946. Its worldwide job was to rescue aircrews, no matter what the cause: pilot error, mechanical failure, hostile action — anything.

During the Korean War, Pararescuemen snatched downed personnel from behind enemy lines and lifted the wounded from near the front to medical facilities in the rear. Often, to achieve the rescue, the Pararescuemen had to exit the transporting helicopter and spend time on the ground amidst enemy forces — in one case, some seventy-two hours. The statistics are impressive. By the end of the three-year Korean War, the Air Rescue Service had saved some eight thousand wounded, and rescued some thousand

men from behind North Korean and Chinese lines.
Pararescuemen were often called upon to leave the helicopters that carried them in order to assist the personnel they were sent to rescue. This might call for an extended stay on the ground behind enemy lines and overland travel of several miles. The longest of these 'Lone Wolf' missions lasted seventy-two hours.
On September 19, 1950, Capt. John C. Shumate was awarded the Silver Star, with the following citation:

> Captain John C. Shumate, United States Air Force, distinguished himself by gallantry in action against the enemy on 10 October 1950, by rescuing an injured British fighter pilot from his downed aircraft, deep in enemy territory north of Seoul, Korea.
>
> Captain Shumate, in the capacity of para-doctor as part of a helicopter team, left the helicopter upon landing near the crashed aircraft, and rushed to the aid of the pilot. Enemy forces from a nearby farm house opened fire with small arms in an attempt to prevent any aid by Captain Shumate. At the risk of his life, Captain Shumate leaped to the wing of the aircraft and attempted to lift the pilot out of the cockpit.
>
> The pilot, paralyzed from the waist down and unable to help, was pinned to the wreckage by his flying suit. Still under enemy small arms fire, Captain Shumate lifted and held the pilot with one arm and with his free hand cut away the pilot's flight suit, freeing the pilot. Practically exhausted, Captain Shumate managed to carry and drag the pilot to safety from the small arms fire.
>
> Assisted by the helicopter pilot, the injured British fighter pilot was placed aboard the helicopter and flown to a hospital. The gallantry under enemy fire and devotion to duty displayed by Captain Shumate on this occasion are in keeping with the highest traditions of the military service, and reflect great credit upon himself and the United States Air Force.

Vietnam changed almost everything for the Pararescuemen because the role of air power was far greater than it had been in Korea.

> The Air Force's scope of operations became so large that demand for Pararescue teams expanded as well. The use of helicopters caused new tactics utilizing the speed, distance, and support they could provide. Rescue "packages" were created utilizing FACs (Forward Air Controllers), rescue escorts (such as AH-1 Cobras or A-1 Sandys), protective fighter CAP (Combat Air Patrol), and the HH-3 Jolly Green Giant and HH-53 Super Jolly Green Giant helicopters to provide fast rescue for pilots shot down far behind enemy lines. Pararescue personnel were part of these packages to provide medical assistance for injured aircrew as well as the ability to patrol for missing aircrew that might have been unconscious or dead.
>
> Pararescue team members would be inserted to conduct LSO (Limited Surface Operations) searches while the escorts maintained an aggressive patrol to provide instantaneous support. Sometimes they would be inserted to search for personnel who were being forced to escape and evade; in such cases, the mission might last for days. The Pararescue teams racked up an impressive record; during the conflict only 19 Airmen were awarded the Air Force Cross. Ten of those were awarded to Pararescuemen.[286]

William H. Pitsenbarger was the first airman to be awarded the Air Force Cross — posthumously — for service in Vietnam. On December 8, 2000, Airman Pitsenbarger's Air Force Cross was upgraded to the Medal of Honor, making him the Air Force's second enlisted man to have received that award since the Air Force became a separate service in 1947.[287] Airman Pitsenbarger's Medal of Honor Citation reads as follows:

> Airman First Class Pitsenbarger distinguished himself by extreme valor on 11 April 1966 near Cam My, Republic of Vietnam, while assigned as a Pararescue Crew Member, Detachment 6, 38th Aerospace Rescue and Recovery Squadron.

On that date, Airman Pitsenbarger was aboard a rescue helicopter responding to a call for evacuation of casualties incurred in an on-going firefight between elements of the United States Army's 1st Infantry Division and a sizable enemy force approximately 35 miles east of Saigon.

With complete disregard for personal safety, Airman Pitsenbarger volunteered to ride a hoist more than one hundred feet through the jungle, to the ground. On the ground, he organized and coordinated rescue efforts, cared for the wounded, prepared casualties for evacuation, and insured that the recovery operation continued in a smooth and orderly fashion. Through his personal efforts, the evacuation of the wounded was greatly expedited. As each of the nine casualties evacuated that day were recovered, Pitsenbarger refused evacuation in order to get one more wounded soldier to safety.

After several pick-ups, one of the two rescue helicopters involved in the evacuation was struck by heavy enemy ground fire and was forced to leave the scene for an emergency landing. Airman Pitsenbarger stayed behind, on the ground, to perform medical duties.

Shortly thereafter, the area came under sniper and mortar fire. During a subsequent attempt to evacuate the site, American forces came under heavy assault by a large Viet Cong force. When the enemy launched the assault, the evacuation was called off and Airman Pitsenbarger took up arms with the besieged infantrymen. He courageously resisted the enemy, braving intense gunfire to gather and distribute vital ammunition to American defenders.
As the battle raged on, he repeatedly exposed himself to enemy fire to care for the wounded, pull them out of the line of fire, and return fire whenever he could, during which time, he was wounded three times. Despite his wounds, he valiantly fought on, simultaneously treating as many wounded as possible. In the

> vicious fighting which followed, the American forces suffered 80 percent casualties as their perimeter was breached, and airman Pitsenbarger was finally fatally wounded.
>
> Airman Pitsenbarger exposed himself to almost certain death by staying on the ground, and perished while saving the lives of wounded infantrymen. His bravery and determination exemplify the highest professional standards and traditions of military service and reflect great credit upon himself, his unit, and the United States Air Force.

The exploits of Pararescuers didn't end with the conclusion of hostilities in Southeast Asia. Here's a snapshot of what happened in faraway Somalia on October 3-4, 1993:

> In connection with military operations against an opposing armed force in Mogadishu, Somalia, 24th Special Tactics Squadron Pararescuemen were directed to a situation where an [American] assault helicopter had been downed in a congested urban area. After fast roping from a helicopter and assaulting through heavy enemy small arms fire from three directions, the Pararescuemen established a casualty collection point and made their way to the wreckage to conduct an assessment, provide emergency medical treatment to the survivors, and to extract all on board.
>
> While freeing these survivors, a Pararescueman was wounded and sent to the ground. Ignoring the traumatic effects of the gunshot wound, he treated his own wound and moved back to the casualty collection point and continued to triage and treat the survivors of the crash.
>
> At this time, a Ranger element 45 meters from their location was engaged and were suffering casualties in an intense fire fight. A Pararescueman, on his own initiative, broke cover and ran through a thick barrage of small arms fire, shrapnel, and RPGs [Rocket Propelled Grenades] to reach the Ranger position.

> Once there, he pulled the wounded one by one into the safety of a covered position and began immediate medical treatment of the seriously wounded Rangers. For eighteen hours, these Pararescuemen rendered emergency medical services to the wounded and repeatedly took up security positions and returned fire to suppress enemy forces.[288]

When one reads the Pitsenbarger citation and what he endured, and glimpses the heroism of Pararescuemen in Somalia, it is nothing short of blasphemous for a Fake Warrior to claim that he was a Pararescueman (let alone was awarded the Medal of Honor).

To identify Fake Warriors claiming to have been, or to be, Pararescuemen, see Robert Lapointe's site (www.pjsinnam.com/VN_History/db_home.htm). It contains all air rescue missions flown in the Vietnam War, and includes names of the pilots, crews, Pararescuemen, call signs, type of aircraft employed, and more.

The main source for checking Pararescue claims is (retiredpj@hotmail.com). While pre-2003 data is not 100 % complete, former Pararescueman K. J. Jones is confident that his data is 100 % accurate from 2003 to the present, and for all those who served in Vietnam, Panama, and certain other years and actions. It is called the "PJ Roster."

Pararescue training is lengthy and extensive, and takes about two years. "Of the many who begin the process, only the most determined will graduate; sometimes as few as four to six from a class of nearly 100. From start to finish, the dropout rate is about 90 percent from each class, the highest training dropout rate in the entire US Special Operations community. Pararescue trainees are required to attend the Pararescue Indoctrination Course. Following that is a long string of courses including Combat Dive School, Army Airborne, National Registry for Paramedic, Survival (SERE), and Military Free-fall Parachutist. Upon completing the aforementioned, a Pararescue trainee is required to then complete the Pararescue Apprentice Course, which combines all the prior skills and adds a few more. Once a Pararescueman has completed the pipeline, they are assigned to a Rescue or Special Tactics team where they will receive informal on-the-job training. Additionally, if a Pararescueman is assigned to a special tactics team, they will receive additional training along with Air Force Combat Controllers in what is known as Advanced Skills Training."[289]

This information is important in identifying a Fake Warrior making a Pararescue claim because a phony will not have knowledge of the schooling requirements.

When confronted with a suspected Fake Warrior who claims to be, or have been, a Pararescueman, here are some of the questions aimed at getting the truth:

- What specialized training did he receive, at what schools, when and where?
- How long did it last?
- How many rescue missions was he on, where, and when?
- Who was the first airman to be awarded the Air Force Cross and then Medal of Honor for pararescue service in Vietnam?
- What do the initials "LSO" stand for?
- What are the names of five pilots, co-pilots, and crew members he flew with?
- What are the names of at least three of his commanding officers?
- What do the letters "FAC" stand for?
- How many men were in his first class, and how many finished?
- Is there a Pararescue motto and, if there is, what is it?
- Where was he based, and for how long?
- What type of aircraft did he fly in on Pararescue missions?

<u>Central Intelligence Agency</u>

Unlike false claims involving POWs, SEALs, LLRPs, Rangers, Special Forces, Air Commandos, or SOG, someone who says he worked for the CIA has the advantage of being able to dodge even rudimentary questions about his alleged service. Once a Fake Warrior says the magic words — "I was with the Company" or "I'd have to kill you if I revealed what I did" — he (or she) is in a position not only to avoid questions that might trip him up, but also to "justify" why his name isn't on any official list. The CIA, after all, really does not comment on its people or its hush-hush activities. Be assured that impostors are well aware of their advantage in this situation. The CIA will not comment about anything or anyone — real or fake.

However, there are five potentially efficacious ways to identify such impostors.

First, are the suspected impostor's stories on their face so incredible as to defy belief? Most of the time, they will be. No one person working for the CIA, for example, infiltrated Laos, assassinated top Communist generals, hijacked a plane, and bombed Pathet Lao headquarters on his way back to Da Nang — where he was awarded the Medal of Honor.[290]

Second, a phony "Company" man is just as prone as any other Fake Warrior to mix up his dates, times, and places. If they don't jibe, glaring inconsistencies can easily be picked apart. If an alleged American CIA agent claims to have posed as a POW in Hanoi in 1975, for example, he's going to be pretty red-faced when you inform him that all POWs were repatriated two years earlier during 1973's Operation Homecoming.

Third, usually CIA employment tales are spun together with other false claims. For example, the impostor claims he not only worked for the CIA, but also was a SEAL and earned two Purple Hearts. Anyone who lies about his duties and medals is also lying about having worked for the CIA.

Fourth, no operators who were strictly CIA, as compared to military personnel detailed to the agency, were ever awarded military combat awards. However, the latter were eligible to receive awards and decorations through their own chain of command based on information forwarded by

CIA.

Fifth, former CIA agents who plied their tradecraft in Indochina are not the kind of people who brag about their exploits, even were they legally allowed to do so — which they are not.[291]

Sniper

The first recorded use of snipers in American history is in September 1777, at the battle of Saratoga. Colonists hid in the trees and used early model rifles to shoot British officers.
After that, United States military forces (and the Confederacy during the Civil War) used snipers in every war and near-war they've been engaged in. Today, snipers are found in all the armed service branches.

> A sniper is a highly trained marksman who operates in one to two man teams which maintain close visual contact with the enemy and engage targets from concealed positions or physical distances exceeding the detection capabilities of the enemy personnel, without being detected. These sniper teams operate independently, with little combat asset support from their parent units. Snipers typically have highly selective and specialized training and possess high-precision rifles, optics, and many times, sophisticated communication assets to feed valuable combat information back to their units.
> In addition to marksmanship, military snipers are trained in camouflage, field craft, infiltration, reconnaissance, and observation. Snipers are especially effective when deployed within the terrain of urban warfare, or jungle warfare.[292]

With all the recent publicity about snipers in the United States Armed Forces, especially those serving in SEAL and other special operations units, it's no wonder that the number of Fake Warrior claiming they were snipers has increased considerably.

Just as with other Fake Warriors, it is not difficult to smoke out a Fake Warrior claiming to have been a sniper.

- Where did he train, with whom, for how long, and where?
- What was the number of his class?
- What rifle(s) and ammunition did he use?
- What other equipment did he have?
- What skills was he taught?
- What is the most accurate firing position?
- What is the significance of the sniper heart?
- What considerations go into aiming?
- What is meant by "zeroing" a weapon, and how is it done?
- What is a "mil dot reticle"?
- What does the word "ghillie" mean?
- What is the preferred part of the target's anatomy to place the shot?
- What is "sound masking"?
- Who was Carlos Hatchcock?
-

Usually, the questioner's familiarity with these questions and others will be enough to spook the Fake Warrior into cutting and running.

<u>Medal of Honor</u>

Vietnam vet convicted of lying about Medal of Honor
By ELAINE SILVESTRINI | *The Tampa Tribune*
Published: February 10, 2010

TAMPA —

For two years, Vietnam War veteran Gary Amster drove around Florida with a license plate that said he had been awarded the Medal of Honor, the nation's highest military award.

But Amster never received the Medal of Honor.

A federal jury today convicted Amster, 62, of three charges — a felony count of lying to a federal agency about having the medal and two misdemeanor counts of falsely representing that he had won the medal. The felony carries up to five years in prison and the misdemeanors each carry up to a year behind bars. * * *

Defense attorney Michael P. Maddux said Amster wrongly thought he had been given the honor because of a form that was mailed to him by the Army. "He believed that he was a hero," Maddux told jurors in his closing argument. "Some people need to believe that they're heroes. That doesn't make them a criminal. You shouldn't make him a criminal."

But a federal prosecutor said Amster fraudulently altered the Army form and then used it to fool authorities; he filed the form with the Brevard County Clerk of the Court and then used a copy with the State of Florida seal. "We don't prosecute people for wrong beliefs in the United States," said Assistant U.S. Attorney Robert Mosakowski. "We do prosecute them for telling lies in important matters."

The medal Amster claimed to have received represents "the thanks of a grateful nation," Mosakowski said. "It's against the law for someone who never earned that to claim that he did."

He said Amster claimed he was a sergeant leading a patrol that was ambushed by the Viet Cong and that he fought them off with his bayonet and lost a kidney as a result of battle wounds. But the prosecutor said there was no evidence Amster ever saw combat;

> a fellow soldier testified they were stationed in headquarters with radios. Amster lost his kidney as the result of an infection brought about by a congenital condition, Mosakowski said. "If the Viet Cong was responsible for him losing his kidney, they would have had to have beaten up his mother," he said.
>
> Maddux said Amster had a good faith reason to believe he had been given the award, pointing out that his client never received any money from the government because of his claims. "They're here after him because of a license plate," he said. Maddux said Amster already has been punished by having to go through the trial. "It's time to let this veteran go home," he said. "Humiliated? Yes. I'm asking you to display your own mighty acts of individual valor in this case. Acquit Mr. Amster."
>
> But Mosakowski urged a conviction. "We're protecting the honor of our Medal of Honor winners, or our bravest of the brave and our heroes," he said.

For a Fake Warrior to claim he was a POW, SEAL, LRRP/LRP/Ranger, Special Forces, SOG, Force Recon, Air Commando, Pararescue, Sniper, or CIA, is bad enough, but to falsely lay claim to our nation's highest decoration, the Medal of Honor, is the most outrageous imposture of all. Federal law spells out what it takes to earn the Medal of Honor:

> The President may award, and present in the name of Congress, a medal of honor . . . to a person who, while a member of the Air Force, distinguished himself conspicuously *by gallantry and intrepidity at the risk of his life above and beyond the call of duty*. . . ."[293]

Note that the statutory language lacks specificity. In order to grasp the enormity of the injustice being done by impostors who glibly award themselves the Medal of Honor, ponder for a moment what legitimate wearers of this decoration endured. The following example of a Marine's action in Afghanistan powerfully makes the point:

Corporal [Dakota] Meyer maintained security at a patrol rally point while other members of his team moved on foot with two platoons of Afghan National Army and Border Police into the village of Ganjgal for a pre-dawn meeting with village elders. Moving into the village, the patrol was ambushed by more than 50 enemy fighters firing rocket propelled grenades, mortars, and machine guns from houses and fortified positions on the slopes above.

Hearing over the radio that four US team members were cut off, Corporal Meyer seized the initiative. With a fellow Marine driving, Corporal Meyer took the exposed gunner's position in a gun-truck as they drove down the steeply terraced terrain in a daring attempt to disrupt the enemy attack and locate the trapped US team. Disregarding intense enemy fire now concentrated on their lone vehicle, Corporal Meyer killed a number of enemy fighters with the mounted machine guns and his rifle, some at near point blank range, as he and his driver made three solo trips into the ambush area.

During the first two trips, he and his driver evacuated two dozen Afghan soldiers, many of whom were wounded. When one machine gun became inoperable, he directed a return to the rally point to switch to another gun-truck for a third trip into the ambush area where his accurate fire directly supported the remaining US personnel and Afghan soldiers fighting their way out of the ambush.

Despite a shrapnel wound to his arm, Corporal Meyer made two more trips into the ambush area in a third gun-truck accompanied by four other Afghan vehicles to recover more wounded Afghan soldiers and search for the missing US team members.

Still under heavy enemy fire, he dismounted the vehicle on the fifth trip and moved on foot to locate and recover the bodies of

> his team members. Corporal Meyer's daring initiative and bold fighting spirit throughout the 6-hour battle significantly disrupted the enemy's attack and inspired the members of the combined force to fight on. His unwavering courage and steadfast devotion to his US and Afghan comrades in the face of almost certain death reflected great credit upon himself and upheld the highest traditions of the Marine Corps and the United States Naval Service.[294]

To verify if someone was awarded the Medal of Honor, one can consult the Medal of Honor Society (www.cmohs.org), Appendix E (the official list of those awarded the Medal of Honor in the Vietnam War), Appendix F (the official list of those awarded the Medal of Honor since the Vietnam War), or (www.militarytimes.com/citations-medals-awards).

<u>Distinguished Service Cross, Navy Cross, Air Force Cross</u>

Second only to the Medal of Honor, the favorite self-awarded medals of Fake Warriors are the Army Distinguished Service Cross, and the Navy and Air Force Crosses. These three are the next-highest decorations that the United States military can bestow, signifying valorous conduct on the part of authentic heroes.

Under federal law, "The President may award an Air Force Cross . . . to a person who, while serving in any capacity with the Air Force, distinguishes himself by *extraordinary heroism* not justifying the award of a medal of honor . . . ."[295] The following examples demonstrate what it cost six Americans to earn, respectively, the Distinguished Service Cross, the Navy Cross, and the Air Force Cross.[296]

<u>Distinguished Service Cross</u>

> Captain [Stanley] Blunt distinguished himself while leading his company during a search and clear operation through enemy controlled territory several kilometers south of the Demilitarized Zone in the northern area of I Corps Tactical Zone.
>
> On 11 November [1969], his company was participating in a

> coordinated battalion attack on elements of the 27th North Vietnamese Army Regiment defending heavily fortified bunker positions. When his company's advance was halted by intense suppressive fire, Captain Blunt single handedly charged a heavily fortified machine gun emplacement and completely destroyed the position. In this same assault, he killed four other enemy soldiers at close range by hurling hand grenades into their positions.
> In the early morning hours of l3 November, in a continuation of the same operation, Captain Blunt infiltrated a seven-man patrol through some twelve hundred meters of closely defended enemy terrain under cover of darkness in order to reinforce and extract besieged friendly elements. He conducted this perilous mission without incident and undoubtedly saved the lives of the twenty-two trapped American soldiers. Captain Blunt's extraordinary heroism and devotion to duty were in keeping with the highest traditions of the military service and reflect great credit upon himself, his unit, and the United States Army.[297]

A more recent example of the conduct necessary to warrant award of the Distinguished Service Cross is this:

> Specialist Felipe Pereira distinguished himself with heroism and exceptionally meritorious service on 1 November, 2010, while under heavy enemy fire as a team leader with Alpha Company, 1st Battalion, 502nd Infantry Regiment, 101st Airborne Division Air Assault while service in Senjaray, Zhari District, Kandahar Province, Afghanistan.
>
> Specialist Pereira and his squad were returning from a dismounted patrol in Senjaray, when a suicide motorcycle borne explosive device detonated in the middle of his squad as they attempted to enter their combat outpost. Two Soldiers were killed instantly, while four others were severely wounded including his squad leader and fellow team leader. Specialist Pereira sustained shrapnel wounds to his spleen, liver, and left lung.

While Soldiers struggled to gain situational awareness, the enemy initiated a complex ambush, firing on the patrol from an estimated seven fighting positions with small arms and rocket-propelled grenades. His lung beginning to collapse, he struggled to breathe. With little regard for his own safety or care, Specialist Pereira refused medical treatment and instead commandeered an all-terrain vehicle and moved back into heavy enemy fire to provide an evacuation platform for his wounded comrades. Specialist Pereira was able to move the vehicle within 20 meters of his fellow Soldiers who were pinned down by enemy fire, but was unable to gain effective cover.

Specialist Pereira immediately provided suppressive fires from the vehicle, allowing two of his fellow Soldiers to move two casualties to the vehicle. As bullets ricocheted off the vehicle and narrowly missed Specialist Pereira, he continued to provide fire direction for the remaining Soldiers on the ground. Specialist Pereira then quickly pulled the vehicle back into the entrance of the outpost, where medics were standing by to receive the casualties. Specialist Pereira helped move the casualties to care then moved back into enemy fire a second time to continue evacuating and directing his fellow Soldiers.

Specialist Pereira is credited with saving the lives of two of his fellow Soldiers, while risking his own multiple occasions. Only after all of the wounded Soldiers had been evacuated and were receiving medical care, did he accept treatment himself. Specialist Pereira's actions during the suicide attack in Senjaray, Zhari District, Afghanistan on Nov. 1, 2010, are what define heroes. He is truly a professional who understands his commitment to duty and his fellow Soldiers despite great odds and risk of life.

Navy Cross

As a forward machine gunner . . . during a combat patrol on

> Bassac River [in Vietnam] . . . [Terrence] Freund was instrumental in preventing an enemy battalion from crossing the river, and assisted in the dispersal of that force. By determinate and accurate gunfire, he repeatedly suppressed enemy fire from the river banks during the hotly-contested action. When an attempt to capture an enemy craft resulted in the recovery party being forced into the river by hostile fire . . . Freund's covering fire was instrumental in their rescue. Although mortally wounded, he continued to fire into enemy positions so that his craft and other friendly forces could be extricated from their perilous positions close to the enemy.
>
> By his heroic conduct, he enabled his unit to retire from the action without further loss of life or damage. Freund's performance distinguished him among his gallant comrades, contributed to a victory over the enemy, and was in keeping with the highest traditions of the United States Naval Service.[298]

Among the Navy Crosses awarded for service in Iraq during Operation Steel Curtain in 2005 is this one:

> The President of the United States of America takes pleasure in presenting the Navy Cross to Lance Corporal Joshua R. Mooi, United States Marine Corps, for extraordinary heroism as Grenadier, Second Platoon, Company F, Battalion Landing Team 2/1, Thirteenth Marine Expeditionary Unit (Special Operations Capable), Regimental Combat Team TWO, SECOND Marine Division, II Marine Expeditionary Force (Forward), in support of Operation IRAQI FREEDOM in New Ubaydi, Iraq, on 16 November 2005.
>
> During Operation Steel Curtain, 21 enemy engaged Corporal Mooi's platoon with grenades and automatic fire from several fortified buildings. Lance Corporal Mooi repeatedly exposed himself to reinforce engaged Marines in one of the heavily fortified buildings. He attacked the enemy at close range with grenades

and his rifle to personally recover four wounded Marines and destroy fierce adversaries who were determined to fight to their death.

On six occasions, Lance Corporal Mooi willingly entered an ambush site to pursue the enemy and extricate injured Marines. Often alone in his efforts, he continued to destroy the enemy and rescue wounded Marines until his rifle was destroyed by enemy fire and he was ordered to withdraw.

Lance Corporal Mooi's relentless and courageous actions eliminated at least four insurgents while permitting the immediate care and evacuation of more than a dozen Marines who lay critically or mortally wounded. His valiant efforts were essential to saving the lives of ten Marines and inspired the Company to destroy 18 insurgents in the battle that ended further enemy resistance during Operation STEEL CURTAIN.

Lance Corporal Mooi's outstanding display of decisive leadership, courageous actions, and total devotion to duty reflected great credit upon himself and were in keeping with the highest traditions of the Marine Corps and the United States Naval Service.

Air Force Cross

The following description reveals more about Airman William H. Pitsenbarger's heroism than does the citation issued when his Air Force Cross was upgraded to the Medal of Honor.

By April 1966, 21-year-old A1C William H. Pitsenbarger, then in the final months of his enlistment, had seen more action than many a 30-year veteran. Young Pitsenbarger had gone through long and arduous training for duty as a pararescue medic with the Aerospace Rescue and Recovery Service and had completed more than 300 rescue missions in Vietnam, many of them under heavy enemy fire.[[299]] He wore the Air Medal with five oak leaf clusters; recommendations for four more were pending. A few days earlier, he had ridden a chopper winch line into a minefield to save a wounded ARVN soldier.

His service with ARRS convinced Pitsenbarger that he wanted a career as a medical technician. He had applied to Arizona State University for admission in the fall. But that was months away. He had a job to do in Vietnam and, as rescue pilot Capt. Dale Potter said, Pitsenbarger "was always willing to get into the thick of the action where he could be the most help."

On April 11 at 3 p.m., while Pitsenbarger was off duty, a call for help came into his unit, Detachment 6, 38th ARR Squadron at Bien Hoa. Elements of the Army's 1st Infantry Division were surrounded by enemy forces near Cam My, a few miles east of Saigon, in thick jungle with the tree canopies reaching up to 150 feet. The only way to get the wounded out was with hoist-equipped helicopters.

Pitsenbarger asked to go with one of the two HH-43 Huskies scrambled on this hazardous mission. Half an hour later, both choppers found an area where they could hover and lower a winch line to the surrounded troops. Pitsenbarger volunteered to go down the line, administer emergency treatment to the most seriously wounded, and explain how to use the Stokes litter that would hoist casualties up to the chopper. It was standard procedure for a pararescue medic to stay down only long enough to organize the rescue effort. Pitsenbarger decided, on his own, to remain with the wounded.

In the next hour and a half, the HH-43s came in five times, evacuating nine wounded soldiers. On the sixth attempt, Pitsenbarger's Huskie was hit hard, forced to cut the hoist line, and pull out for an emergency landing at the nearest strip. Intense enemy fire and friendly artillery called in by the Army made it impossible for the second chopper to return. Heavy automatic weapons and mortar fire was coming in on the Army defenders

> from all sides while Pitsenbarger continued to care for the wounded. In case one of the Huskies made it in again, he climbed a tree to recover the Stokes litter that his pilot had jettisoned.
>
> When the C Company commander, the unit Pitsenbarger was with, decided to move to another area, Pitsenbarger cut saplings to make stretchers for the wounded. As they started to move out, the company was attacked and overrun by a large enemy formation. By this time, the few Army troops able to return fire were running out of ammunition. Pitsenbarger gave his pistol to a soldier who was unable to hold a rifle. With complete disregard for his own safety, he scrambled around the defended area, collecting rifles and ammunition from the dead and distributing them to the men still able to fight.
>
> It had been about two hours since the HH-43s were driven off. Pitsenbarger had done all he could to treat the wounded, prepare for a retreat to safer ground, and rearm his Army comrades. He then gathered several magazines of ammunition, lay down beside wounded Army Sgt. Fred Navarro, one of the C Company survivors who later described Pitsenbarger's heroic actions, and began firing at the enemy. Fifteen minutes later, as an eerie darkness fell beneath the triple-canopy jungle, Pitsenbarger was hit and mortally wounded. The next morning, when Army reinforcements reached the C Company survivors, a helicopter crew brought Pitsenbarger's body out of the jungle. Of the 180 men with whom he fought his last battle, only 14 were uninjured.

The best way to verify if someone was awarded the Distinguished Service Cross, the Navy Cross or the Air Force Cross, is to consult (www.militarytimes.com/citations-medals-awards). While not a perfect reference source, still, it's useful.[300]

Letting a suspected impostor know that you're familiar with what heroism is required to support the award of one of these hard-won medals can quickly fluster many a Fake Warrior. But if he persists, press him to produce a copy of the order making the award, together with a copy of the citation accompanying it.[301]

Limitations on awards

Thanks to several little-known provisions of the United States Code, you can easily identify Vietnam era Fake Warriors, and those in recent decades, who claim — let alone wear — multiple medals and decorations.

For every branch of the Armed Forces — Army, Air Force, Navy, Marine Corps, and Coast Guard — there are *express* federal statutes which impose limitations on how many medals of a particular kind can be awarded.

The limitation language is identical for the Army, Air Force, Navy, and Marine Corps, with only the references to each branch's particular medals being different.

Title 10, United States Code, Section 3744, pertaining to the Army, provides: "No more than one medal of honor, distinguished-service cross, or distinguished-service medal may be awarded to a person."

Title 10, United States Code, Section 8744, pertaining to the Air Force, refers to the "medal of honor, Air Force Cross, or distinguished-service medal."

Title 10, United States Code, Section 6247, pertaining to the Navy and Marine Corps, refers to the "medal of honor, Navy Cross, distinguished-service medal, distinguished flying cross, or Navy and Marine Corps medal."

Although the Coast Guard statute (Title 14, United States Code, Section 494) is worded slightly differently, the limitation is the same: "No more than one medal of honor, distinguished service medal, distinguished flying cross, or one Coast Guard medal shall be issued to any one person . . . ."

This limitation of medal awards applies, as well, to the award of the Purple Heart. Section 5 of the Kennedy Executive Order, provides that ". . . not more than one Purple Heart [medal] shall be awarded to any person . . . ."

In the event that an individual becomes entitled to an additional award, the Army and Air Force statutes provide: "For each succeeding act that would otherwise justify the award of such a medal or cross, the President may award a suitable bar or other device to be worn as he directs."

The Navy wording is "bar, emblem, or insignia to be worn with the decoration and corresponding rosette or other device," and the Coast Guard language is "... but for each succeeding deed or service sufficient to justify the awarding of a medal of honor, distinguished service medal, distinguished flying cross, or Coast Guard medal, the President may award a suitable emblem or insignia to be worn with the decoration and a corresponding rosette or other device."

As to the Purple Heart, the same "additional award" provision has been made: "[B]ut for each subsequent award a Gold Star, or other suitable device, shall be awarded to be worn with the Purple Heart [medal]."[302]

But no matter how restrictive the statutory limitation language, and regardless of how additional meritorious recognition is manifested from branch to branch of the services, *no member of the Armed Forces can legitimately wear more than one of the enumerated awards.* He can have only one medal/ribbon, and one or more "devices." We've seen that Fake Warriors typically gild the lily by wearing and/or producing false documentation for multiple medals — say, two Navy Crosses, four Silver Stars, six Purple Hearts. Documents to this effect constitute more than lies. They amount to criminal forgeries as well.[303]

<u>Phony uniforms</u>

The story is told of Wilhelm Voight — "The Captain of Kopenick" — a quintessential tale of how far an imposter can go in life through the simple device of adorning oneself with a uniform.

> One out of three men in the streets of Potsdam [Germany], the

> cradle of Prussian militarism, wore a uniform — the bright blue uniform of Kaiser Wilhelm's soldiers. Wherever you looked there was saluting, standing to attention, presenting arms; officers were riding past on horseback or in carriages, or marching at the head of their columns of men. Every now and then you could hear the brassy, aggressive music of military bands, and the barking voices of sergeant-majors training their recruits in the barrack yards to perform that supreme feat of the uniformed human machine, the Prussian goose-step. The time was autumn 1906.[304]

Voigt was a factory worker in his mid-fifties. One day he spotted in the window of a second-hand clothes store the uniform of a Prussian officer, a captain. Soon after, he wore the uniform in public. People reacted as though he were a captain in the Prussian guards. Soldiers of lesser rank saluted. Civilians toadied.

Emboldened, Voigt commandeered a small body of troops in Berlin and they journeyed to the nearby town of Kopenick. There, 'Captain' Voight intimidated everyone, after which he proceeded to empty the town's treasury. How could a mere factory worker have pulled off such a scam? "No one had questioned his authority. How could they? Disobeying an officer in uniform would have been the deadliest of all sins in Kaiser Wilhelm's Germany."[305]

The self-willed blindness of Voight's victims extended even to the impostor's costume:

> [N]ot only the captain himself had been false, but even the cockades on his peaked cap had been placed the wrong way round, the Prussian insignia above instead of below the black, white, and red one of Imperial Germany—and no one had noticed it![306]

In a telling observation that could be made about many Fake Warriors from the Vietnam War era and later decades, Egon Larsen, author of *The Deceivers, Lives of the Great Impostors*, notes with exasperation that "[T]he Captain of

Kopenick was really an old gaolbird [jailbird], a bow-legged cobbler who had not even served in the army!"[307] Sound familiar?

Modern-day Captains of Kopenick are very much with us:

> The Saturday weekend of Memorial Day, at the dedication of a Veterans Memorial, Mr. McKeaque showed up in full Naval uniform as a Captain. But upon a closer look, the four stripes and command stars were of bright gold, a shiny thread, the kind used on women's clothing, sewn on unevenly. His hat was that of a Naval officer, but the scrambled eggs was the iron-on kind that is used for a ball cap.[308]

<u>Spotting forged DD-214s</u>

According to a United States Department of Justice press release concerning a Fake Warrior who was recently brought to justice,

> Robert E. Neener, 65, of Smithville, Tennessee, pleaded guilty on March 12, 2012, to possessing and selling federal agency seals, and pretending to be a federal officer or employee, announced Jerry E. Martin, US Attorney for the Middle District of Tennessee. The guilty plea is pursuant to a plea agreement which includes a three-year prison sentence and the payment of restitution to defrauded victims.
>
> As part of the plea agreement, Neener admits that from January 2007 through December 2008 he operated a document vending business from his residence in Smithville, Tenn. which he advertised via the Internet. In these advertisements, Neener falsely represented that he could provide customers with "authentic" military replacement documents which were "exact reproductions" of those originally issued, and that he had contracts with military branches of the government.
>
> *Neener received more than $200,000 from customers who ordered*

> *thousands of documents, which included honorable discharges and various military awards.*[309]

We have emphasized this sentence of the Department of Justice press release because it staggers the imagination that a nobody in a small town using the Internet could develop a fake document business so large that Fake Warriors would spend $200,000 on counterfeit "honorable discharges and various military awards." It staggers the imagination even more to extrapolate Neener's activities across the country and even abroad. The United States is awash in counterfeit military documents, with no end in sight.

As we saw in Chapter 4 (and as Neener can probably attest), the essential building block upon which Fake Warrior claims are based is the DD-214. But there's an irony here. Although forged DD-214s are the documents most often used, it is through his forged DD-214 that a Fake Warrior often can be identified.

At least as far back as the Korean War, the United States military has, from time to time, slightly altered the structure and content of the DD-214 form. So while it's not fruitful to analyze each of the various editions of that form here — especially since content
has remained essentially the same — it is worth identifying some red flags that could alert a questioner to telltale discrepancies or doctoring.

> Correlating dates. During the Korean War era, the DD-214 version of January 1, 1950 became obsolete with the issuance of a version that went into effect on July 1, 1952 — the version issued to this book's co-author, Henry Mark Holzer, when he was separated from service in July, 1956.
>
> Professor Holzer's DD-214 — and every other veteran's — provides a "floor" for when his military service *had* to have begun: in his case, sometime *after* July 1, 1952 when the new form was first used. If Professor Holzer's DD-214 had contained dates of service, promotion, awards, schooling, and the like, *pre-dating*

the effective date of his DD-214, these entries would have been bogus on their face. Had Professor Holzer's DD-214 — effective July 1, 1952 — stated that he had been promoted on June 5, 1951, the document would have been, *prima facie*, a forgery.[310]

Other uncorrelated dates can also be a tip-off to a forged DD-214. For example, if the dates on a DD-214 show that a veteran went from induction or enlistment to a specialty school, such as SEAL training, in just a few months, the document is clearly a forgery.

Spelling. For whatever reason, Fake Warriors are, for the most part, rotten spellers. Even allowing for legitimate clerical errors, the mistakes in forged DD-214s tend to be glaring: "amphious" instead of "amphibious," "Distinguish" Flying Cross instead of "Distinguished" Flying Cross, "shrapernel" instead of "shrapnel."

Signatures. Every DD-214 has a block for two different signatures: one for the "officer authorized to sign" the form, the other for the service person being separated or discharged. Often, even to the untutored eye, the handwriting is identical.

Case and fonts. Frequently, without any apparent justification, a doctored DD-214 will be typed in an obvious mixture of upper and lower case characters, as well as in more than one font — often several. Yet virtually every legitimate DD-214 that we've seen from the Vietnam War era and since is typed in a consistent case and font.

Decorations. While some service personnel have served in more than one military branch — Army, Navy, Air Force, Marine Corps — the number is comparatively small.[311] Forged DD-214s, on the other hand, often lay claim to medals and awards from more than one branch. For example, it would be virtually impossible for someone to have been awarded both a Navy Cross and the Distinguished Service Cross for service in Vietnam.

Misidentifying one's alleged decoration is a dead giveaway. For example, Marines don't earn a Combat Infantryman Badge; it's a Combat Action Ribbon.

Sometimes, merely inserting an unearned decoration in a place where it doesn't belong can undo a Fake Warrior. The POW designation is virtually never shown on a DD-214.[312] And because the POW medal was not even authorized until 1985 (by Title 10, *United States Code,* Section 1128), no veteran could lay claim to the award prior to that time.[313]

Another glaring mistake Fake Warriors are prone to make concerning medals stems from simple greed. They award themselves too many! While we've seen DD-214s laced with an unbelievable number of medals, an alleged SEAL won the prize for awarding himself — all in capital letters on his DD-214 — no less than the "Navy Cross, Silver Star (2) Dis. Ser. Medal, Bronze Star (3), Purple Heart (6) [!], Navy Comm. Good Conduct (2) Prisoner of War, Navy Exp. National Defense Combat Action Vietnam Ser. United Nat. Ser. Rep. Vietnam Com. Navy Unit Co. Pres. Unit Cit. Merit Unit Comm. Navy 'E' Rib.Rep. Vietnam Cross Gal."[314]

Then there are the Fake Warriors who describe a medal erroneously, referring to the Purple Heart Medal, say, as the Purple Heart 'Award'.

Units. Occasionally there has been some branch crossover. But common sense dictates that it would be virtually impossible for someone in Vietnam to have been a Navy SEAL *and* an Air Commando.

Vietnam service. Block 19 of the DD-214, effective November 1, 1972, contains the sentence "INDOCHINA OR KOREA SERVICE SINCE AUGUST 5, 1964," and provides a 'yes or no' box to check. Sometimes, the 'yes' box is checked, but nowhere else on the DD-214 is his service in Vietnam or Korea indicated — a glaring omission. Sometimes, although an impostor will check the 'no' box, he later contradicts himself by claiming elsewhere in his DD-214 that he did indeed serve in Vietnam or Korea.

Alterations. For quite a while[315] it was not been easy (although not impossible) to obtain a blank DD-214 form — especially one dating from the Vietnam War period — the preferred *modus operandi* of Fake Warriors who have done at least some military service has been to alter their own DD-214. It's a crude technique, but it works.

As Richard Davis told us in Chapter 4, he used white-out to obliterate the authentic information in certain DD-214 boxes, after which he photocopied the altered form. On his partially blank copy, he typed in new information — decorations, POW status, whatever — then photocopied his doctored DD-214. Voila, a hero is born. Not all impostors are as deft as was Davis in making alterations, and some of them are downright sloppy. Look for inconsistent entries, careless misspellings, even telltale differences in ink density.

Wounds. How about this on a DD-214? "AK-47 gun shot, left knee, 1963, Quang Tri, Vietnam; AK-47 gunshot, right leg (thigh), Kien Hoa, Vietnam; gunshot left temple." Apparently, it never occurred to this gung-ho impostor that the description of wounds never appears on a legitimate DD-214, let alone the weapon that caused them, where on the body they occurred, and the exact geographical location of the incident![316]

A final, important point about DD-214s and other military records needs to be made, and an unpleasant one at that. Even though the DD-214 is often crucial in identifying and exposing a Fake Warrior, and even though it would appear that DD-214 information provided by the NPRC in St. Louis is *prima facie* correct and reliable, unfortunately that's not always the case. DD-214s are based entirely on information in the service member's file. What's in that file, and how it got there, can be a substantial problem.

NPRC is only the *custodian* of military records. That facility cannot edit, alter, correct or in any other manner make changes to a military record in its custody. (There are formal military "correction of records" procedures.)

Regrettably, however, it is not unusual to find a record that contains false information. This occurs, because in the past and perhaps even now, active, reserve, and retired military personnel were permitted actual hands-on access to their records (for example, in their unit) *before* they were archived at NPRC. Under those circumstances, it was easy for a Fake Warrior to doctor a file manually by hand or by substituting a page or more. How do we know? Because in a case handled by the authors and P.O.W. Network, the damning evidence was right there in the NPRC file: The Fake Warrior not only added to his file an entirely new page chock full of false information, but *the fool negligently left the original page in the file.*[317] The anomalous result of this kind of counterfeiting of records is a 'legitimate' DD-214 containing underlying information that is, itself, false.

There have been cases in which veterans have spent years helpfully providing 'lost' documents to records centers, which turned out to be false — sometimes having based the information and documents on another veteran's service.

The only solution to this aspect of the Fake Warrior problem is cross-checking even documents received from government records centers, using information provided in this book.

EXPOSING FAKE WARRIORS

Once a Fake Warrior has been identified, the next step is exposure. Some of the most active Phony Busters have shared with us certain of their techniques.

P.O.W. Network sends information about an impostor, via e-mail, to every non-profit organization, church, veterans organization, newspaper, radio and television station, city hall, court, government office, VA installation, and law enforcement agency — all within one-hundred miles of where the Fake Warrior lives.

Other Phony Busters use the phone, e-mail, and/or snail mail, when they tip off spouses, lovers, parents, children, friends, employers, and veterans groups to which the Fake Warrior belongs.[318]

One Phony Buster, a Navy veteran, calls impostors on the telephone:

> I've personally called several dozen. It's amazing what a badass you can be on the phone! Most of the phonies back right down. . . . A few still stick to their stories; then one must take more severe methods, like calling an employer or girlfriend or newspaper reporter. Once I called a US Senator's office to inform the senator that he had been bamboozled by a phony constituent in Iowa."[319]

This same Phony Buster "shotgunned faxes to a company headquarters, letting a Fake Warrior's cohorts in on his little secret."[320]

Television tabloid shows and talk radio (especially those dominated by conservative voices) can be powerful tools in exposing Fake Warriors.

Using the Internet can be a real time-saver, with information traveling worldwide in mere seconds.

One of the most effective ways to expose a Fake Warrior is through the wide circulation afforded by the print media.[321] In mid-2002, the conscientious publisher of the *McCurtain Gazette*, an Oklahoma newspaper, wrote to P.O.W. Network:

> Dan Corley, Okemah, Oklahoma, appeared on podium Sunday in Idabel, Okla., for opening service of Vietnam Memorial Moving Wall. Was announced as one of only 14 POWs in Vietnam who escaped. Said to have been in tiger cage for 18 months. I would appreciate any info you have on him. I am a newspaper editor

> and will be writing a story for Tuesday's paper."

The Phony Busters' response was quick and to the point: "PLEASE DO NOT RUN THE STORY NOTING HIM AS A POW. HE IS A LIAR, FRAUD, PHONY." Details were supplied.

The publisher contacted Fake Warrior Corley, asking for corroboration of his claims. After Corley launched into the usual excuses (e.g., "advice of counsel") and the braggadocio threat of a lawsuit ("It will be interesting to see what changes I make when I own your local newspaper"), the following story appeared in the *McCurtain Gazette*:

> The Vietnam Memorial Moving Wall is so renowned that it draws tens of thousands each place it visits to honor those on the wall, those who made the ultimate sacrifice for their country. Unfortunately, the wall is also so renowned that it draws another type of visitor: phonies that prey on the emotions of others.
>
> Among those who visited Sunday's opening ceremony for the wall in Idabel was a man who wasn't listed on the program, because organizers didn't know in advance that he was going to attend. That man, Dan Corley, told organizers he was a prisoner-of-war during Vietnam; in fact, that he was one of only a handful of Americans who escaped from his captors.
>
> He also told of the horrors of his captors torturing him, of keeping him in a 4-foot by 4-foot tiger cage, of stabbing split bamboo pieces into his skin, then dousing them with diesel and setting them afire.
>
> But is his story true?
>
> "Please do not run a story denoting him as a POW. He is a liar, a fraud, a phony," say the keepers of a web site that lists biographies of POWS in Vietnam. The site also has a list of those said to be POW phonies. On that list is the name Dan Corley, but not on the list

of real POWs. Chuck and Mary Schantag, who maintain the site, minced no words when this newspaper, trying to find Corley's biography, told them of his appearance at the opening ceremony of the moving wall here.

"According to all available records from the U.S. government, posted publicly on the Internet (www.pownetwork.org) and on numerous sites, Mr. Corley was never captured, detained, missing in action for two hours nor any amount of time during the Vietnam War," they write. "He wasn't rescued and did not escape. He was never on covert ops, secret missions, his papers were not burned in St. Louis, his mission wasn't classified nor did he beg to be kept off the lists for privacy sake. He is not a "lost sheep" nor a member of the group of legitimate returnees. His statements to this effect, since 2000, have disgraced the honor of the many that served, the families that still wait, and those that have returned," the Schantags write.

But could the couple be mistaken? After getting their e-mailed response, this newspaper then checked U.S. Department of Defense websites, which list all Southeast Asia POWs and MIAs, along with specific details on each. The Department of Defense even breaks down POWs by state. Corley's name is not to be found, appearing to bolster the Schantags' claim. Further, a crosscheck of the information on the Schantags' site against information on government websites verifies at least the accuracy of their POW listings.

Later, a spokesman from the Pentagon returned a call, saying the information on the Department of Defense website was accurate. Corley was at the wall Tuesday morning, talking with those who visited. Asked about the claims of his being a phony, Corley became livid and threatened litigation. Corley indicated he was aware of the website listing of POW biographies, but was unaware he was listed on their list of phonies. He left Tuesday morning after this newspaper asked him about the Schantags' web site,

> the Department of Defense information and about the comments made by the newspaper publisher at Okemah. Corley said his records had been lost in St. Louis, and that it took him over a year to get his DD 214 (military discharge papers). He offered to fax them to this newspaper, but later e-mailed, saying after talking with an attorney, he had changed his mind.
>
> The paper also contacted Corley's hometown paper at Okemah. Ironically,
>
> Corley had actually worked at the paper as a reporter. Publisher Guy Mason said he was not surprised at this newspaper's discovery when trying to find a biography on him. "He was real active in the American Legion here and some of the members got suspicious and ran a check on him," Mason said. That's when Mason said he thought Corley was first exposed as a fraud. "I guess the guy can't help it," he said. "He lies about everything." Corley said he did indeed work as a reporter at the Okemah paper. Asked to explain why the publisher there would say such things (he was shown the direct quotes), Corley responded, "He's a liar."
>
> Mary Schantag wasn't bothered by Corley's litigation threats against either her web site or this newspaper. She said phonies typically respond in this way when confronted with the truth. Schantag said a suit would allow the opportunity to discover if Corley has received any government money improperly, as they have found to be the case several times with others making false claims about military service.[322]

Despite Corley's threadbare excuses, despite all the bluster and the threats, eventually he caved in.[323]

The despicable conduct by Fake Warriors spelled out in this Chapter raises an important question: How can these people be punished?

CHAPTER 6

HOW CAN FAKE WARRIORS BE PUNISHED?

"Wherever a Knave is not punished, an honest man is laughed at." [324]

Before we examine the weapons available to punish Fake Warriors, it's necessary to explain a controlling principle that's as important as the legal distinction between *motive* and *intent*, explained earlier.

The First Amendment to the Constitution of the United States provides that "Congress shall make no law . . . abridging the freedom of speech. . . ." Similar prohibitions apply to the states through the due process clause of the Fourteenth Amendment and in each state's Bill of Rights.

Constitutional jurisprudence makes an important distinction between what is called *pure speech*, such as the contents of a book, and speech which accompanies action, such as denouncing the Vietnam War while burning a draft card.

Ever since the Bill of Rights was ratified in 1791, the Supreme Court of the United States has held repeatedly (often in the face of forceful dissents) that the protection of even pure speech is not *absolute*. Despite the textual —

and unequivocal — protection of free speech embodied in our Constitution, government can limit even *pure speech*, such as hard-core pornography. As to speech accompanied by action, such as protest marches, much of that also can be regulated.

Fortunately, however, most pure speech is still protected. An excellent example is found in the case of *Cohen* v. *California*.

The year was 1968. Protest against the Vietnam War was raucous and widespread. Paul Robert Cohen opposed both the war and the draft. One day, he showed up at the Los Angeles County Court where a policeman noticed him in the corridor outside one of the courtrooms. Cohen wore a jacket on the back of which were the words: "Fuck the Draft." Entering the courtroom, Cohen removed his jacket and stood with it folded over his arm. Meanwhile, the offended policeman sent a note to the court's presiding judge, suggesting that Cohen be held in contempt of court. The judge declined to do so.

Cohen had not threatened, or engaged in, violence. He had not caused any disturbance. Nevertheless, he was arrested as soon as he emerged from the courtroom. Charged with violation of California Penal Code Section 415 — prohibiting "maliciously and willfully disturb[ing] the peace or quiet of any neighborhood or person . . . by . . . offensive conduct . . ." — Cohen testified that although he'd worn the jacket knowing what was displayed on the back, he had done so merely as a way of informing the public of how strongly he felt about the war and the draft.

Cohen's defense was unavailing. Convicted under the California statute and sentenced to thirty days in jail, he appealed to the California Court of Appeals. The conviction was affirmed. The California Supreme Court refused to take the case.

Cohen sought review in the Supreme Court of the United States — which was granted.

Justice John M. Harlan, writing for a 7-2 majority, began the Court's opinion with a pointed observation: "This case may seem at first blush too inconsequential to find its way into our books, but the issue it presents is of no small constitutional significance."[325] Indeed, the *Cohen* case is significant as well, regarding what legal options may — and may not — be available to Phony Busters seeking to expose Fake Warriors.

Justice Harlan started his analysis with what, in the Court's view, the *Cohen* case was *not* about. It did not involve any *conduct* on Cohen's part, only speech. There was no showing of an intent by Cohen to incite disobedience, no evidence that he'd attempted to disrupt the draft.

Moreover, Harlan reasoned, the words "Fuck the Draft" on Cohen's jacket were not obscene.[326] Nor, Harlan continued, could Cohen's three-word display be construed as "fighting words" — those "personally abusive epithets which, when addressed to the ordinary citizen, are, as a matter of common knowledge, inherently likely to provoke violent reaction."[327] Moreover, the facts of the *Cohen* case did not present the Court with a *captive audience* situation, where a speaker forces unwelcome words on another person's private space.

In other words, Cohen's *message* did not fall into any of the categories of *pure speech* which the Court in other cases had ruled could be regulated, or even prohibited, by the government. Accordingly, the Supreme Court of the United States ruled that the 'expression' on the back of Cohen's jacket was protected speech.

In discussing the *Cohen* case in the first edition some nine years ago, we wrote that "[w]hile the facts of *Cohen* v. *California* narrowly involved the public display of a crude vulgarity, the *principle* for which the decision stands is applicable to a *pure speech* situation involving a Fake Warrior. A military impostor's mere *words* — no matter how exaggerated, no matter how completely false they may be — are not *legally* actionable." We made this statement years before enactment of the federal *Stolen Valor Act* and the Supreme Court's 2012 ruling on its constitutionality in *United States* v. *Alvarez*, which is discussed in the next chapter.

In the meantime, in this chapter, we want to make a related point: Regardless of whether a Fake Warrior's *pure speech* is constitutionally protected, an imposter's lies will not protect him in all situations, because usually there is more involved. If his false statements are made under oath, or if he obtains someone else's property through fraud, or if his words are accompanied by action, the likelihood is that he's violating some state and/or federal law. Nor does the *Cohen* case rule out the possibility that an impostor can be punished in other *non-legal* ways.

As we approach our examination of both legal and non-legal weapons through which Fake Warriors can be punished, it's important to reiterate the lesson of Chapter 1: No matter what the Fake Warrior's *motive,* it is no defense to a criminal charge. What determines criminal guilt is *intent.*[328]

STATE CRIMES

It's understandable, especially because of the Stolen Valor Act, for people to mistakenly assume that any crimes committed by a Fake Warrior falls within the exclusive jurisdiction of federal authorities.[329] After all, their conduct involves the military. But, as we'll soon see, while a host of federal crimes *do* arise from the imposture of Fake Warriors, there are at least four major *state* criminal laws that an impostor can have violated.

For example, the key document most utilized by Fake Warriors is a doctored DD-214, and in Chapter 4 we saw how Richard Davis falsified his DD-214 to give himself a service history, military assignments and activities, and medals he didn't deserve. We've also seen some other uses to which doctored DD-214s have been put. Let's assume the following scenario:

A Fake Warrior doctors his DD-214.[330]

He files the document with the County Clerk.[331]

Then he applies for a special automobile license plate — POW, Purple Heart, whatever — using the doctored DD-214 as proof of entitlement. To obtain the license plate, he must first sign his name to an Applicant's Certification, representing that the information he has provided, and any accompanying documentation, "is true and correct to the best of my knowledge."[332]

From the Motor Vehicle Bureau, the impostor proceeds to the Civil Service Department. There, he files yet another application — this one for employment — and claims a preference based upon his military service. What does he use as proof of entitlement? His doctored DD-214.

The Fake Warrior has just committed at least *four* separate crimes under the laws of most states.[333]

Doctoring a DD-214, without more, constitutes forgery:

> A person is guilty of forgery . . . when, with intent to defraud [or] deceive . . . he falsely makes, completes or alters a written instrument which is or purports to be, or which is calculated to become, or to represent if completed: (1) A[n] . . . instrument which does or may evidence, create, transfer, terminate or otherwise affect a legal right, interest, obligation or status; or (2) A public record, or an instrument filed or required or authorized by law to be filed in or with a public office or public servant; or (3) A written instrument officially issued or created by a public office, public servant or governmental instrumentality . . . . *Forgery* [*in this degree*] *is a class D felony.*[334]

The moment the Fake Warrior doctors the DD-214, he commits an additional crime, a class A misdemeanor: "A person is guilty of criminal possession of a forged instrument [the doctored DD-214] . . . when, with knowledge that it is forged and with intent to defraud [or] deceive . . . he utters [uses], or *possesses* a forged instrument.[335]

The moment the Fake Warrior files his forged DD-214 with the New York County Clerk, he commits a class A misdemeanor: "A person is guilty of *offering* [as distinguished from merely possessing] a false instrument for filing . . . when, knowing that a written instrument contains a false statement or false information, he presents it to a public office or public servant with the knowledge or belief that it will be filed with, registered or recorded in or otherwise become a part of the records of such public office or public servant."[336]

The moment the Fake Warrior applies for the license plates, he commits another class A misdemeanor under the same statute, New York Penal Law Section170.20: "A person is guilty of criminal possession of a forged instrument . . . when, with knowledge that it is forged and with intent to defraud [or] deceive . . . he *utters* or possesses a forged instrument.[337] In other words, mere possession of the doctored DD-214 violates *one* part of the statute. Attaching it to the license plate application — what the statute calls "uttering" — is a violation of the other part.[338]

There are other state-level statutory crimes a Fake Warrior is likely to violate.

Claiming a civil service preference is one. In some jurisdictions, this constitutes the crime of larceny. New York law defines larceny as the wrongful obtaining of property accompanied by the intent to deprive the owner of it. There are various ways to commit this crime. One traditional way is named *false pretenses* (a legal term for lying). Clearly, using a forged DD-214 to obtain civil service preferences — getting the job itself, or a higher position, or more than normal salary — constitutes the intentional use of false pretenses to obtain property to which the Fake Warrior is not otherwise entitled.

In situations where no doctored DD-214s are involved, a Fake Warrior may jeopardize himself in other ways. An example is the Fake Warrior discussed in the Introduction. Recall 'Colonel' Connolly and his habit of donning military uniforms, wearing unearned medals, and parading himself at patriotic events? Most states criminalize this conduct:

> A person is guilty of criminal impersonation . . . when he: (1) Impersonates another and does an act in such assumed character with intent to obtain a benefit . . . ; or (2) Pretends to be a representative of some . . . organization and does an act in such pretended capacity with intent to obtain a benefit . . .

> ; or (3) (a) Pretends to be a public servant, or wears or displays without authority any uniform, badge, insignia or facsimile thereof by which such public servant is lawfully distinguished, or falsely expresses by his words or actions that he is a public servant or is acting with approval or authority of a public agency or department; and (b) so acts with intent to induce another to submit to such pretended official authority, to solicit funds or to otherwise cause another to act in reliance upon that pretense.[339]

As useful as these state statutes are in punishing Fake Warriors, they pale in comparison with the weapons available to the federal government (putting aside for the moment the Stolen Valor Act discussed in Chapters 7 and 8, and the Fake Warrior Act discussed in Chapter 9).

FEDERAL CRIMES

There have been relatively few federal prosecutions of Fake Warriors (even after enactment of the Stolen Valor Act), although at least seven federal criminal statutes exist which can be violated by imposter conduct.

Analogous to the typical state crime of impersonation is Title 18, *United States Code*, Section 912, which deals with "False personation — officer or employee of the United States":

> Whoever falsely assumes or pretends to be an officer or employee acting under the authority of the United States or any department, agency or officer thereof, and acts as such . . . shall be fined under this title or imprisoned not more than three years, or both.

Lest anyone wonder whether this federal criminal statute applies to modern-day

Captains of Kopenick who parade around in military uniforms and adorn their thrusting chests with rows of unearned medals, the 1949 case of *United States* v. *Wight*[340] is instructive.

Wight was indicted under Section 912 for "masquerading as an enlisted man of the Air Force." He pleaded guilty, and neither the trial court nor the federal Court of Appeals had any difficulty in concluding that the statute's intent and language unmistakably applied to a civilian impostor claiming to be a serviceman: "[O]ne who falsely impersonated an enlisted man in the Air Force was holding himself out as an employee of the United States and . . . he was within the condemnation of the statute. An enlisted man is no less chargeable under the statute merely because, by its language, it also includes officers."

Although Wight was prosecuted and convicted only for the crime of impersonation,[341] he could have been prosecuted for other related crimes. Usually, impersonating a member of the United States military requires wearing an unauthorized uniform and unearned medals (like 'Colonel' Connolly). So, it's likely that a Fake Warrior could be prosecuted under multiple federal criminal statutes.

Indeed, because the Section 912 violation, as in *Wight*, almost invariably involves the wearing of a military uniform and medals, two *other* federal criminal statutes come into play.

Title 18, *United States Code*, Section 702 provides:

> Whoever, in any place within the jurisdiction of the United States . . . without authority, wears the uniform or a distinctive part thereof or anything similar to a distinctive part of the uniform of any of the armed forces of the United States . . . shall be fined . . . [$250] or imprisoned not more than six months, or both.[342]

Section 704 of that same title — "Military medals or decorations" — provides:

> In general. — Whoever knowingly wears, manufactures, or sells any decoration or medal authorized by Congress for the armed forces of the United States, or any of the service medals or badges awarded to the members of such forces, or the ribbon, button, or

rosette of any such badge, decoration or medal, or any colorable imitation thereof, except when authorized under regulations made pursuant to law, shall be fined under this title or imprisoned not more than six months, or both.

(a) Congressional Medal of Honor. —

(1) In general. — If a decoration or medal involved in an offense under subsection (a) is a Congressional Medal of Honor, in lieu of the punishment provided in that subsection, the offender shall be fined under this title, imprisoned not more than one year, or both.

(2) Definitions. — (A) As used in subsection (a) with respect to a Congressional Medal of Honor, "sells" includes trades, barters, or exchanges for anything of value. (B) As used in this subsection, "Congressional Medal of Honor" means a medal awarded under sections 3741, 6241, or 8741 of title 10.

Both Sections 702 and 704 came into play in the case of Roger Dale Dinsmore. The case arose in 1999, and it was one of the rare occasions — prior to enactment of the Stolen Valor Act — where a federal statute was invoked against the serious lies of a Fake Warrior. We obtained Dinsmore's official records from the United States District Court for the Eastern District of Tennessee:

> Roger Dale Dinsmore, age 53, of Church Hill, Tennessee, served in the United States Army from 1966 to February 1969. Dinsmore's military occupational specialty (MOS) was 51B20, carpentry and masonry specialist.
>
> Dinsmore served in the Republic of Vietnam (South Vietnam) from February 1966 to February 1967; Dinsmore reported that he served with an engineer unit. Dinsmore's military records reflect that during that period, he was awarded the National Defense

Service Medal, the Republic of Vietnam Commendation Medal, two overseas service ribbons, the Vietnam Service Medal, the Vietnam Cross of Gallantry (a unit award)[343], the Sharpshooter badge, and the Expert Hand Grenade Badge.[344]

Dinsmore states that he also was awarded the Good Conduct Medal during this period. Dinsmore held the rank of Specialist Four (E-4) at the time of his discharge. Dinsmore re-enlisted in the Army in 1976, but was discharged due to physical limitations from injuries Dinsmore reported he had received in a vehicle accident in Vietnam.

Over the past decade or more, Dinsmore has misrepresented his military service and has worn unauthorized uniforms, decorations, awards, and badges in furtherance of those misrepresentations.

Dinsmore has represented himself to be a "war hero" and has been sought as a preacher and inspirational speaker at churches and veteran's ceremonies throughout east Tennessee. At eleven separate churches in Anderson, Cocke, Sevier, Loudon, Hawkins, and Union Counties, between March 1998 to November 1998, Dinsmore appeared wearing a United States Army officer's dress green uniform with "U.S." insignia and Chaplain Corp[s] branch insignia affixed to the lapels and Major or Lieutenant Colonel rank insignia affixed to the epaulets.

Dinsmore falsely represented that he had re-entered military service in 1985 as a chaplain. Additionally, Dinsmore wore numerous medals, awards, and decorations for which he was not authorized, to include the Silver Star, the Purple Heart, the Distinguished Flying Cross, the Soldier's Medal, the Meritorious Service Medal, the Air Medal, the U.S. Army Aviator Badge, the U.S. Army Parachutist Badge, the U.S. Army Combat Infantryman's Badge, the U.S. Army Pathfinder Badge, the U.S. Army Special Forces tab, the U.S. Army Ranger tab, and the U.S. Army Special Forces unit patch.

Recall that the Silver Star is awarded for extreme heroism. The Purple Heart for combat wounds. The qualifications for these medals and all the other awards for valor falsely claimed by Dinsmore are spelled out in Chapter 5.[345]

The court continued:

> In his sermons to local churches and in interviews for area newspapers, Dinsmore falsely represented that he had received U.S. Army Special Forces (Green Beret) training and had served with the Special Forces in Vietnam. Dinsmore falsely stated that he had been on a "classified" Special Forces mission when he was captured and held as a prisoner of war (POW).
>
> Dinsmore falsely claimed to have been wounded in combat and to have been awarded the Purple Heart for his injuries. Dinsmore wore a Silver Star, which he falsely represented was awarded to him for having saved the life of his co-pilot when his helicopter was shot down in Cambodia.
>
> Dinsmore falsely claimed that some of his awards and decorations had been presented to him personally by President Reagan in 1986.
>
> Dinsmore appeared in the Army green uniform with the unauthorized decorations at Antioch Baptist Church, Clinton, Tennessee in March 1998; at Riverview Baptist Church, Newport, Tennessee in March-April 1998; at Fellowship Chapel Baptist Church, Sevierville, Tennessee in April 1998; at Vaughn Baptist Church, Lenoir City, Tennessee in May 1998; at Carter Town Baptist Church, Sevierville, Tennessee in May 1998; at Bethel Baptist Church, Sevierville, Tennessee in June 1998; at Calvary Baptist Church, Oak Ridge, Tennessee in June 1998; at East Rogersville Baptist Church, Rogersville, Tennessee in July 1998; at First Baptist Church, Maynardville, Tennessee, in July 1998; at New Bethel Baptist Church, Sevierville, Tennessee, in October 1998; at a

> Veteran's Day service at Resthaven Memorial Gardens, Jefferson County, Tennessee in November 1998; and at Providence Baptist Church, Seymour, Tennessee, in November 1998.

Apparently, although Dinsmore's tales were literally incredible on their face, he was more adept than most Fake Warriors at fooling gullible people by spinning tall tales about his military exploits. His success, while it lasted, may have been due to his targeted audience: religious men and women to whom it would never have occurred that their chaplain would lie to them.

How was Dinsmore finally identified and exposed?

Ironically, by another chaplain. Said the court:

> In late 1998, retired military officers and non-commissioned officers (NCOs) in east Tennessee reported to the post chaplain at Fort Campbell, Kentucky that Dinsmore was representing himself to be an Army chaplain. The post chaplain referred the matter to the Army Criminal Investigation Detachment (CID) at Fort Campbell. Dinsmore was interviewed by a CID special agent in early January 1999, at which time Dinsmore admitted that he had misrepresented his military service and had worn unauthorized uniforms, decorations, awards, and badges. Because Dinsmore was a civilian (i.e. "Colonel" Connolly), the matter was subsequently referred to the Federal Bureau of Investigation.
>
> Dinsmore was re-interviewed on February 17, 1999.[[346]] Dinsmore again admitted he had misrepresented his military service and had worn the uniform, decorations, awards, and badges without authorization. Dinsmore stated that the only pecuniary gain he had received from his deception was approximately $3,500 in "love offerings" he received from the churches at which he spoke. Dinsmore expressed remorse for his misconduct and indicated his desire to apologize to those persons he had deceived.[347]

It's apparent that Dinsmore had a strong desire to reveal his masquerade.

When he appeared at the office of the United States Attorney in response to the government's invitation for him to come in for a discussion, even before Dinsmore spoke to the lawyers, "he confessed to the receptionist."[348]

Roger Dale Dinsmore was charged with two federal crimes.[349] Count One charged a violation of Title 18, *United States Code*, Section 702:

> [T]hat Dinsmore "did, without authority, wear the uniform and distinctive parts thereof of an armed force of the United States, to wit, a United States Army officer's green uniform with U.S. insignia and Chaplain Corps branch insignia affixed to the labels and Lieutenant Colonel rank insignia affixed to the epaulets. . . ."

Count Two charged a violation of Title 18, *United States Code*, Section 704:

> [T]hat Dinsmore "did, without authority, knowingly wear decorations and medals authorized by Congress for the armed forces of the United States and service medals and badges awarded to members of such forces, to wit, the Silver Star, the Purple Heart, the Distinguished Flying Cross, the Soldier's Medal, the Meritorious Service Medal, the Air Medal, the U.S. Army Aviator Badge, the U.S. Army Parachutist Badge, the U.S. Army Combat Infantryman's Badge, the U.S. Army Pathfinder Badge, the U.S. Army Special Forces tab, the U.S. Army Ranger tab, and the U.S. Army Special Forces unit patch. . . ."[350]

On March 3, 1999, Dinsmore appeared before United States Magistrate Judge Dennis Inman. Some of the local veterans who had exposed Dinsmore were in attendance. Dinsmore, wearing a sports jacket and turtleneck sweater, was "shaking like a leaf." Choosing to represent himself, he admitted that he was guilty "before you [the judge] and God almighty." Although he never explained *why* for ten years he had been a Fake Warrior, or *why* he had purchased a uniform,[351] the Assistant United States Attorney informed the court that the defendant had admitted to investigators his "desire to get the respect that would be accorded a war hero."[352]

At the sentencing, Judge Inman — after making sure Dinsmore knew his rights before he forfeited them by pleading guilty — accepted his plea.

Unfortunately, the judge's sentence of this Fake Warrior — facing a year in jail, six months on each of the two counts — who had benefited from his brazen imposture for a decade was unconscionably lenient: a $4,000 fine to be paid over a four-year period, and five years supervised probation.

Magistrate Judge Inman was apparently more comfortable with imposing soft penalties rather than punitive ones. In addition to the fine and probation, Dinsmore was ordered to continue with his psychotherapy for as long as his therapist and probation officer thought it necessary.[353]

The judge also issued a list of activities Dinsmore was forbidden to engage in: no more lying about his military record, no more participating in any veteran-related affairs, no more wearing a military uniform or phony decorations. [354] It's more than likely Judge Inman included these conditions because the government attorney had made sure Inman knew how deeply offended many veterans were by Dinsmore's conduct. Accordingly, the Judge required Dinsmore to send written corrections of his misrepresentations to everyone who'd been misled by his lies. When Dinsmore made his final statement — "I apologize to the court" — the judge replied, appropriately, "It's not me that you need to apologize to."[355] Clearly, he had been sobered by the prosecutor's statement that a lot of veterans felt strongly about how Dinsmore's lies had cheapened "the value of true military honors."[356]

Although in the *Dinsmore* case there didn't appear to be any falsification of documents, as noted earlier, counterfeiting DD-214s and other military-related papers is one of the Fake Warriors' tools. Understandably, we tend to associate the crime of counterfeiting with shifty-eyed criminals bent over a printing press and cranking out phony hundred-dollar bills. Most people aren't aware that, for Fake Warriors, counterfeiting is yet another serious pitfall.

Title 18, *United States Code*, Section 498—"Military or naval discharge certificates"—provides:

> Whoever forges, counterfeits, or falsely alters any certificate of discharge from the military or naval service of the United States, or uses, unlawfully possesses or exhibits any such certificate, knowing the same to be forged, counterfeited, or falsely altered, shall be fined under this title or imprisoned not more than one year, or both.

In late 1999, the United States Attorney for the Middle District of Pennsylvania charged that Raymond Eduard Aucker — a former Pennsylvania district superintendent of schools who claimed he had been a SEAL[357] — "did use, unlawfully possess and exhibit military and naval discharge certificates, knowing the same to be forged, counterfeited, or falsely altered, in that they identified decorations, commendations, and awards that he had not received, including, but not limited to a Vietnam Service Ribbon, Vietnam Campaign Medal, Seal Medal,, and Purple Heart," in violation of Title 18, U.S.C. Section 498."[358]

When Aucker pleaded guilty, he faced a substantial fine and up to a year in a federal prison for his transgressions.

What did the sentencing judge give this fake SEAL? In a word, leniency: two years' probation and two-hundred hours of "community service."

Even in a case that combined violations of *three* U.S.C. provisions (Sections 702, 704, and 498), as with Dinsmore the same slap-on-the-wrist "justice" was meted out.

Neither of these cases was unique. Donald R. Nicholson, a retired Ohio police chief, claimed to have been Special Forces *and* a POW. Nicholson had even prevailed upon a National Guard battalion commander to pin on the Distinguished Service Cross at an armory ceremony.[359] A typically gullible journalist not only characterized Nicholson as a war hero, but also took a potshot at the Department of the Army:

> [U]ntil 1997, the federal government refused to recognize Mr.

> Nicholson's heroic action because the mission that led to his capture was classified. * * * Mr. Nicholson was nominated in 1970 for the Medal of Honor, the country's highest military award, but the Department of the Army denied the nomination.

Less than a month later, the reporter was forced to eat his words. The headline of his article read:

> EX-POLICE CHIEF FAKED WAR RECORD
> "Medal Bought to Try to Get More [VA] Benefits."[360]

Charged with the unauthorized wearing of military medals and decorations, as well as with unlawful use of a false military discharge certificate, Nicholson pleaded guilty. His sentence? A paltry three years' probation.

Perhaps the most egregious Fake Warrior conduct punishable under federal criminal law is larceny — whether committed by fraud or otherwise. The victim is usually the Veterans Administration. The VA, incidentally, has lost incalculable sums in the past half-century alone. The usual scenario is summed up in the following press release issued by the VA:

> Man indicted for claiming to be a veteran in order to receive medical care from VA. Richard J. Griffin, Inspector General, Department of Veterans Affairs (VA) announced today that in U.S. District Court, St. Louis, MO, James C. Brown was indicted by a Federal grand jury for theft of Government services.
>
> Griffin stated that the indictment resulted from an investigation conducted by his Central Field Office. The indictment alleges that in June 1993, Brown, who is not a veteran, presented an altered military discharge form to the VA Medical Center, St. Louis, in order to receive medical care to which he was not entitled. From June 1993, until December 1998, *he continued to receive fraudulently over $285,000 worth of medical care.* If convicted, Brown faces up to 10 years' imprisonment and a fine of up to $250,000.[361]

Although very few larceny/fraud cases involving the Veterans Administration are actually brought, and although the sentences imposed when the VA does go to court are mostly disgracefully lenient, there is a positive side to this otherwise depressing situation: At least statutory tools do exist through which prosecutors might be persuaded to pursue thieving Fake Warriors.

Three other federal criminal statutes can be used to great effect against the machinations of Fake Warriors.

Title 18, *United States Code*, Section 1001, is one of the most deadly of all federal criminal statutes. This law applies to everyone who deals with the federal government in any capacity. Section 1001 provides:

> [W]hoever, in any manner within the jurisdiction of the executive, legislative, or judicial branch of the Government of the United States, knowingly and willfully — (1) falsifies, conceals, or covers up by any trick, scheme, or device a material fact; (2) makes any materially false, fictitious, or fraudulent statement or representation; or (3) makes or uses any false writing or document knowing the same to contain any materially false, fictitious, or fraudulent statement or entry; *shall be fined under this title, imprisoned not more than 5 years or, if the offense involves international or domestic terrorism . . . imprisoned not more than 8 years, or both. . . .* [362]

Consider this: The statute reaches *virtually every contact anyone could possibly have with the entire federal government.* It applies to every conceivable material fact, every statement and document. And it punishes, as a felony, prevarications of every kind — even if the impostor doesn't lie under oath, or otherwise swear under penalty of perjury.[363] The simplest example is lying to an FBI agent about something *material.*

There are thousands of these Section 1001 cases. But the bad news is that *not a single reported case involves lying about military service,*[364] notwithstanding that the essence of Fake Warrior conduct falls precisely within Section 1001 prohibitions. In virtually every case we refer to in this book, the Fake

Warrior has falsified, concealed, or covered up by trick, scheme, or device, some material fact. Either that, or he has made a *materially* false, fictitious, or fraudulent statement or representation, or made or used a false writing or document, knowing it contained materially false, fictitious, or fraudulent statements or entries.

Even as we were completing this chapter in the first edition, a Section 702/ Section 704 case arose in the Western District of Missouri that had, as well, a Section 1001 element.

An FBI Special Agent had submitted an affidavit to a federal court in support of his request for a criminal complaint and arrest warrant charging Ralph Ervin Crowder, also known as Roy A. Toups, with violations of Title 18, United States Code, Sections 702 (unauthorized wearing of the uniform of the Armed Forces of the United States) and Section 704 (a) (unauthorized wearing of the Congressional Medal of Honor).

A Kansas City veteran of the Navy had seen in someone's office "a photograph of a white male . . . wearing a United States Navy (USN) Admiral's summer white uniform and numerous military decorations including the Congressional Medal of Honor (CMH)."

The veteran's examination of the photograph revealed "that a Navy Expeditionary Medal and a Prisoner of War Medal were incorrectly placed in order of their precedence. The man in the photograph was also wearing a Command at Sea Badge on his left breast pocket" — which Admirals do not wear. The vet informed the FBI. The Bureau seized the incriminating photograph. The FBI then checked out Toups, but was unable to find anyone by that name in any of the databases they searched. The Special Agent then concluded: "It appeared likely that he ['Toups'] was an impostor."

Toups was arrested. He provided the FBI Special Agents with "United States of America Special Identification" indicating his affiliation with the NSA (the super-secret National Security Agency). The identification was immediately recognized as fraudulent." At the FBI office, Toups admitted his imposture and "was advised that record checks on the identifying information he had provided indicated that he was concealing his true identity. After some time, he reluctantly admitted his true name was Ralph Ervin Crowder. . . . Record checks on Crowder identified an outstanding Cole County, Missouri, warrant from 1979 for Parole Violation on an underlying charge of Fraudulent Checks."[365]

It is clear from these facts that Crowder apparently had violated at least four federal criminal statutes: Section 702, for wearing the uniform;[366] Section 704, for wearing the Medal of Honor; Section 912, for false personation; and Section 1001, for false statements and documentation.

But what was he actually charged with in a criminal complaint filed on July 10, 2002, in the United States District Court for the Western District of Missouri? Only the following two counts:

> Count 1. . . . defendant did knowingly and willfully and without authority, wear the uniform of an officer in the United States Navy, in violation of Title 18, United States Code, Section 702.
>
> Count 2. . . . defendant did knowingly and willfully and without authority . . . wear a decoration or medal authorized by Congress for the armed forces of the United States, that being the Congressional Medal of Honor, in violation of Title 18, United States Code, Section 702.[367]

While these Section 702 and Section 704 charges are entirely appropriate, it seemed to us inappropriate that Crowder was not charged, as well, with Section 912 and Section 1001 violations.

So we queried the United States Attorney in Missouri. Perhaps coincidentally, on the same day of our inquiry, the government filed an amended complaint adding a third count: possession of a false government ID card that identified Crowder as a member of the National Security Agency. This charge was under Title 18, *United States Code*, Section 1028 (a) (6):

> Defendant did knowingly possess an identification document

> of the United States, to wit a false government identification document identifying the defendant as a member of the United States National Security Agency, which document was produced without lawful authority, knowing that such document was so produced without such authority. . . ."[368]

Crowder was not, however, charged with either a Section 912 or a Section 1001 violation, and despite our explicit query, we never did receive an explanation of why not.

An important issue lurking just beneath the surface in the *Crowder* case — and many if not most other Fake Warrior cases — is whether the fraud (or other crime) involved the impostor *alone*, or whether he had active help from someone else, a co-conspirator. For example, when the FBI was investigating Crowder, they also contacted a woman friend of Crowder's about the photograph:

> She advised that the individual in the photo was . . . Roy A. Toups . . . . She produced the photo . . . and stated Toups was a retired Admiral in the United States Navy. She explained that Toups had recently retired from the USN . . . . She stated he had been a highly decorated Navy SEAL in Vietnam. . . . [S]he indicated that Toups worked for the National Security Agency (NSA). She stated Toups had shown her documents and identification from the NSA."

So, while the conversation about Ralph Ervin Crowder/aka Roy A. Toups concentrated on Crowder, no apparent effort was made by the FBI to extend its investigation to a woman who had access to the incriminating photograph, and at the very least, an awareness of his retired Admiral/decorated SEAL/NSA story. Since two other federal criminal statutes apply to persons who may have aided and abetted the imposture of a Fake Warrior, and since the woman may have been in league with Crowder, it was incumbent upon the FBI to try to ascertain either her innocence or complicity.

The two additional federal criminal statutes which might have applied to this woman, had she been thoroughly investigated and found complicit, are

Title 18, *United States Code*, Sections 2 and 371.

Section 2 provides:

> (a)Whoever commits an offense against the United States or aids, abets, counsels, commands, induces or procures its commission, is punishable as a principal.
>
> (b)Whoever willfully causes an act to be done which if directly performed by him or another would be an offense against the United States, is punishable as a principal.

Section 371 provides:

> If two or more persons conspire either to commit any offense against the United States, or to defraud the United States, or any agency thereof in any manner or for any purpose, and one or more of such persons do any act to effect the object of the conspiracy, each shall be fined under this title, or imprisoned not more than five years, or both. If, however, the offense, the commission of which is the object of the conspiracy, is a misdemeanor only, the punishment for such conspiracy shall not exceed the maximum punishment provided for such misdemeanor.

Applying these two sections to the *Crowder* case — and, by implication, to many other cases that we covered in earlier chapters — this question should have been raised by the investigators: What did a person other than the Fake Warrior have to do with his imposture, and why?

If Crowder's woman friend had, for example, obtained the uniform and medals for the Fake Warrior, or if she had knowingly conspired with him in his imposture, she could and should have been charged under either Section 2, or Section 371, or both. She was not charged. For all we know, she was not even investigated. Rarely, if ever, is an *enabler* charged with either aiding and abetting or conspiracy.

INVESTIGATORS AND PROSECUTORS

As we've seen, there is a powerful arsenal — both state and federal — with which to punish Fake Warriors, *if* a prosecutor is so disposed. The preliminary step is obvious: a thorough investigation of the suspected impostor's claims and conduct by the appropriate investigatory agency.

In most states, criminal investigations are conducted by local law enforcement - usually county sheriffs or district attorneys.[369] But despite the availability of laws that punish larceny, forgery, and other Fake Warrior conduct, *rarely do investigators at the local level concern themselves if those crimes are committed by military impostors* (unless vast sums of money are involved).

Even when an investigation of a military impostor *is* conducted — either by an official investigator, or by a Phony Buster acting on his own — there is a significant hurdle between a fruitful investigation and a recommended prosecution. It is called the doctrine of *prosecutorial discretion*.

The courts have repeatedly held that the decision to bring charges — or *not* to bring them — against someone who may have committed a crime, rests exclusively in the discretion of the prosecutor.[370] Neither the courts, nor the legislature, nor the governor, can force a prosecutor to prosecute. Even if some detective attached to the District Attorney's office puts together an ironclad case and strongly recommends prosecution, he can't make the DA take action.

What accounts for a decision not to prosecute a Fake Warrior? There are a number of possible explanations. The DA, understandably, may be unwilling to put scarce resources into a case he deems unimportant compared to, say, murder or rape. Or, the DA may feel sympathy for an impostor — maybe having told a few whoppers himself. Or, the DA may be unsure of obtaining a conviction, and thus reluctant to proceed without conclusive evidence (which is not always available). Or, the DA may be uneasy about how a jury might react to a Fake Warrior case. Or, the DA may be subject to local political pressures if a suspected impostor has standing in the community.

Can the District Attorney's office — without any discernable reason — arbitrarily decline to prosecute? It happens all the time.

Getting the federal government to investigate and then prosecute can be just as problematic — and in those cases prosecutorial discretion is only part of the problem. More often than not, the investigating authority is the Federal Bureau of Investigation.[371] Sometimes a Special Agent will do his job, sometimes not. We can hope that the FBI agent who chided Captain Mike McGrath for wanting to "embarrass an old man" was atypical.

But even if the FBI, as the investigatory agency, does put together a solid case, and even if the Bureau does strongly recommend prosecution, the United States Attorney for that federal district is under no obligation to prosecute.

LEGISLATURES

The role that legislatures, state and federal, could play in coping with the out-of-control problem of Fake Warriors is crucial. Legislatures make the laws, both those specifically addressed to Fake Warrior behavior (such as wearing unauthorized medals), and those that apply to *all* citizens but can also ensnare an impostor who, say, creates a forged document.

Since there seem to be more than enough laws that could be used to suppress the epidemic of False Warriors, why do we regard the legislature's role as so important?

The answer is because together with enacting laws — which is only one part of the legislature's job — that branch of government's responsibility is to provide *oversight*. Legislators are obliged to make sure that the laws they have enacted remain adequate to the task. That's why legislatures have the power to hold hearings and call expert witnesses in a public forum. If a particular law needs more teeth, or if it's deficient in some way, it's incumbent upon the legislature to amend that law.

As we will see in the next chapter, that was why the Stolen Valor Act was enacted.

THE EXECUTIVE BRANCH

As a practical matter, the President of the United States doesn't directly have anything to do with the problems posed by Fake Warriors, which, compared to his other concerns, are of little concern. But it is the President who appoints the Attorney General (with the consent of the Senate). And it is the Attorney General who can — and should — have a great deal to do with seeing that Fake Warriors are investigated, prosecuted, and punished through United States Attorneys everywhere in this country.

In a properly functioning legal system, word should come down from the top — if not from the Attorney General himself, then at least from the chief of the Criminal Division of the United States Department of Justice. The federal mandate ought to be this one: Alleged Fake Warrior cases are to be fully investigated and — if warranted — prosecuted to the fullest extent of the law.

On the state level, the situation is more flexible, and in theory, easier to implement. Governors can and should have much more of a hands-on role where Fake Warriors are concerned. After all, they appoint parole and clemency boards — and sometimes even the state's Attorney General. They also routinely deliver State of the State messages, in which they propose legislation. Often, governors have substantial leverage over local district attorneys — especially within their own political party. They appoint the head of the state police — an agency that usually possesses broad investigative power.[372]

In short, state governors are empowered — if they are so inclined — to strike a considerable blow against the Fake Warrior phenomenon.

But, the sad fact is that few of these elected officials are inclined to confront, let alone effectively deal with, the Fake Warrior problem.

PRIVATE LAWYERS

Lawyers in this country have their hands on the levers of power. They know how to construct arguments to legislators, many of whom are fellow lawyers. They know how to invoke the power of courts in which they, alone, are allowed to practice. They know how to make presentations to governors, whose political buttons they know how to push. For better or worse, lawyers hold the keys to the kingdom.

This fact alone enables private lawyers to make unparalleled contributions to the fight against Fake Warriors.

Take the unwillingness of investigators to investigate, or of prosecutors to prosecute. Not only can lawyers attempt to convince the appropriate authorities that investigation and prosecution is warranted, but they can also 'package' cases for the government by providing such crucial information as witness statements, copies of documents, and even photographs of Fake Warriors in uniform.

What else can a conscientious lawyer do?

- He can prepare written briefs for prosecutors, laying out the facts of a particular Fake Warrior's imposture and analyzing what law(s) that imposture violates;
- He can oppose clemency applications for convicts seeking to be released from prison because of false claims of military connected problems;
- He can draft and analyze legislation which would create new crimes — or, more important, stiffen the penalties for military imposture, based on laws already on the books;
- He can zealously defend Phony Busters when they are victimized by the "best-defense-is-a-good-offense" tactic of an unrepentant and aggressive Fake Warrior;

- He can assist in preparing Freedom of Information Act requests to obtain military records of those suspected of being Fake Warriors;
- He can lobby elected officials to lean on recalcitrant prosecutors, urging the latter to order proper investigations and, where justified, commence prosecutions;
- He can draft informative petitions that alert the public to a suspected Fake Warrior and, simultaneously, demand action against him;
- He can explain Fake Warrior behavior to the press and discuss the subject on radio, TV, or other available platforms;
- He can review proposed paid advertisements designed to expose Fake Warriors, making sure that the sponsors of such ads have not opened themselves up to a libel action.

Lawyers, in short, have an integral — indeed, indispensable — role to play in the identification, exposure, and punishment of Fake Warriors. We can hope that more of them step up to the plate, eager to exercise their considerable knowledge and skill on behalf of this important cause.

PRIVATE INITIATIVE

Even though state and federal investigators don't have to investigate, and state and federal prosecutors don't have to prosecute, still, there are ways to force their hand.

State investigators work for prosecutors — and prosecutors are elected.

The President of the United States appoints the Attorney General, who must be confirmed by the Senate — and the Senate is an elected body.

The President appoints the hundreds of United States Attorneys throughout the country — and every one of these US Attorneys must be confirmed by the Senate.

Special Agents of the Federal Bureau of Investigation not only work for the Attorney General, but also prepare cases for the United States Attorneys. So FBI agents' jobs are ultimately dependent on voter approval.

All of these people are political animals, and are, therefore, risk-adverse to bad publicity. *This makes them subject to political pressure which can be aimed at getting them to do their jobs.*

How to best exert that pressure?

One approach has the merit of being both easy and cost-free. Aroused private citizens — veterans in particular — should bombard the appropriate prosecutor with demands for investigation and prosecution of a suspected Fake Warrior. On the state level, telephone calls, e-mail, and snail mail should be directed to the county District Attorney. On the federal level, try to influence the United States Attorney for the federal district where the suspected imposture occurred.

Another approach — for those who can afford to spend a little money and a lot of time — is publicity. Consider taking out paid advertisements in local newspapers. Everyone is familiar with ads promoting a local politician or soliciting stockholder proxies or espousing a particular cause. Running an ad that exposes a Fake Warrior where he lives and works can be very effective.[373] The last thing an impostor wants to be subjected to is the shock or disappointment of friends and neighbors, let alone an employer.

But a word of caution. People make mistakes. A *supposed* Fake Warrior may be the real McCoy.[374] So, if you're the slightest bit unsure of your facts, running a false or misleading ad not only exposes you to civil liability, but it can have devastating consequences for an innocent person who turns out *not* to be an impostor. No well-meaning but mistaken Phony Buster wants to be the precipitating cause of job loss, a ruptured romantic relationship, the breakup of a marriage, or community censure. Even if you're convinced that your proposed ad is accurate, and even though truth is an absolute defense to a defamation lawsuit, you would be well advised to consult a qualified lawyer in advance and clear the text of your ad with him before running it.[375]

Even if you are sure of your facts and your lawyer gives you the go-ahead, you might want to consider an alternative — especially in a situation where the Fake Warrior is only sounding off, but has not, to your knowledge, broken any laws. Copy the suspected impostor with your *proposed* advertisement and a demand that he cease and desist. Chances are he'll get the message without further prodding.

Petition drives, talk radio, rallies and demonstrations, Op Ed articles, getting the ear of a sympathetic reporter or an investigative journalist — these are other excellent ways to focus public attention on a Fake Warrior. This kind of high profile public agitation has been successful in the past, and often results in investigations being conducted, prosecutions being brought, and convictions being obtained.

CHAPTER 7[376]
STOLEN VALOR ACT

Stolen: "Acquired, or possessed, as a result of some wrongful or dishonest act or taking, whereby a person willfully obtains . . . possession of property which belongs to another . . . and with the intent to deprive the owner of the benefit of ownership(or possession) permanently."[377]

Introduction

The Fake Warrior phenomenon is nothing new. It has a long and dishonorable history in the United States.

When George Washington established the first military medal in 1782,[378] the Purple Heart, he knew that it needed to be protected from people falsely claiming to be recipients.[379] He stated, "[s]hould any who are not entitled to these honors have the insolence to assume the badges of them, they shall be severely punished."[380] Today, Washington would be saddened and offended by the nature and extent of military imposters.

During American history, efforts have been made to expand the coverage of federal statutes punishing military imposture, and to increase their penalties. The most recent attempt at this was the enactment of the Stolen Valor Act of 2005.

This chapter discusses anti-Fake Warrior legislation prior to the Stolen Valor Act of 2005, the Act's legislative history, lower court challenges to it, and the case in which the Supreme Court of the United States answered the question of whether the SVA was constitutional, *U.S. v. Alvarez.*

Legislative History

a. Legislation pre-Stolen Valor Act

The Stolen Valor Act of 2005 was not the first attempt by Congress to impose criminal penalties on individuals falsely claiming to have received war medals.[381] The act that originally established Section 704 of title 18 of the United States Code, which the SVA modified, was based on Title 10, Section 1425 of the 1940 version of the United States Code.[382] That section entitled "Unlawful wearing, manufacture, or sale of medals, etc." provided:

> The *wearing, manufacturing, or sale* of the Congressional Medal of Honor, distinguished-service cross, distinguished-service medal, distinguished-flying cross, soldier's medal, or any other decoration or medal which has been, or may be, authorized by Congress for the military forces of the United States, or any of the service medals or badges which have been, or may hereafter be, awarded by the War Department, or the ribbon, button, or rosette of any of the said medals, badges, or decorations, of the form as is or may hereafter be prescribed by the Secretary of War, or of any colorable imitation thereof, is prohibited, except when authorized under such regulations as the Secretary of War may prescribe.
>
> Any person who knowingly offends against the provisions of this section shall, on conviction, be punished by a fine not exceeding $250 or by imprisonment not exceeding six months, or by both such fine and imprisonment.[383]

It's important to note that Section 1425, unlike the Stolen Valor Act of 2005, was expressly aimed not at speech, but at *conduct*: wearing, manufacturing, or sale. This distinction would loom large some sixty decades later when the Supreme Court ruled on the SVA.

A section of the federal code was created in 1948 to include war medals relating to the Navy and War Department.[384] The following year, the section was further expanded to include any service decoration awarded to any branch of the military.[385]

After these two changes, in 1952 Title 18 of the United States Code, Section 704, was codified.[386] It stated:

> Whoever knowingly *wears, manufactures, or sells* any decoration or medal authorized by Congress for the armed forces of the United States, or any of the service medals or badges awarded to the members of such forces, or the ribbon, button, or rosette of any such badge, decoration or medal, or any colorable imitation thereof, except when authorized under regulations made pursuant to law, shall be fined not more than $250 or imprisoned not more than six months, or both.[387]

Note the continuation of the *conduct* element of the crime: "*wears, manufactures, or sells.*"

After the 1952 codification, as 18 United States Code, Section 704, the statute remained substantively unchanged for many years.[388] The first significantly amended version appears in the 1994 United States Code. The 1994 version of 18 United States Code, Section704 divided the law into two sections; one dealt with general provisions including improper wearing, manufacturing, or selling of military decorations, and the other dealt with provisions specifically focused on the Congressional Medal of Honor.[389] Still, the statute punished *conduct*, not pure speech.

The provisions dealing with the Medal of Honor increased the possible incarceration penalty from six months to twelve months.[390] Another significant change in Congress's attempt to protect the Medal of Honor against unacceptable conduct was an increase of the fine from $250 to

$100,000.[391] Additionally, this section defined "sells" to mean, "trades, barters, or exchanges for anything of value."[392]

The Congressional Medal of Honor is the highest honor a member of the military can receive.[393] It has only been awarded approximately 3,500 times.[394] Compared to the next highest ranking medals awarded for valor, the Navy Cross, the Distinguished Service Cross (for the Army), and the Air Force Cross which combined have been awarded almost 20,000 times, the significance of the Medal of Honor is substantial.

The law remained unchanged in the updated publication of the United States Code in 2000.[395]

Eventually, because of the Vietnam, Kuwait, Afghanistan, and Iraq Wars and other military conflicts around the world, because of a marked increase in patriotism early in the Twenty-First Century, and more of a public awareness about how widespread and unpatriotic the Fake Warrior phenomenon had become, there was growing agitation for tougher legislation.

b. Legislative History of the Stolen Valor Act

On July 12, 2005, Representative John Salazar addressed the House of Representatives to discuss the importance of the Medal of Honor and express his respect for past recipients.[396] Salazar noted there were only 121 living recipients of the Medal of Honor.[397] He went on to assert "[t]he Nation's highest award is facing a serious challenge to its meaning and symbol."[398] Salazar expressed his disapproval of the current situation by stating, "I am outraged by the impostors who claim they have received this and other honors the military awards for deeds and actions of soldiers. These criminals not only dishonor themselves, but they dishonor the sacrifice that true recipients have made."[399]

Bravo! Salazar was right to be outraged, mostly.[400]

Soon after, Salazar announced his intention to introduce the Stolen Valor Act of 2005 into the House during the coming week.[401] He asserted that the

legislation would
better allow law enforcement officers to prosecute people who falsely *alleged* they received military medals and "restore the true meaning of these illustrious awards."[402]
He then urged the rest of the members of the house to join his effort "to reclaim the meaning of honor and bravery and sacrifice in these United States."[403]

Note Salazar's use of the word *alleged,* the clear meaning of which was 'spoken'. Salazar's proposal would make a sea change from the earlier statutes' criminalization of *conduct* to punishment of mere *speech.*

Salazar followed through on his promise and introduced the Stolen Valor Act of 2005 in the United States House of Representatives on July 19, 2005.[404] The bill included findings that asserted false claims of receiving military medals harmed the reputation and intrinsic meaning of the medals.[405] The findings also included a claim that federal law enforcement officers were "currently limited in their ability to prosecute fraudulent claims of receipt of military medals."[406] Finally, the findings asserted that changes in the current provisions were needed in order to better allow law enforcement officers to "protect the reputation and meaning of these medals."[407]

Pure speech was to be criminalized in the name of protecting against harm to medals' reputation and meaning, and because of difficulty in law enforcement.

The Stolen Valor Act of 2005 amended section 704 of title 18 of the United States Code.[408] The changes greatly expanded the punishable activities contained subsection (a) from the original text from only "wears, manufactures, or sells" to "purchases, attempts to purchase, solicits for purchase, mails, ships, imports, exports, produces black certificate of receipt."[409] Additionally, the bill sought to add "attempts to sell, advertises for sale, trades, barters, or exchanges for anything of value" after 'sells'.[410] These two changes more than quadrupled punishable conduct under the provision.[411]

The next major change was the addition of text to criminalize false claims about receipt of medals.[412] This section made it a crime to falsely represent oneself "verbally or in writing, to have been awarded any decoration or medal authorized by Congress for the armed forces of the United States, or any of the service medals or badges awarded to members of such forces . . . or any colorable imitation thereof."[413] The punishment for this offense included either a fine, imprisonment for six months, or both.[414] The new bill also sought to add specific punishments for some of the most distinguished military awards.[415] In these cases, the maximum punishment allowed was increased from six months in jail to a year in jail.[416]

Kent Conrad introduced the act in the United States Senate on November 10, 2005.[417] The findings listed in the Senate version were not significantly different than those listed in the House version, except for a few minor changes in wording.[418] The Senate version expanded the general criminal offense to cover the same activities as the House version.[419] However, the Senate called for a change in the definition portion of the Medal of Honor subsection of 18 United States Code, Section 704 to include duplicate Medals of Honor and replacement Medals of Honor.[420]

The Senate passed this version of the bill unanimously on September 7, 2006.[421] Following this, the Senate version moved to the House Judiciary Committee, which was reviewing the House version.

The House passed the Senate's version of the Act on December 6, 2006.[422]

President George W. Bush signed the SVA into law.

Professor Henry Mark Holzer, co-author of this book, had for months been telling the SVA's proponents and supporters that the false claims provisions were a violation of the free speech provision of the First Amendment.

c. Early Challenges to the Stolen Valor Act

It did not take long after the passage of the Stolen Valor Act to see cases challenging its constitutionality popping up in courts across the United

States. Soon after the Act became law, various United States Attorneys began bringing charges against individuals in violation of it.

Many of these individuals challenged the constitutionality of the Act, and courts throughout the United States varied in their decisions regarding the constitutional question.

In examining those cases, much of the commentary — lay and professional alike — has been wide of the mark, and thus misleading. Sloppy references have been to "the Stolen Valor Act" generally, rather than to the specific section of that Act the government charged was violated.

It was, and is, necessary to understand that *there is nothing unconstitutional about Section 702* (a)*, which criminalizes "wearing" unearned medals.*[423] Yet commentary about Section 702 (a) frequently referred not to this *conduct*, but to the "Stolen Valor Act" generically, which also contains Section 702 (*b*).

It is this section which punishes pure speech:

> FALSE CLAIMS ABOUT RECEIPT OF MILITARY DECORATIONS OR MEDALS. — Whoever *falsely represents himself or herself, verbally or in writing*, to have been awarded any decoration or medal authorized by Congress for the Armed Forces of the United States, any of the service medals or badges awarded to the members of such forces, the ribbon, button, or rosette of any such badge, decoration, or medal, or any colorable imitation of such item shall be fined under this title, imprisoned not more than six months, or both."[424]
>
> Which brings us to the two principal Section 702 (b) cases.
>
> The first case we want to discuss is *United States* v. *Strandlof.*[425]

Strandlof had never served in the armed forces, but had founded a veterans group and told its members he was a Marine captain, was wounded in Iraq, and earned a Purple Heart and a Silver Star.[426] Because Standlof's claims didn't ring true, some veterans questioned their legitimacy. As a result, Section 702 (b) charges were brought against Strandlof for violating the "Stolen Valor Act."[427]

Strandlof filed a motion to dismiss the charges. The federal district judge ruled that "[t]he Stolen Valor Act is . . . facially unconstitutional [on its face, as written, no matter how applied] as a content-based restriction on speech that does not serve a compelling government interest, and consequently . . . the Act is invalid as violative of the First Amendment."[428] Moreover, the judge ruled that the speech regulated by section 702 (b) did not fall within any of the few categories of pure speech that could constitutionally be punished (e.g., pornography, defamation).[429]

The government appealed. The United States Court of Appeals for the Tenth Circuit reversed the district court, ruling that the Stolen Valor Act was constitutional.[430] It stated "[w]e disagree with this reading [by the trial judge] of Supreme Court precedent and reverse. As the Supreme Court has observed time and again, false statements of fact do not enjoy constitutional protection, except to the extent necessary to protect more valuable speech."[431]

The Court of Appeals added, "the Stolen Valor Act survives [constitutional] scrutiny because (1) it restricts only knowingly false statements of fact, and (2) specific characteristics of the statute, including its *mens rea* [knowledge, intent] requirement, ensure it does not overreach so as to chill protected speech."[432] Conceding that Section 702 (b) of the Stolen Valor Act does criminalize a specific category of speech, and thus was inescapably a content-based restriction,[433] the Court of Appeals recognized the section did have the potential to be too far-reaching, but noted that "it has limits."[434]

This view of *limits* was crucial to the court's finding that Section 702 (b) was constitutional.

The *Strandlof* court ruled that the first limitation in the Act was the "falsely represents" language of the statute.[435]

The second limitation was that "the Stolen Valor Act [expressly] does not criminalize any satirical, rhetorical, theatrical, literary, ironic, or hyperbolic statements that qualify as protected speech."[436] The court noted this limitation negated the "slippery slope" argument that Congress could regulate any speech at all and concluded, "[r]ead with these two limitations, only outright lies — not ideas, opinions, artistic statements, or unwitting misstatements of fact — are punishable under the Act."[437]

The court then analyzed the constitutional framework of Section 702 (b) by examining past Supreme Court precedent,[438] concluding that "[s]ince the 1960s, the Supreme Court has repeatedly declared that knowingly false statements of fact, as a category of speech, are not generally entitled to full First Amendment protection."[439]

The Court of Appeals noted that a Supreme Court precedential three-part analysis did exist by which it could be determined whether a statute unconstitutionally suppresses speech: "First, we must assess whether a law punishes only *knowingly* false statements. If this is the case, the court must then decide whether the law leaves adequate 'breathing space' for truthful and other fully protected speech. And, if a statute survives both of these inquiries but still chills some speech, it is constitutional so long as it reaches no further than necessary to protect the government's legitimate interest."[440]

As to the 'breathing space' standard, "[a] restriction on knowingly false factual statements is constitutional so long as it has some limiting characteristic that prevents it from suppressing constitutionally valuable opinions and true statements."[441] The court further explained that the "breathing space analysis recognizes that false statements of fact are categorically unprotected for their own sake, and then asks courts to consider whether the challenged legislation impinges on or chills core speech." It then noted "the standard of review is straightforward: so long as the legislature leaves breathing space for valuable speech, it may restrict knowingly false statements of fact."[442]

Accordingly, Section 704 (b) "simply does not encroach on any protected speech" and "even were we to assume the Stolen Valor Act chills some speech, it 'reach[es] no farther than is necessary to protect the legitimate interest involved.'"[443] The court recognized the strong governmental interest in protecting the reputation of military medals and, compared to the risk that the challenged section chilled speech, found that strong interest was adequate to save the section constitutionally.[444]

The Court of Appeals then reversed the trial court's ruling, held that Section 702 (b) survived strict scrutiny, and declared it *constitutional.*[445]

United States v. *Alvarez* — another Section 704(b) pure speech case, which would
become *the* precedent — also presented the constitutional question. The following is an edited version of Cornell University Law School's Legal Information Institute's description of the case.[446] It contains a clear statement of the lower court proceedings, and has the added benefit of explaining the policy reasons for and against the statute.

It is an excellent preface to the Supreme Court's opinions in *United States* v. *Alvarez,* discussed in the next chapter.

> In 2007, Respondent Xavier Alvarez was serving as an elected member of the Board of Directors of the Three Valleys Water District in Claremont, California. During a board meeting, Alvarez stated to his fellow members: "I'm a retired marine of 25 years. I retired in the year 2001. Back in 1987, I was awarded the Congressional Medal of Honor. I got wounded many times by the same guy. I'm still around." This statement was a lie — he never served in the Marines or received a Medal of Honor. In fact, Alvarez had frequently lied about his accomplishments in the past, often fabricating sensationalistic stories about his purported military service.
>
> After Alvarez made his untruthful statement in the board meeting, the Federal Bureau of Investigation received a recording of the statement, and initiated a proceeding against Alvarez in the United States District Court for the Central District of California for

violating the Stolen Valor Act. Specifically, Alvarez was charged with violating provisions 18 United States Code, Sections 704(b) and (c)(1) of the Act. Alvarez was subsequently convicted of these violations. The charge against Alvarez emphasized the fact that he knew he was lying when he stated that he had received a Medal of Honor.

Alvarez filed a motion to dismiss the indictment, attacking the constitutionality of [Section 704(b) of the Stolen Valor Act; he asserted that the [section] was unconstitutional both as written and as applied to him under the First Amendment. The district court denied his motion and sentenced him to probation for three years, 416 hours of community service, and a fine of $5000. Alvarez conditionally pled guilty to the first count [Section 704(b)] and appealed the First Amendment issue to the United States Court of Appeals for the Ninth Circuit.

The Ninth Circuit reversed Alvarez's conviction, holding that the Stolen Valor Act violated the First Amendment. The court determined that the broad prohibition articulated in the Act unconstitutionally limited free speech — it was not narrow enough to meet a "compelling government interest."[[447]] The United States appealed this ruling, and the United States Supreme Court granted certiorari on October 17, 2011 to address whether the Stolen Valor Act is, on its face, an unconstitutional violation of the First Amendment.

In this case, the Supreme Court [was called upon to] determine whether the First Amendment's protection of free speech extends to lying about receiving military awards. Petitioner, the United States, argue[d] that, because the Stolen Valor Act only prohibits knowingly false factual statements, it is subject to a relatively deferential "breathing space" inquiry, and that, under this test, there is a compelling government interest enabling the Act to survive. Respondent, Xavier Alvarez, counter[ed] that the Act should be subject to strict scrutiny because it imposes a content-

> based restriction [on speech], and that, since it is not narrowly tailored to achieve a compelling government interest, the [Section 704(b) of the] Act cannot survive this test.

Not surprisingly, in addition to the two parties to the case, many other individuals and organizations were interested in both the military awards and First Amendment issues presented by the case. Hence, they submitted *amicus curiae* (friend-of-the-court) briefs to the Supreme Court of the United States. Those briefs and the submissions of the parties — the United States government, and Mr. Alvarez — paint a clear picture of the policy and jurisprudential stakes on the table before the Supreme Court of the United States.

> The American Legion argue[d] that the Stolen Valor Act's criminalization of lies is crucial to preserving the integrity of military awards. The American Legion argue[d] that many benefits are available to recipients of military awards, and that, without some kind of prohibition, imposters could wrongfully access government disability payments, tax breaks, and other social benefits. Military awards like the Medal of Honor also have inherent value, conferring respect and status on the recipients, the Congressional Medal of Honor Foundation ("CMOHF") contend[ed]. The Legion of Valor and the Criminal Justice Legal Foundation argue[d] that individuals who lie about receiving these awards reduce the value of military awards by causing other people in society to doubt the real recipients.
>
> The National Association of Criminal Defense Lawyers (NACDL) counter[ed] that individuals, like Alvarez, who lie about receiving military awards do not dilute the meaning and prestige of these awards. Indeed, NACDL argues, the very fact that people like Alvarez falsely claim to have received awards indicates that they still have great value. Alvarez himself asserts that the military knows who the true recipients are and can confer benefits on these people without being hampered by false claims. Additionally, the American Civil Liberties Union and the ACLU of Southern California

(collectively ACLU) argue[d] that there are better ways to preserve the status of awards than restricting speech, such as maintaining a searchable database of award recipients or initiating a public campaign to promote respect for military honors.

CMOHF contend[ed] that limiting false representations about military awards is beneficial to society. CMOHF argue[ed] that ensuring the meaningfulness of awards inspires troops and encourages citizens to join the armed forces. The Legion of Valor and the Criminal Justice Legal Foundation explain[ed] that the value of awards is mostly psychological, and that, in order for medals to foster morale in this way, recognition must be based on real merit. Furthermore, twenty states contend[ed] that, since a military award is a verifiable fact, there is no risk that the speaker will be punished for expressing an opinion or making an honest mistake. Additionally, the states argue, it is acceptable for society to limit a lie about a verifiable fact because the lie cannot contribute to the public's search for truth.

The American Booksellers Foundation for Free Expression and eight other media groups (Media Coalition) counter[ed] that judging the acceptability of speech by the social harm it might cause is not desirable for society. The Media Coalition argue[ed] that lying is valuable in order to expose truth. There is also value, the First Amendment Lawyers Association contend[ed], in having people figure out for themselves why a statement is wrong. The ACLU add[ed] that our society values the freedom to lie in asserting individual autonomy and achieving self-fulfillment. Allowing [Section 704(b) of] the Stolen Valor Act to limit lies, the ACLU contend[ed], could set a precedent for Congress to enact laws criminalizing dishonest acts like the posting of 'puffed-up' profile information on dating sites and false qualifications on resumes.

In this case, the Supreme Court will decide whether the Stolen Valor Act, which criminalizes false claims of receiving military honors, violates the First Amendment of the United States Constitution. The United States argues that a compelling state interest in protecting the integrity of the military awards program necessitates a prohibition on knowingly false claims to military awards. In contrast, Alvarez argues that the United States failed to demonstrate any connection between false claims to receiving military awards and reduced morale in the military, and also that the Stolen Valor Act criminalizes speech protected under the First Amendment.

The United States argue[d] that, because the Court treats false statements differently than true ones, the Court should review the Stolen Valor Act under a lower standard than for other content-based restrictions. The United States argues[d] that the validity of the Stolen Valor Act should depend on the strength of the state interest in protecting official military awards, and that the Act should be reviewed from a perspective that focuses on the provision of a 'breathing space' for protected speech within legislative restrictions. Remarking that the Court has not recognized constitutional value in false statements, the United States argue[d] that a restriction on a knowingly false statement is valid if the restriction does not inhibit or 'chill' legitimate statements that the First Amendment protects. The United States argue[d] that a valid restriction on speech leaves 'breathing space' for protected speech. The United States note[d] that the Court used the 'breathing space' analysis in categories such as fraud, intentional infliction of emotional distress through false statements, false promises during political campaigns, and tortious statements depicting a person in a 'false light'. The United States contend[ed] that, because the Stolen Valor Act restricts the same kind of knowingly false speech as these categories, the Court should review [Section 704(a) of] the Stolen Valor Act with the same 'breathing space' test.

Additionally, the United States argue[d] that applying the highest standard of review — strict scrutiny — would depart from the Court's previous treatment of federal restrictions on false statements. The United States offer[ed] the example of 18 United States Code, Section 1001(a), a valid law, which prohibits fraud against the government through false statements, regardless of intent to deceive. The United States claim[ed] that the Court has not required knowledge of falsehood in other laws that restrict false statements because a sufficiently strong state interest supported each law.

In contrast, Alvarez argue[d] that the First Amendment requires the United States to demonstrate that the Stolen Valor Act is the least restrictive way to solve a significant societal problem. Alvarez maintain[d] that, under the First Amendment, any law restricting the content of speech is facially invalid, with only a few exceptions. Alvarez list[ed] the historically unprotected speech categories as: obscenity, defamation, and fraud. Alvarez argue[d] that this list of exceptions excludes lying about receiving awards for military service. Alvarez argue[d] that, because [Section 704(a) of]the Stolen Valor Act restricts the content of speech and does not target a historically unprotected category of speech, the Court should find [that section] invalid under a strict scrutiny test. Alvarez also argue[d] that a lower standard of review balancing the value of speech against its costs should not be applied in this instance. Alvarez claim[ed] that the United States' test would weaken the requirement that a state interest in restricting speech be compelling, and would allow less important state interests to suffice. Alvarez contend[ed] that the United States' test is fundamentally the same as the test that the Court rejected in *United States v. Stevens*. According to Alvarez, both the United States' current test and the rejected test in *Stevens* disregard historical categories of unprotected speech and grant the government the unjustifiable power to decide which speech to protect and which to prohibit. Further, Alvarez argue[d] that the United States distorts the 'breathing space' test for restrictions on historically unprotected categories of speech. Alvarez claim[ed] that, for restrictions on historically unprotected categories of speech, explicit elements — e.g., scienter [knowledge] and materiality — permit 'breathing space' for protected speech. The Stolen Valor Act, according to Alvarez, fatally lacks these elements.

The United States argue[d] that the state interest in military service is so strong and compelling that the narrowly tailored [Section 704(a) of the] Stolen Valor Act survives even the highest level of scrutiny. Military awards, according to the United States, not only encourage valor and service, but also educate the public about honorable actions. Additionally, the United States contend[ed] that the program of military awards motivates service members to be brave and act honorably.

The United States contend[ed] that the criteria for conferring an award are stringent; only the most deserving candidates receive honors. The United States argues[ed] that, because the exclusion of undeserving candidates makes the award valuable to the exceptional few who receive it, false claims to military awards dilute and depreciate the value of true awards. Further, according to the United States, [Section 704(b) of] the Stolen Valor Act, while prohibiting knowingly false claims to military awards, does not deter legitimate, hyperbolic assertions of valor or other false, self-aggrandizing claims. The United States argues that the implied scienter or knowledge requirement of the Stolen Valor Act avoids deterrence of truthful or mistakenly false speech. Noting that the Stolen Valor Act permits criticism of the military awards program and false descriptions of valor, the United States argue[d] that the Stolen Valor Act is narrowly tailored to the state interest in preserving the integrity of the military awards program by targeting only knowingly false claims to military awards.

Alvarez question[ed] the extent to which medals and ribbons actually cause praiseworthy behavior, and argue[d] that the United States fail[ed] to offer a sufficiently strong or important interest to justify the broad restriction on speech, even under the 'breathing space' test. Rejecting the United States' categorization

> of false speech as valueless, Alvarez contend[ed] that the United States mischaracterize[ed] the harm of the challenged section on society by drastically undervaluing false speech.
>
> Alvarez invoked the 'marketplace of ideas' theory, in which the competition of statements sharpens distinctions between facts and falsehoods and enhances participants' analytical abilities. Alvarez assert[ed] that, under this theory, the mere capacity to enter the marketplace has great societal value, and the capacity to lie facilitates individual autonomy. Contending that the Stolen Valor Act criminalizes more than the United States alleges, Alvarez argue[d] that the Act would prohibit irony, hyperbole, and parody. In response to the United States' claim that the Act is narrowly tailored, Alvarez suggest[ed] that other governmental measures could address the problem of devaluing the military award program without threatening First Amendment protections.
> As examples, Alvarez cited a public database of award recipients, educational programming about service and honor, and prosecuting false recipients of official benefits for fraud. Further, Alvarez argue[d] that the United States undervalued the role of the public in attacking false claims to military awards, and overstated the difficulties involved in a private citizen's attempt to access public records in a database of award recipients.

Following this extensive recitation by the Legal Information Institute of the nature of the *Alvarez* case and the various arguments on both sides, LII's conclusion was that . . .

> [t]his case will determine whether the Stolen Valor Act's prohibition of falsely claiming to have received a military award is valid under the First Amendment. In addition to deciding whether to apply the strict scrutiny or the 'breathing space' test, the Court will decide whether the Stolen Valor Act targets a historically unprotected category of speech. Further, the Court will decide whether the United States has demonstrated a sufficiently strong governmental interest to justify the restriction of false claims to

receiving military awards.

On February 22, 2012, the Supreme Court of The United States heard oral arguments in the *Alvarez* case.

The justices appeared to be divided, or at least troubled, regarding the constitutionality of Section 704(b) of the Act.[448] Some seemed in accord with the reasoning suggested by Judge Bybee's dissent in the Ninth Circuit: First Amendment protection does not extend to the kind of false statements punished by Section 704(b), especially when considering the harm Congress found that the false statements caused.[449]

Justice Kennedy, however, seemed to be concerned about the proverbial 'slippery slope' which might result if the Court allowed these kinds of these false statements to be punished.[450] Nevertheless, he recognized that "[o]n the other hand, I have to acknowledge that this [lying about military medals] does diminish the medal in many respects."[451]

Justice Kagan acknowledged that the government has a strong interest in family stability and asked if the line of reasoning used in support of Section 704 (b) could be used to "prevent everybody from telling lies about their extramarital affairs." Solicitor General Verrilli was quick to note, politely, that Justice Kagan's hypothetical was very different from the case at hand.

Justice Scalia appeared to be a strong advocate of upholding the challenged section, and seemed to agree with Congress that false statements about receiving military medals dull the luster of those medals.[452] Indeed, some comments during oral argument could be construed as support for Solicitor General Verrilli's argument that the government has a compelling interest in protecting the integrity of the military medals.[453]

Justice Roberts noted people such as Alvarez do benefit from lying about the receipt of military medals, asking, "[d]oesn't it help a politician to have a Congressional Medal of Honor?"[454]

At least one justice seemed to discredit Alvarez's argument that Section

704(b) could be invoked to punish parody or satire, with Justice Ginsburg stating "[b]ut the government has said, 'that's not how we read the statute,' and the courts read statutes to avoid constitutional collision."[455]

In June 2012, the Supreme Court of the United States decided *United States* v. *Alvarez,* and no one had to wonder any longer whether Section 704(b) of the Stolen Valor Act was constitutional or unconstitutional.

CHAPTER 8[456]

***United States* v. *Alvarez*:**

What was the Supreme Court's ruling on the constitutionality of the Stolen Valor Act's Section 704(b)?

The remedy for speech that is false is speech that is true.
—Associate Justice Anthony Kennedy, *U.S.* v. *Alvarez*

Opinion

Justice Kennedy announced the judgment of the Court and delivered an opinion, in which The Chief Justice, Justice Ginsburg, and Justice Sotomayor join. **This is important. To hold Section 704 (b) of the Stolen Valor Act unconstitutional, of the nine justices five votes were required. So far, we are told that Justice Kennedy authored the opinion and in it only three of his colleagues joined: Chief Justice Roberts and Justices Ginsburg and Sotomayor. That made four. That is not a majority; it is a plurality. Where was the fifth vote? We'll see.**

Lying was his habit. Xavier Alvarez, the respondent here, lied when he said that he played hockey for the Detroit Red Wings and that he once married a starlet from Mexico. But when he lied in announcing he held the Congressional Medal of Honor, respondent ventured onto new ground; for that lie violates a federal criminal statute, the Stolen Valor Act of 2005. 18 U. S. C. §704. **As detestable as the latter lie was, given the actual valor required for an award of the Medal of Honor, Alvarez had engaged only**

in "pure speech."

In 2007, respondent attended his first public meeting as a board member of the Three Valley Water District Board. The board is a governmental entity with headquarters in Claremont, California. He introduced himself as follows: "I'm a retired marine of 25 years. I retired in the year 2001. Back in 1987, I was awarded the Congressional Medal of Honor. I got wounded many times by the same guy." 617 F. 3d 1198, 1201–1202 (CA9 2010). None of this was true. For all the record shows, respondent's statements were but a pathetic attempt to gain respect that eluded him. The statements do not seem to have been made to secure employment or financial benefits or admission to privileges reserved for those who had earned the Medal. **The last sentence is at the core of the decision in this case, and central to the constitutionality of the Fake Warrior Act presented in Chapter 9: Alvarez had engaged in pure speech with no intention, said Justice Kennedy, "to secure employment or financial benefits or admission to privileges reserved for those who had earned the Medal." In other words, Alvarez did not seek, nor did he receive, any *tangible or material* benefit from his lie about the Medal of Honor.**

Respondent was indicted under the Stolen Valor Act for lying about the Congressional Medal of Honor at the meeting. The United States District Court for the Central District of California rejected his claim that the statute is invalid under the First Amendment. Respondent pleaded guilty to one count, reserving the right to appeal on his First Amendment claim. The United States Court of Appeals for the Ninth Circuit, in a decision by a divided panel, found the Act invalid under the First Amendment and reversed the conviction. *Id.*, at 1218. With further opinions on the issue, and over a dissent by seven judges, rehearing en banc was denied. 638 F. 3d 666 (2011). This Court granted certiorari. 565 U. S. ___ (2011).

After certiorari was granted, and in an unrelated case, the United States Court of Appeals for the Tenth Circuit, also in a decision by a divided panel, found the Act constitutional. *United States* v. *Strandlof*, 667 F. 3d 1146 (2012). So there is now a conflict in the Courts of Appeals on the question of the Act's validity.

This is the second case in two Terms requiring the Court to consider speech that can disparage, or attempt to steal, honor that belongs to those who fought for this Nation in battle. See *Snyder* v. *Phelps*, 562 U. S. ___ (2011) (hateful protests directed at the funeral of a serviceman who died in Iraq). Here the statement that the speaker held the Medal was an intended, undoubted lie.

It is right and proper that Congress, over a century ago, established an award so the Nation can hold in its highest respect and esteem those who, in the course of carrying out the "supreme and noble duty of contributing to the defense of the rights and honor of the nation," *Selective Draft Law Cases,* 245 U. S. 366, 390 (1918), have acted with extraordinary honor. And it should be uncontested that this is a legitimate Government objective, indeed a most valued national aspiration and purpose. **It is an understandably legitimate function of government to honor the valorous. OK, so far.** This does not end the inquiry, however. Fundamental constitutional principles require that laws enacted to honor the brave must be consistent with the precepts of the Constitution for which they fought. **However, when so honoring the valorous, we can't ignore "fundamental constitutional principles," here the Free Speech Clause of the First Amendment.**

The Government contends the criminal prohibition is a proper means to further its purpose in creating and awarding the Medal. When content-based speech regulation is in question, however, *exacting scrutiny* is required. **The emphasis is supplied by the authors, because in using these two words Justice Kennedy is invoking the Supreme Court's test by which it evaluates whether government restraints on pure speech are constitutional. Usually called the "strict scrutiny" test, it requires that to survive constitutional scrutiny a government restraint on speech must (1) be supported by a "compelling" (really, really important) government interest, and (2) be "narrowly tailored" to further that interest.** Statutes suppressing or restricting speech must be judged by the sometimes inconvenient principles of the First Amendment. *By this measure, the statutory provisions under which respondent was convicted must be held invalid, and his conviction must be set aside*. **(Our emphasis.)**

I

Respondent's claim to hold the Congressional Medal of Honor was false. There is no room to argue about interpretation or shades of meaning. On this premise, respondent violated §704(b); and, because the lie concerned the Congressional Medal of Honor, he was subject to an enhanced penalty under subsection (c). Those statutory provisions are as follows:

> (b) False Claims About Receipt of Military Decorations or Medals.––Whoever falsely represents himself or herself, verbally or in writing, to have been awarded any decoration or medal authorized by Congress for the Armed Forces of the United States . . . shall be fined under this title, imprisoned not more than six months, or both.
>
> (c) Enhanced Penalty for Offenses Involving Congressional Medal of Honor.––
>
> (1) In General.––If a decoration or medal involved in an offense under subsection (a) or (b) is a Congressional Medal of Honor, in lieu of the punishment provided in that subsection, the offender shall be fined under this title, imprisoned not more than 1 year, or both.

Respondent challenges the statute as a content-based suppression of pure speech, speech not falling within any of the few categories of expression where content-based regulation is permissible. **"The few categories of expression where content-based regulation is permissible" includes, for example, adult and child pornography and defamation.** The Government defends the statute as necessary to preserve the integrity and purpose of the Medal, an integrity and purpose it contends are compromised and frustrated by the false statements the statute prohibits. It argues that false statements "have no First Amendment value in themselves," and thus "are protected only to the extent needed to avoid chilling fully protected speech." Brief for United States 18, 20. Although the statute covers respondent's speech, the Government argues that it leaves breathing room for protected speech, for example speech which might criticize the idea of the Medal or the importance of the military. The Government's arguments cannot suffice to save the statute. **Remember, the Court is considering "pure speech," suppression of which comes with a heavy burden of presumed unconstitutionality.**

II

"[A]s a general matter, the First Amendment means that government has no power to restrict expression because of its message, its ideas, its subject matter, or its content." *Ashcroft* v. *American Civil Liberties Union*, 535 U. S. 564, 573 (2002) (internal quotation marks omitted). As a result, the Constitution "demands that content-based restrictions on speech be presumed invalid ... and that the Government bear the burden of showing their constitutionality." *Ashcroft* v. *American Civil Liberties Union*, 542 U. S. 656, 660 (2004).

In light of the substantial and expansive threats to free expression posed by content-based restrictions, this Court has rejected as "startling and dangerous" a "free-floating test for First Amendment coverage . . . [based on] an ad hoc balancing of relative social costs and benefits." *United States* v. *Stevens*, 559 U. S. ___, ___ (2010) (slip op., at 7). Instead, content-based restrictions on speech have been permitted, as a general matter, only when confined to the few " 'historic and traditional categories [of expression] long familiar to the bar,' " *Id.*, at ___ (slip op., at 5) (quoting *Simon & Schuster, Inc.* v. *Members of N. Y. State Crime Victims Bd.*, 502 U. S. 105, 127 (1991) (Kennedy, J., concurring in judgment)). Among these categories are advocacy intended, and likely, to incite imminent lawless action, see *Brandenburg* v. *Ohio*, 395 U. S. 444 (1969) *(per curiam);* obscenity, see, *e.g., Miller* v. *California*, 413 U. S. 15 (1973); defamation, see, *e.g., New York Times Co.* v. *Sullivan*, 376 U. S. 254 (1964) (providing substantial protection for speech about public figures); *Gertz* v. *Robert Welch, Inc.*, 418 U. S. 323 (1974) (imposing some limits on liability for defaming a private figure); speech integral to criminal conduct, see, *e.g., Giboney* v. *Empire Storage & Ice Co.*, 336 U. S. 490 (1949); so-called "fighting words," see *Chaplinsky* v. *New Hampshire*, 315 U. S. 568 (1942); child pornography, see *New York* v. *Ferber*, 458 U. S. 747 (1982); fraud, see

Virginia Bd. of Pharmacy v. *Virginia Citizens Consumer Council, Inc.*, 425 U. S. 748, 771 (1976); true threats, see *Watts* v. *United States*, 394 U. S. 705 (1969) *(per curiam);* and speech presenting some grave and imminent threat the government has the power to prevent, see *Near* v. *Minnesota ex rel. Olson*, 283 U. S. 697, 716 (1931), although a restriction under the last category is most difficult to sustain, see *New York Times Co.* v. *United States*, 403 U. S. 713 (1971) *(per curiam).* **This paragraph amounts to a summary of Free Speech 101, by providing a laundry list of cases, and their rulings, which have permitted suppression or limitation of speech.** These categories have a historical foundation in the Court's free speech tradition. The vast realm of free speech and thought always protected in our tradition can still thrive, and even be furthered, by adherence to those categories and rules.

Absent from those few categories where the law allows content-based regulation of speech is any general exception to the First Amendment for false statements. **Kennedy is saying that despite the suppression/limitation of speech allowed for the ten or so categories discussed above, none of them include *false* statements—arguing that they have not been suppressed/limited, and should not be. He continues:** This comports with the common understanding that some false statements are inevitable if there is to be an open and vigorous expression of views in public and private con-versation, expression the First Amendment seeks to guarantee. See *Sullivan, supra,* at 271 ("Th[e] erroneous statement is inevitable in free debate").

The Government disagrees with this proposition. It cites language from some of this Court's precedents to support its contention that false statements have no value and hence no First Amendment protection. See also Brief for Eugene Volokh et al. as *Amici Curiae* 2–11. These isolated statements in some earlier decisions do not support the Government's submission that false statements, as a general rule, are beyond constitutional protection. That conclusion would take the quoted language far from its proper context. For instance, the Court has stated "[f]alse statements of fact are particularly valueless [because] they interfere with the truth-seeking function of the marketplace of ideas," *Hustler Magazine, Inc.* v. *Falwell*, 485 U. S. 46, 52 (1988), and that false statements "are not protected by the First

Amendment in the same manner as truthful statements," *Brown* v. *Hartlage*, 456 U. S. 45, 60–61 (1982). See also, *e.g., Virginia Bd. of Pharmacy, supra*, at 771 ("Untruthful speech, commercial or otherwise, has never been protected for its own sake"); *Herbert* v. *Lando*, 441 U. S. 153, 171 (1979) ("Spreading false information in and of itself carries no First Amendment credentials"); *Gertz, supra*, at 340 ("[T]here is no constitutional value in false statements of fact"); *Garrison* v. *Louisiana*, 379 U. S. 64, 75 (1964) ("[T]he knowingly false statement and the false statement made with reckless disregard of the truth, do not enjoy constitutional protection").

These quotations all derive from cases discussing defamation, fraud, or some other legally cognizable harm associated with a false statement, such as an invasion of privacy or the costs of vexatious litigation. See Brief for United States 18–19. In those decisions the falsity of the speech at issue was not irrelevant to our analysis, but neither was it determinative. *The Court has never endorsed the categorical rule the Government advances: that false statements receive no First Amendment protection.* **Our emphasis. False statements can be protected.** Our prior decisions have not confronted a measure, like the Stolen Valor Act, that targets falsity and nothing more.

Even when considering some instances of defamation and fraud, moreover, the Court has been careful to instruct that falsity alone may not suffice to bring the speech outside the First Amendment. The statement must be a knowing or reckless falsehood. See *Sullivan, supra*, at 280 (prohibiting recovery of damages for a defamatory falsehood made about a public official unless the statement was made "with knowledge that it was false or with reckless disregard of whether it was false or not"); see also *Garrison, supra*, at 73 ("[E]ven when the utterance is false, the great principles of the Constitution which secure freedom of expression . . . preclude attaching adverse consequences to any except the knowing or reckless falsehood"); *Illinois ex rel. Madigan* v. *Telemarketing Associates, Inc.*, 538 U. S. 600, 620 (2003) ("False statement alone does not subject a fundraiser to fraud liability"). **False statements have long been protected, and in various contexts.**

The Government thus seeks to use this principle for a new purpose. It seeks to convert a rule that limits liability even in defamation cases where the law permits recovery for tortious wrongs into a rule that expands liability in a different, far greater realm of discourse and expression. That inverts the rationale for the exception. The requirements of a knowing falsehood or reckless disregard for the truth as the condition for recovery in certain defamation cases exists to allow more speech, not less. A rule designed to tolerate certain speech ought not blossom to become a rationale for a rule restricting it. **The government is seeking to extend suppression/limitation of speech by use of precedents that protect speech.**

The Government then gives three examples of regulations on false speech that courts generally have found permissible: first, the criminal prohibition of a false statement made to a Government official, 18 U. S. C. §1001; second, laws punishing perjury; and third, prohibitions on the false representation that one is speaking as a Government official or on behalf of the Government, see, *e.g.,* §912; §709. These restrictions, however, do not establish a principle that all proscriptions of false statements are exempt from exacting First Amendment scrutiny. **Next, Kennedy will distinguish those three situations from this case.**

The federal statute prohibiting false statements to Government officials punishes "whoever, in any matter within the jurisdiction of the executive, legislative, or judicial branch of the Government . . . makes any materially false, fictitious, or fraudulent statement or representation." §1001. Section 1001's prohibition on false statements made to Government officials, in communications concerning official matters, does not lead to the broader proposition that false statements are unprotected when made to any person, at any time, in any context.

The same point can be made about what the Court has confirmed is the "unquestioned constitutionality of perjury statutes," both the federal statute, §1623, and its state-law equivalents. *United States* v. *Grayson*, 438 U. S. 41, 54 (1978). See also *Konigsberg* v. *State Bar of Cal.*, 366 U. S. 36, 51, n. 10 (1961). It is not simply because perjured statements are false that they lack First Amendment protection. Perjured testimony "is at war with justice" because it can cause a court to render a "judgment not resting on truth." *In re Michael,*

326 U. S. 224, 227 (1945). Perjury undermines the function and province of the law and threatens the integrity of judgments that are the basis of the legal system. See *United States* v. *Dunnigan*, 507 U. S. 87, 97 (1993) ("To uphold the integrity of our trial system . . . the constitutionality of perjury statutes is unquestioned"). Unlike speech in other contexts, testimony under oath has the formality and gravity necessary to remind the witness that his or her statements will be the basis for official governmental action, action that often affects the rights and liberties of others. Sworn testimony is quite distinct from lies not spoken under oath and simply intended to puff up oneself.

Statutes that prohibit falsely representing that one is speaking on behalf of the Government, or that prohibit impersonating a Government officer, also protect the integrity of Government processes, quite apart from merely restricting false speech. Title 18 U. S. C. §912, for example, prohibits impersonating an officer or employee of the United States. Even if that statute may not require proving an "actual financial or property loss" resulting from the deception, the statute is itself confined to "maintain[ing] the general good repute and dignity of . . . government . . . service itself." *United States* v. *Lepowitch*, 318 U. S. 702, 704 (1943) (internal quotation marks omitted). The same can be said for prohibitions on the unauthorized use of the names of federal agencies such as the Federal Bureau of Investigation in a manner calculated to convey that the communication is approved, see §709, or using words such as "Federal" or "United States" in the collection of private debts in order to convey that the communication has official authorization, see §712. These examples, to the extent that they implicate fraud or speech integral to criminal conduct, are inapplicable here.

As our law and tradition show, then, there are instances in which the falsity of speech bears upon whether it is protected. Some false speech may be prohibited even if analogous true speech could not be. This opinion does not imply that any of these targeted prohibitions are somehow vulnerable. But it also rejects the notion that false speech should be in a general category that is presumptively unprotected.

Although the First Amendment stands against any "freewheeling authority to declare new categories of speech outside the scope of the First Amendment," *Stevens*, 559 U. S., at ___ (slip op., at 9), the Court has acknowledged that perhaps there exist "some categories of speech that have been historically unprotected . . . but have not yet been specifically identified or discussed . . . in our case law." *Ibid*. Before exempting a category of speech from the normal prohibition on content-based restrictions, however, the Court must be presented with "persuasive evidence that a novel restriction on content is part of a long (if heretofore unrecognized) tradition of proscription," *Brown* v. *Entertainment Merchants Assn.*, 564 U. S. ___, ___ (2011) (slip op., at 4). The Government has not demonstrated that false statements generally should constitute a new category of unprotected speech on this basis. **Here, Kennedy is rejecting the government's argument that the Court should create yet another category of unprotected false speech, although it has the power to do so.**

III

The probable, and adverse, effect of the Act on freedom of expression illustrates, in a fundamental way, the reasons for the Law's distrust of content-based speech prohibitions.

The Act by its plain terms applies to a false statement made at any time, in any place, to any person. **That's pretty broad. Three "anys."** It can be assumed that it would not apply to, say, a theatrical performance. See *Milkovich* v. *Lorain Journal Co.*, 497 U. S. 1, 20 (1990) (recognizing that some statements nominally purporting to contain false facts in reality "cannot reasonably be interpreted as stating actual facts about an individual" (internal quotation marks and brackets omitted)). Still, the *sweeping*, quite *unprecedented* reach of the statute puts it in conflict with the First Amendment. **Note the italicized words, and those that follow in this paragraph.** Here the lie was made in a public meeting, but the statute would apply with equal force to *personal, whispered conversations within a home*. The statute seeks to control and suppress all false statements on this one subject in almost *limitless* times and settings. And it does so entirely without regard *to whether the lie was made for the purpose of material gain*. See *San Francisco Arts & Athletics, Inc.* v. *United States Olympic Comm.*, 483 U. S. 522, 539–540

(1987) (prohibiting a nonprofit corporation from exploiting the "commercial magnetism" of the word "Olympic" when organizing an athletic competition (internal quotation marks omitted)). **See also the authors' Fake Warrior Act, presented in Chapter 9.**

Permitting the government to decree this speech to be a criminal offense, whether shouted from the rooftops or made in a barely audible whisper, would endorse government authority to compile a list of subjects about which false statements are punishable. That governmental power has no clear limiting principle. Our constitutional tradition stands against the idea that we need Oceania's Ministry of Truth. See G. Orwell, Nineteen Eighty-Four (1949) (Centennial ed. 2003). Were this law to be sustained, there could be an endless list of subjects the National Government or the States could single out. *Where false claims are made to effect a fraud or secure moneys or other valuable considerations, say offers of employment, it is well established that the Government may restrict speech without affronting the First Amendment.* See, *e.g., Virginia Bd. of Pharmacy*, 425 U. S., at 771 (noting that fraudulent speech generally falls outside the protections of the First Amendment). But the Stolen Valor Act is not so limited in its reach. Were the Court to hold that the interest in truthful discourse alone is sufficient to sustain a ban on speech, *absent any evidence that the speech was used to gain a material advantage,* it would give government a broad censorial power unprecedented in this Court's cases or in our constitutional tradition. The mere potential for the exercise of that power casts a chill, a chill the First Amendment cannot permit if free speech, thought, and discourse are to remain a foundation of our freedom. **Our emphasis.**

IV

The previous discussion suffices to show that the Act conflicts with free speech principles. But even when examined within its own narrow sphere of operation, the Act cannot survive. **Here comes Kennedy's discussion of the "strict scrutiny/narrowly tailored" test.** In assessing content-based restrictions on protected speech, the Court has not adopted a free-wheeling approach, see *Stevens*, 559 U. S., at ___ (slip op., at 7) ("The First Amendment's guarantee of free speech does not extend only to categories of speech that survive an ad hoc balancing of relative social costs and benefits"), but rather has applied the "most exacting scrutiny." *Turner Broadcasting System, Inc.* v. *FCC*, 512 U. S. 622, 642 (1994). Although the objectives the Government seeks to further by the statute are not without significance, the Court must, and now does, find the Act does not satisfy exacting scrutiny.

The Government is correct when it states military medals "serve the important public function of recognizing and expressing gratitude for acts of heroism and sacrifice in military service," and also "'foste[r] morale, mission accomplishment and esprit de corps' among service members." Brief for United States 37, 38. General George Washington observed that an award for valor would "cherish a virtuous ambition in . . . soldiers, as well as foster and encourage every species of military merit." General Orders of George Washington Issued at Newburgh on the Hudson, 1782–1783 (Aug. 7, 1782), p. 30 (E. Boynton ed. 1883). Time has not diminished this idea. In periods of war and peace alike public recognition of valor and noble sacrifice by men and women in uniform reinforces the pride and national resolve that the military relies upon to fulfill its mission.

These interests are related to the integrity of the military honors system in general, and the Congressional Medal of Honor in particular. Although millions have served with brave resolve, the Medal, which is the highest military award for valor against an enemy force, has been given just 3,476 times. Established in 1861, the Medal is reserved for those who have distinguished themselves "conspicuously by gallantry and intrepidity at the risk of his life above and beyond the call of duty." 10 U. S. C. §§3741 (Army), 6241 (Navy and Marine Corps), 8741 (Air Force), 14 U. S. C. §491 (Coast Guard). The stories of those who earned the Medal inspire and fascinate, from Dakota Meyer who in 2009 drove five times into the midst of a Taliban ambush to save 36 lives, see Curtis, President Obama Awards Medal of Honor to Dakota Meyer, The White House Blog (Sept. 15, 2011) (all Internet materials as visited June 25, 2012, and available in Clerk of Court's case file); to Desmond Doss who served as an army medic on Okinawa and on June 5, 1945, rescued 75 fellow soldiers, and who, after being wounded, gave up his own place on a stretcher so others could be taken to safety, see America's Heroes 88–90 (J. Willbanks ed. 2011); to William Carney who sustained multiple gunshot wounds to the head, chest, legs, and arm, and yet carried the flag to ensure it did not touch the ground during the Union army's assault on Fort Wagner in July 1863, *id.,* at 44–45. The rare acts of courage the Medal celebrates led President Truman to say he would "rather have that medal round my neck than . . . be president of the United States." Truman Gives No. 1 Army Medal to 15 Heroes, Washington *Post,* Oct. 13, 1945, p. 5. The Government's interest in protecting the integrity of the Medal of Honor is beyond question. **Translation: The government's interest in what Section 704 (b) seeks to accomplish is "compelling." All true, and a welcome recognition by a justice of the Supreme Court of the United States.**

But to recite the Government's compelling interests is not to end the matter. The First Amendment requires that the Government's chosen restriction on the speech at issue be "actually necessary" to achieve its interest. *Entertainment Merchants Assn.,* 564 U. S., at ___ (slip op., at 12). There must be a direct causal link between the restriction imposed and the injury to be prevented. See *ibid.* The link between the Government's interest in protecting the integrity of the military honors system and the Act's restriction on the false claims of liars like respondent has not been shown. **Section 704(b) is not "narrowly tailored."** Although appearing to concede that "an isolated misrepresentation by itself would not tarnish the meaning of military honors," the Government asserts it is "common sense that false representations have the tendency to dilute the value and meaning of military awards," Brief for United States 49, 54. It must be acknowledged that when a pretender claims the Medal to be his own, the lie might harm the Government by demeaning the high purpose of the award, diminishing the honor it confirms, and creating the appearance that the Medal is awarded more often than is true. Furthermore, the lie may offend the true holders of the Medal. From one perspective it insults their bravery and high principles when falsehood puts them in the unworthy company of a pretender.
Yet these interests do not satisfy the Government's heavy burden when it seeks to regulate protected speech. See *United States* v. *Playboy Entertainment Group, Inc.,* 529 U. S. 803, 818 (2000). **Our emphasis.** The Government points to no evidence to support its claim that the public's general perception of military awards is diluted by false claims such as those made by Alvarez. Cf. *Entertainment Merchants Assn., supra,* at ___–___ (slip op.,

at 12–13) (analyzing and rejecting the findings of research psychologists demonstrating the causal link between violent video games and harmful effects on children). As one of the Government's *amici* notes "there is nothing that charlatans such as Xavier Alvarez can do to stain [the Medal winners'] honor." Brief for Veterans of Foreign Wars of the United States et al. as *Amici Curiae* 1. This general proposition is sound, even if true holders of the Medal might experience anger and frustration.

The lack of a causal link between the Government's stated interest and the Act is not the only way in which the Act is not actually necessary to achieve the Government's stated interest. *The Government has not shown, and cannot show, why counter-speech would not suffice to achieve its interest.* **Our emphasis.** The facts of this case indicate that the dynamics of free speech, of counter-speech, of refutation, can overcome the lie. Respondent lied at a public meeting. Even before the FBI began investigating him for his false statements "Alvarez was perceived as a phony," 617 F. 3d, at 1211. Once the lie was made public, he was ridiculed online, see Brief for Respondent 3, his actions were reported in the press, see Ortega, Alvarez Again Denies Claim, Ontario, CA, Inland Valley Daily Bulletin (Sept. 27, 2007), and a fellow board member called for his resignation, see, *e.g.,* Bigham, Water District Rep Requests Alvarez Resign in Wake of False Medal Claim, San Bernardino Cty., CA, The Sun (May 21, 2008). There is good reason to believe that a similar fate would befall other false claimants. See Brief for Reporters Committee for Freedom of the Press et al. as *Amici Curiae* 30–33 (listing numerous examples of public exposure of false claimants). Indeed, the outrage and contempt expressed for respondent's lies can serve to reawaken and reinforce the public's respect for the Medal, its recipients, and its high purpose. The acclaim that recipients of the Congressional Medal of Honor receive also casts doubt on the proposition that the public will be misled by the claims of charlatans or become cynical of those whose heroic deeds earned them the Medal by right. See, *e.g.,* Well Done, Washington *Post,* Feb. 5, 1943, p. 8 (reporting on Pres-ident Roosevelt's awarding the Congressional Medal of Honor to Maj. Gen. Alexander Vandegrift); Devroy, Medal of Honor Given to 2 Killed in Somalia, Washington *Post,* May 24, 1994, p. A6 (reporting on President Clinton's awarding the Congressional Medal of Honor to two special forces soldiers killed during operations in Somalia).

The remedy for speech that is false is speech that is true. **Our emphasis.** This is the ordinary course in a free society. The response to the unreasoned is the rational; to the uninformed, the enlightened; to the straight-out lie, the simple truth. See *Whitney* v. *California*, 274 U. S. 357, 377 (1927) (Brandeis, J., concurring) ("If there be time to expose through discussion the falsehood and fallacies, to avert the evil by the processes of education, the remedy to be applied is more speech, not enforced silence"). The theory of our Constitution is "that the best test of truth is the power of the thought to get itself accepted in the competition of the market," *Abrams* v. *United States*, 250 U. S. 616, 630 (1919) (Holmes, J., dissenting). The First Amendment itself ensures the right to respond to speech we do not like, and for good reason. Freedom of speech and thought flows not from the beneficence of the state but from the inalienable rights of the person. And suppression of speech by the government can make exposure of falsity more difficult, not less so. Society has the right and civic duty to engage in open, dynamic, rational discourse. These ends are not well served when the government seeks to orchestrate public discussion through content-based mandates.

Expressing its concern that counter-speech is insufficient, the Government responds that because "some military records have been lost . . . some claims [are] unverifiable," Brief for United States 50. This proves little, however; for without verifiable records, successful criminal prosecution under the Act would be more difficult in any event. So, in cases where public refutation will not serve the Government's interest, the Act will not either. In addition, the Government claims that "many [false claims] will remain unchallenged." *Id.*, at 55. The Government provides no support for the contention. And in any event, in order to show that public refutation is not an adequate alternative, the Government must demonstrate that unchallenged claims undermine the public's perception of the military and the integrity of its awards system. This showing has not been made.

It is a fair assumption that any true holders of the Medal who had heard of Alvarez's false claims would have been fully vindicated by the community's expression of outrage, showing as it did the Nation's high regard for the Medal. The same can be said for the Government's interest. The American people do not need the assistance of a government prosecution to express their high regard for the special place that military heroes hold in our tradition. Only a weak society needs government protection or intervention before it pursues its resolve to preserve the truth. Truth needs neither handcuffs nor a badge for its vindication.

In addition, when the Government seeks to regulate protected speech, the restriction must be the "least restrictive means among available, effective alternatives." *Ashcroft*, 542 U. S., at 666. There is, however, at least one less speech-restrictive means by which the Government could likely protect the integrity of the military awards system. A Government-created database could list Congressional Medal of Honor winners. Were a database accessible through the Internet, it would be easy to verify and expose false claims. It appears some private individuals have already created databases similar to this, see Brief for Respondent 25, and at least one data- base of past winners is online and fully searchable, see Congressional Medal of Honor Society, Full Archive, (www.cmohs.org/recipient-archive.php). The Solicitor General responds that although Congress and the Department of Defense investigated the feasibility of establishing a database in 2008, the Government "concluded that such a database would be impracticable and insufficiently comprehensive." Brief for United States 55. Without more explanation, it is difficult to assess the Government's claim, especially when at least one database of Congressional Medal of Honor winners already exists.
The Government may have responses to some of these criticisms, but there has been no clear showing of the necessity of the statute, the necessity required by exacting scrutiny.

* * *

The Nation well knows that one of the costs of the First Amendment is that it protects the speech we detest as well as the speech we embrace. Though few might find respondent's statements anything but contemptible, his right to make those statements is protected by the Constitution's guarantee of freedom of speech and expression. The Stolen Valor Act infringes upon speech protected by the First Amendment. **Yes, it's as simple as that.**

The judgment of the Court of Appeals is affirmed.

It is so ordered.

But where is the fifth vote, to make the four vote plurality into a majority of the nine justices?

It's here, in a concurring opinion by the compromisers, for whom it is not enough that the Supreme Court constructed a two-tier test for federal statutes—"strict scrutiny" for "fundamental rights" (e.g., speech) and mere "rational basis" for everything else (e.g., economic regulation). They want "intermediate" scrutiny.

Justice Breyer **(5)**, with whom Justice Kagan **(6)** joins, concurring in the judgment. **These are the fifth and sixth votes for unconstitutionality. But for a different reason.**

I agree with the plurality that the Stolen Valor Act of 2005 violates the First Amendment. But I do not rest my conclusion upon a strict categorical analysis. *Ante,* at 4–10. Rather, I base that conclusion upon the fact that the statute works First Amendment harm, while the Government can achieve its legitimate objectives in less restrictive ways.

I

In determining whether a statute violates the First Amendment, this Court has often found it appropriate to examine the fit between statutory ends and means. In doing so, it has examined speech-related harms, justifications, and potential alternatives. In particular, it has taken account of the seriousness of the speech-related harm the provision will likely cause, the nature and importance of the provision's countervailing objectives, the extent to which the provision will tend to achieve those objectives, and whether there are other, less restrictive ways of doing so. Ultimately the Court has had to determine whether the statute works speech-related harm that is out of proportion to its justifications. **Cutting through the Orwellian ("double-**

speak) justice-speak, Breyer is saying that the Court "balances" all the competing interests—applying "intermediate" scrutiny, also known as "proportionality" review.

Sometimes the Court has referred to this approach as "intermediate scrutiny," sometimes as "proportionality" review, sometimes as an examination of "fit," and sometimes it has avoided the application of any label at all. See, *e.g., Turner Broadcasting System, Inc.* v. *FCC*, 512 U. S. 622, 641–652 (1994) (intermediate scrutiny); *Randall* v. *Sorrell*, 548 U. S. 230, 249 (2006) (plurality opinion) (proportionality); *Board of Trustees of State Univ. of N. Y.* v. *Fox*, 492 U. S. 469, 480 (1989) (requiring a "fit" between means and ends that is " 'in proportion to the interest served' "); *In re R. M. J.*, 455 U. S. 191, 203 (1982) ("[I]nterference with speech must be in proportion to the [substantial governmental] interest served"); *Pickering* v. *Board of Ed. of Township High School Dist. 205, Will Cty.*, 391 U. S. 563, 568 (1968).

Regardless of the label, some such approach is necessary if the First Amendment is to offer proper protection in the many instances in which a statute adversely affects constitutionally protected interests but warrants neither near-automatic condemnation (as "strict scrutiny" implies) nor near-automatic approval (as is implicit in "rational basis" review). **Kind of "strict scrutiny" lite or "rational basis" heavy.** See, *e.g., Turner Broadcasting System, Inc., supra*, at 641–652 ("must-carry" cable regulations); *Central Hudson Gas & Elec. Corp.* v. *Public Serv. Comm'n of N. Y.*, 447 U. S. 557, 566 (1980) (nonmisleading commercial speech); *Burdick* v. *Takushi*, 504 U. S. 428, 433–434 (1992) (election regulation); *Pickering, supra,* at 568 (government employee speech); *United States* v. *O'Brien*, 391 U. S. 367, 377 (1968) (application of generally applicable laws to expressive conduct). I have used the term "proportionality" to describe this approach. *Thompson* v. *Western States Medical Center*, 535 U. S. 357, 388 (2002) (dissenting opinion); see also *Bartnicki* v. *Vopper*, 532 U. S. 514, 536 (2001) (concurring opinion); *Nixon* v. *Shrink Missouri Government PAC*, 528 U. S. 377, 402–403 (2000) (concurring opinion). But in this case, the Court's term "intermediate scrutiny" describes what I think we should do.

As the dissent points out, "there are broad areas in which any attempt by the state to penalize purportedly false speech would present a grave and unacceptable danger of suppressing truthful speech." *Post,* at 14. Laws restricting false statements about philosophy, religion, history, the social sciences, the arts, and the like raise such concerns, and in many contexts have called for strict scrutiny. But this case does not involve such a law. The dangers of suppressing valuable ideas are lower where, as here, the regulations concern false statements about easily verifiable facts that do not concern such subject matter. Such false factual statements are less likely than are true factual statements to make a valuable contribution to the marketplace of ideas. And the government often has good reasons to prohibit such false speech. See *infra,* at 5–7 (listing examples of statutes and doctrines regulating false factual speech). But its regulation can nonetheless threaten speech-related harms. Those circumstances lead me to apply what the Court has termed "intermediate scrutiny" here.

II

A

The Stolen Valor Act makes it a crime "falsely" to "represen[t]" oneself "to have been awarded any decoration or medal authorized by Congress for the Armed Forces of the United States." 18 U. S. C. §704(b). I would read the statute favorably to the Government as criminalizing only false factual statements made with knowledge of their falsity and with the intent that they be taken as true. See *Staples* v. *United States*, 511 U. S. 600, 605 (1994) (courts construe statutes "in light of the background rules of the common law, . . . in which the requirement of some *mens rea* **intent** for a crime is firmly embedded"); cf. *New York Times Co.* v. *Sullivan*, 376 U. S. 254, 279–280 (1964) (First Amendment allows a public official to recover for defamation only upon a showing of " 'actual malice' "). As so interpreted the statute covers only lies. But although this interpretation diminishes the extent to which the statute endangers First Amendment values, it does not eliminate the threat.

I must concede, as the Government points out, that this Court has frequently said or implied that false factual statements enjoy little First Amendment protection. See, *e.g., BE&K Constr. Co.* v. *NLRB*, 536 U. S. 516, 531 (2002) ("[F] alse statements may be unprotected for their own sake"); *Hustler Magazine, Inc.* v. *Falwell*, 485 U. S. 46, 52 (1988) ("False statements of fact are particularly valueless"); *Gertz* v. *Robert Welch, Inc.*, 418 U. S. 323, 340 (1974) ("[T]he erroneous statement of fact is not worthy of constitutional protection").

But these judicial statements cannot be read to mean "no protection at all." False factual statements can serve useful human objectives, for example: in social contexts, where they may prevent embarrassment, protect privacy, shield a person from prejudice, provide the sick with comfort, or preserve a child's innocence; in public contexts, where they may stop a panic or otherwise preserve calm in the face of danger; and even in technical, philosophical, and scientific contexts, where (as Socrates' methods suggest) examination of a false statement (even if made deliberately to mislead) can promote a form of thought that ultimately helps realize the truth. See, *e.g.*, 638 F. 3d 666, 673–675 (CA9 2011) (Kozinski, J., concurring in denial of rehearing en banc) (providing numerous examples); S. Bok, Lying: Moral Choice in Public and Private Life (1999) (same); *New York Times Co., supra*, at 279, n. 19 ("Even a false statement may be deemed to make a valuable contribution to public debate, since it brings about 'the clearer perception and livelier impression of truth, produced by its collision with error' " (quoting J. Mill, On Liberty 15 (Blackwell ed. 1947))).

Moreover, as the Court has often said, the threat of criminal prosecution for making a false statement can inhibit the speaker from making true statements, thereby "chilling" a kind of speech that lies at the First Amendment's heart. See, *e.g., Gertz, supra*, at 340–341. Hence, the Court emphasizes *mens rea* requirements that provide "breathing room" for more valuable speech by reducing an honest speaker's fear that he may accidentally incur liability for speaking.

Further, the pervasiveness of false statements, made for better or for worse motives, made thoughtlessly or deliberately, made with or without accompanying harm, provides a weapon to a government broadly empowered to prosecute falsity without more. And those who are unpopular may fear that the government will use that weapon selectively, say by prosecuting a pacifist who sup- ports his cause by (falsely) claiming to have been a war hero, while ignoring members of other political groups who might make similar false claims.

I also must concede that many statutes and common-law doctrines make the utterance of certain kinds of false statements unlawful. Those prohibitions, however, tend to be narrower than the statute before us, in that they limit the scope of their application, sometimes by requiring proof of specific harm to identifiable victims; sometimes by specifying that the lies be made in contexts in which a tangible harm to others is especially likely to occur; and sometimes by limiting the prohibited lies to those that are particularly likely to produce harm.

Fraud statutes, for example, typically require proof of a misrepresentation that is material, upon which the victim relied, and which caused actual injury. See Restatement (Second) of Torts §525 (1976). Defamation statutes focus upon statements of a kind that harm the reputation of another or deter third parties from association or dealing with the victim. See *id.*, §§558, 559. Torts involving the intentional infliction of emotional distress (like torts involving placing a victim in a false light) concern falsehoods that tend to cause harm to a specific victim of an emotional-, dignitary-, or privacy-related kind. See *id.*, §652E.

Perjury statutes prohibit a particular set of false statements—those made under oath—while requiring a showing of materiality. See, *e.g.*, 18 U. S. C. §1621. Statutes forbidding lying to a government official (not under oath) are typically limited to circumstances where a lie is likely to work particular and specific harm by interfering with the functioning of a government department, and those statutes also require a showing of materiality. See, *e.g.*, §1001.

Statutes prohibiting false claims of terrorist attacks, or other lies about the commission of crimes or catastrophes, require proof that substantial public harm be directly foreseeable, or, if not, involve false statements that are very likely to bring about that harm. See, *e.g.*, 47 CFR §73.1217 (2011) (requiring showing of foreseeability and actual substantial harm); 18 U. S. C. §1038(a)

(1) (prohibiting knowing false statements claiming that terrorist attacks have taken, are taking, or will take, place).

Statutes forbidding impersonation of a public official typically focus on *acts* of impersonation, not mere speech, and may require a showing that, for example, someone was deceived into following a "course [of action] he would not have pursued but for the deceitful conduct." *United States* v. *Lepowitch*, 318 U. S. 702, 704 (1943); see, *e.g.*, §912 (liability attaches to "[w]hoever falsely assumes or pretends to be an officer or employee acting under the authority of the United States . . . and *acts as such*" (emphasis added)).

Statutes prohibiting trademark infringement present, perhaps, the closest analogy to the present statute. Trademarks identify the source of a good; and infringement causes harm by causing confusion among potential customers (about the source) and thereby diluting the value of the mark to its owner, to consumers, and to the economy. Similarly, a false claim of possession of a medal or other honor creates confusion about who is entitled to wear it, thus diluting its value to those who have earned it, to their families, and to their country. But trademark statutes are focused upon commercial and promotional activities that are likely to dilute the value of a mark. Indeed, they typically require a showing of likely confusion, a showing that tends to assure that the feared harm will in fact take place. See 15 U. S. C. §1114(1)(a); *KP Permanent Make-Up, Inc.* v. *Lasting Impression I, Inc.*, 543 U. S. 111, 117 (2004); see also *San Francisco Arts & Athletics, Inc.* v. *United States Olympic Comm.*, 483 U. S. 522, 539–540, 548 (1987) (upholding statute giving the United States Olympic Committee the right to prohibit certain *commercial and promotional uses* of the word "Olympic").

While this list is not exhaustive, it is sufficient to show that few statutes, if any, simply prohibit without limitation the telling of a lie, even a lie about one particular matter. Instead, in virtually all these instances limitations of context, requirements of proof of injury, and the like, narrow the statute to a subset of lies where specific harm is more likely to occur. The limitations help to make certain that the statute does not allow its threat of liability or criminal punishment to roam at large, discouraging or forbidding the telling of the lie in contexts where harm is unlikely or the need for the prohibition is small.

The statute before us lacks any such limiting features. It may be construed to prohibit only knowing and intentional acts of deception about readily verifiable facts within the personal knowledge of the speaker, thus reducing the risk that valuable speech is chilled. *Supra,* at 3–4. But it still ranges very broadly. And that breadth means that it creates a significant risk of First Amendment harm. As written, it applies in family, social, or other private contexts, where lies will often cause little harm. It also applies in political contexts, where although such lies are more likely to cause harm, the risk of censorious selectivity by prosecutors is also high. Further, given the potential haziness of individual memory along with the large number of military awards covered (ranging from medals for rifle marksmanship to the Congressional Medal of Honor), there remains a risk of chilling that is not completely eliminated by *mens rea* requirements; a speaker might still be worried about being *prosecuted* for a careless false statement, even if he does not have the intent required to render him liable. And so the prohibition may be applied where it should not be applied, for example, to bar stool braggadocio or, in the political arena, subtly but selectively to speakers that the Government does not like. *These considerations lead me to believe that the statute as written risks significant First Amendment harm.* **Our emphasis.**

B

Like both the plurality **Kennedy, Roberts, Ginsburg, Sotomayor** and the dissent **Alito, Scalia, Thomas**, I **[Breyer]** believe the statute nonetheless has substantial justification. It seeks to protect the interests of those who have sacrificed their health and life for their country. The statute serves this interest by seeking to preserve intact the country's recognition of that sacrifice in the form of military honors. To permit those who have not earned those honors to claim otherwise dilutes the value of the awards. Indeed, the Nation cannot fully honor those who have sacrificed so much for their country's honor unless those who claim to have received its military awards tell the truth. Thus, the statute risks harming protected interests but only in order to achieve a substantial countervailing objective.

C

We must therefore ask whether it is possible substantially to achieve the Government's objective in less burdensome ways. In my view, the answer to this question is "yes." Some potential First Amendment threats can be alleviated by interpreting the statute to require knowledge of falsity, etc. *Supra,* at 3–4. But other First Amendment risks, primarily risks flowing from breadth of coverage, remain. *Supra,* at 4–5, 7–8. As is indicated by the limitations on the scope of the many other kinds of statutes regulating false factual speech, *supra,* at 5–7, it should be possible significantly to diminish or eliminate these remaining risks by enacting a similar but more finely tailored statute. For example, not all military awards are alike. Congress might determine that some warrant greater protection than others. And a more finely tailored statute might, as other kinds of statutes prohibiting false factual statements have done, insist upon a showing that the false statement caused specific harm or at least was material, or focus its coverage on lies most likely to be harmful or on contexts where such lies are most likely to cause harm.

I recognize that in some contexts, particularly political contexts, such a narrowing will not always be easy to achieve. In the political arena a false statement is more likely to make a behavioral difference (say, by leading the listeners to vote for the speaker) but at the same time criminal prosecution is particularly dangerous (say, by radically changing a potential election result) and consequently can more easily result in censorship of speakers and their ideas. Thus, the statute may have to be significantly narrowed in its applications. Some lower courts have upheld the constitutionality of roughly comparable but narrowly tailored statutes in political contexts. See, *e.g., United We Stand America, Inc.* v. *United We Stand, America New York, Inc.*, 128 F. 3d 86, 93 (CA2 1997) (upholding against First Amendment challenge application of Lanham Act to a political organization); *Treasure of the Committee to Elect Gerald D. Lostracco* v. *Fox*, 150 Mich. App. 617, 389 N. W. 2d 446 (1986) (upholding under First Amendment statute prohibiting campaign material falsely claiming that one is an incumbent). Without expressing any view on the validity of those cases, I would also note, like the plurality, that in this area more accurate information will normally counteract the lie. And an accurate, publicly available register of military awards, easily obtainable by political opponents, may well adequately protect the integrity of an award against those who would falsely claim to have earned it. See *ante,* at 17–18. And so it is likely that a more narrowly tailored statute combined with such information-disseminating devices will effectively serve Congress' end.

The Government has provided no convincing explanation as to why a more finely tailored statute would not work. In my own view, such a statute could significantly reduce the threat of First Amendment harm while permitting the statute to achieve its important protective objective. That being so, I find the statute as presently drafted works disproportionate constitutional harm. It consequently fails intermediate scrutiny, and so violates the First Amendment. **As Chapter 9 demonstrates, the authors' Fake Warrior Act is "finely tailored."**

For these reasons, I **[Breyer]** concur in the Court's judgment.

Justice Alito, with whom Justice Scalia and Justice Thomas join, dissenting.

Only the bravest of the brave are awarded the Congressional Medal of Honor, but the Court today holds that every American has a constitutional right to claim to have received this singular award. The Court strikes down the Stolen Valor Act of 2005, which was enacted to stem an epidemic of false claims about military decorations. These lies, Congress reasonably concluded, were undermining our country's system of military honors and inflicting real harm on actual medal recipients and their families.

Building on earlier efforts to protect the military awards system, Congress responded to this problem by crafting a narrow statute that presents no threat to the freedom of speech. **This is surprising coming from Justice Alito. Section 704(b) is not a "narrow statute." It applies to all statements, by whomever and to whoever made, in whatever context, at all times, and everywhere.** The statute reaches only knowingly false statements about hard facts directly within a speaker's personal knowledge.

It does not. There is no "knowingly" language in the statute. These lies have no value in and of themselves, and proscribing them does not chill any valuable speech. **This is a wholly unsupported assertion.**

By holding that the First Amendment nevertheless shields these lies, the Court breaks sharply from a long line of cases recognizing that the right to free speech does not protect false factual statements that inflict real harm and serve no legitimate interest. **As with the absence of "knowingly" language in Section 704(b), there is no requirement, none, in the statute that the false statements cause "harm." Regarding these two limitations, Justice Alito is trying to support a law that does not exist.** I would adhere to that principle and would thus uphold the constitutionality of this valuable law.

I

The Stolen Valor Act makes it a misdemeanor to "falsely represen[t]" oneself as having been awarded a medal, decoration, or badge for service in the Armed Forces of the United States. 18 U. S. C. §704(b). Properly construed, this statute is limited in five significant respects. First, the Act applies to only a narrow category of false representations about objective facts that can almost always be proved or disproved with near certainty. Second, the Act concerns facts that are squarely within the speaker's personal knowledge. Third, as the Government maintains, see Brief for United States 15–17, and both the plurality, see *ante,* at 7, and the concurrence, see *ante,* at 3 (Breyer, J., concurring in judgment), seemingly accept, a conviction under the Act requires proof beyond a reasonable doubt that the speaker actually knew that the representation was false.[1] Fourth, the Act applies only to statements that could reasonably be interpreted as communicating actual facts; it does not reach dramatic performances, satire, parody, hyperbole, or the like.[2] Finally, the Act is strictly viewpoint neutral. The false statements proscribed by the Act are highly unlikely to be tied to any particular political or ideological message. In the rare cases where that is not so, the Act applies equally to all false statements, whether they tend to disparage or commend the Government, the military, or the system of military honors. **Even accepting for the purpose of argument that all these limitations**

do exist, though they are certainly not expressly provided in Section 704(b), still, the law punishes pure speech.

The Stolen Valor Act follows a long tradition of efforts to protect our country's system of military honors. When George Washington, as the commander of the Continental Army, created the very first "honorary badges of distinction" for service in our country's military, he established a rigorous system to ensure that these awards would be received and worn by only the truly deserving. See General Orders of George Washington Issued at Newburgh on the Hudson, 1782–1783, p. 35 (E. Boynton ed. 1883) (reprint 1973) (requiring the submission of "incontestable proof" of "singularly meritorious action" to the Commander in Chief). Washington warned that anyone with the "insolence to assume" a badge that had not actually been earned would be "severely punished." *Id.*, at 34.

Building on this tradition, Congress long ago made it a federal offense for anyone to wear, manufacture, or sell certain military decorations without authorization. See Act of Feb. 24, 1923, ch. 110, 42 Stat. 1286 (codified as amended at 18 U. S. C. §704(a)). Although this Court has never opined on the constitutionality of that particular provision, we have said that §702, which makes it a crime to wear a United States military uniform without authorization, is "a valid statute on its face." *Schacht* v. *United States*, 398 U. S. 58, 61 (1970). **That was decades before enactment of Section 704(b).**

Congress passed the Stolen Valor Act in response to a proliferation of false claims concerning the receipt of military awards. For example, in a single year, *more than 600* Virginia residents falsely claimed to have won the Medal of Honor.3 An investigation of the 333 people listed in the online edition of Who's Who as having received a top military award revealed that fully a third of the claims could not be substantiated.4 When the Library of Congress compiled oral histories for its Veterans History Project, 24 of the 49 individuals who identified themselves as Medal of Honor recipients had not actually received that award.5 The same was true of 32 individuals who claimed to have been awarded the Distinguished Service Cross and 14 who claimed to have won the Navy Cross.6 Notorious cases brought to Congress' attention included the case of a judge who falsely claimed to have been awarded *two* Medals of Honor and displayed counterfeit medals in his courtroom;7 a television network's military consultant who falsely claimed that he had received the Silver Star;8 and a former judge advocate in the Marine Corps who lied about receiving the Bronze Star and a Purple Heart.9 **All true, and more. See Chapter 2.**

As Congress recognized, the lies proscribed by the Stolen Valor Act inflict substantial harm. In many instances, the harm is tangible in nature: Individuals often falsely represent themselves as award recipients in order to obtain financial or other material rewards, such as lucrative contracts and government benefits.10 An investigation of false claims in a single region of the United States, for example, revealed that 12 men had defrauded the Department of Veterans Affairs out of more than $1.4 million in veteran's benefits.11 In other cases, the harm is less tangible, but nonetheless significant.

The lies proscribed by the Stolen Valor Act tend to debase the distinctive honor of military awards. See Stolen Valor Act of 2005, §2, 120 Stat. 3266, note following 18 U. S. C. §704 (finding that "[f]raudulent claims surrounding the receipt of [military decorations and medals] damage the reputation and meaning of such decorations and medals"). And legitimate award recipients and their families have expressed the harm they endure when an imposter takes credit for heroic actions that he never performed. One Medal of Honor recipient described the feeling as a " 'slap in the face of veterans who have paid the price and earned their medals.' "12 **All true, but is a figurative, not literal, slap in the face (whatever that means) to justify criminalizing pure speech?**

It is well recognized in trademark law that the proliferation of cheap imitations of luxury goods blurs the " 'signal' given out by the purchasers of the originals." Landes & Posner, Trademark Law: An Economic Perspective, 30 J. Law & Econ. 265, 308 (1987). In much the same way, the proliferation of false claims about military awards blurs the signal given out by the actual awards by making them seem more common than they really are, and this diluting effect harms the military by hampering its efforts to foster morale and esprit de corps. Surely it was reasonable for Congress to conclude that the goal of preserving the integrity of our country's top military honors is at least as worthy as that of protecting the prestige associated with fancy watches and designer handbags. Cf. *San Francisco Arts & Athletics, Inc.* v. *United States Olympic Comm.*, 483 U. S. 522, 539–541 (1987) (rejecting First Amendment challenge to law prohibiting certain unauthorized uses of the word "Olympic" and recognizing that such uses harm the U. S. Olympic Committee by "lessening the distinctiveness" of the term).

Both the plurality and Justice Breyer argue that Congress could have preserved the integrity of military honors by means other than a criminal prohibition, but Congress had ample reason to believe that alternative approaches would not be adequate. The chief alternative that is recommended is the compilation and release of a comprehensive list or database of actual medal recipients. If the public could readily access such a resource, it is argued, imposters would be quickly and easily exposed, and the proliferation of lies about military honors would come to an end.

This remedy, unfortunately, will not work. The Department of Defense has explained that the most that it can do is to create a database of recipients of certain top military honors awarded since 2001. See Office of Undersecretary of Defense, Report to the Senate and House Armed Services Committees on a Searchable Military Valor Decorations Database 4–5 (2009).13

Because a sufficiently comprehensive database is not practicable, lies about military awards cannot be remedied by what the plurality calls "counter-speech." *Ante*, at 15. Without the requisite database, many efforts to refute false claims may be thwarted, and some legitimate award recipients may be erroneously attacked. In addition, a steady stream of stories in the media about the exposure of imposters would tend to increase skepticism among members of the public about the entire awards system. This would only exacerbate the harm that the Stolen Valor Act is meant to prevent.

The plurality and the concurrence also suggest that Congress could protect the system of military honors by enacting a narrower statute. The plurality recommends a law that would apply only to lies that are intended to "secure moneys or other valuable considerations." *Ante*, at 11. In a similar vein, the concurrence comments that "a more finely tailored statute might . . . insist upon a showing that the false statement caused specific harm." *Ante,* at 9 (opinion of Breyer, J.). But much damage is caused, both to real award recipients and to the system of military honors, by false statements that are not linked to any financial or other tangible reward. Unless even a small financial loss—say, a dollar given to a homeless man falsely claiming to be a decorated veteran—is more important in the eyes of the First Amendment than the damage caused to the very integrity of the military awards system, there is no basis for distinguishing between the Stolen Valor Act and the alternative statutes that the plurality and concurrence appear willing to sustain.

Justice Breyer also proposes narrowing the statute so that it covers a shorter list of military awards, *ante,* at 9 (opinion concurring in judgment), but he does not provide a hint about where he thinks the line must be drawn. Perhaps he expects Congress to keep trying until it eventually passes a law that draws the line in just the right place.

II

A

Time and again, this Court has recognized that as a general matter false factual statements possess no intrinsic First Amendment value. See *Illinois ex rel. Madigan* v. *Telemarketing Associates, Inc.,* 538 U. S. 600, 612 (2003) ("Like other forms of public deception, fraudulent charitable solicitation is unprotected speech"); *BE&K Constr. Co.* v. *NLRB,* 536 U. S. 516, 531 (2002) ("[F]alse statements may be unprotected for their own sake"); *Hustler Magazine, Inc.* v. *Falwell,* 485 U. S. 46, 52 (1988) ("False statements of fact are particularly valueless; they interfere with the truth-seeking function of the marketplace of ideas, and they cause damage to an individual's reputation that cannot easily be repaired by counterspeech, however persuasive or effective"); *Keeton* v. *Hustler Magazine, Inc.,* 465 U. S. 770, 776 (1984) ("There is 'no constitutional value in false statements of fact' " (quoting *Gertz* v. *Robert Welch, Inc.,* 418 U. S. 323, 340 (1974))); *Bill John- son's Restaurants, Inc.* v. *NLRB,* 461 U. S. 731, 743 (1983) ("[F]alse statements are not immunized by the First Amendment right to freedom of speech"); *Brown* v. *Hartlage,* 456 U. S. 45, 60 (1982) ("Of course, demonstrable falsehoods are not protected by the First Amendment in the same manner as truthful statements"); *Herbert* v. *Lando*, 441 U. S. 153, 171 (1979) ("Spreading false information in and of itself carries no First Amendment credentials"); *Virginia Bd. of Pharmacy* v. *Virginia Citizens Consumer Council, Inc.*, 425 U. S. 748, 771 (1976) ("Untruthful speech, commercial or otherwise, has never been protected for its own sake"); *Gertz, supra,* at 340 ("[T]he erroneous statement of fact is not worthy of constitutional protection"); *Time, Inc.* v. *Hill*, 385 U. S. 374, 389 (1967) ("[T]he constitutional guarantees [of the First Amendment] can tolerate sanctions against *calculated* falsehood without significant impairment of their essential function"); *Garrison* v. *Louisiana*, 379 U. S. 64, 75 (1964) ("[T] he knowingly false statement and the false statement made with reckless disregard of the truth, do not enjoy constitutional protection").

Consistent with this recognition, many kinds of false factual statements have long been proscribed without " 'rais[ing] any Constitutional problem.' " *United States* v. *Stevens*, 559 U. S. ___, ___ (2010) (slip op., at 6) (quoting *Chaplinsky* v. *New Hampshire*, 315 U. S. 568, 571–572 (1942)). Laws prohibiting fraud, perjury, and defamation, for example, were in existence when the First Amendment was adopted, and their constitutionality is now beyond question. See, *e.g., Donaldson* v. *Read Magazine, Inc.*, 333 U. S. 178, 190 (1948) (explaining that the government's power "to protect people against fraud" has "always been recognized in this country and is firmly established"); *United States* v. *Dunnigan*, 507 U. S. 87, 97 (1993) (observing that "the constitutionality of perjury statutes is unquestioned"); *Beauharnais* v. *Illinois*, 343 U. S. 250, 256 (1952) (noting that the "prevention and punishment" of libel "have never been thought to raise any Constitutional problem").

We have also described as falling outside the First Amendment's protective shield certain false factual statements that were neither illegal nor tortious at the time of the Amendment's adoption. The right to freedom of speech has been held to permit recovery for the intentional infliction of emotional distress by means of a false statement, see *Falwell, supra,* at 56, even though that tort did not enter our law until the late 19th century, see W. Keeton, D. Dobbs, R. Keeton, & D. Owen, Prosser and Keeton on Law of Torts §12, p. 60, and n. 47. (5th ed. 1984) (hereinafter Prosser and Keeton). And in *Hill, supra,* at 390, the Court concluded that the free speech right allows recovery for the even more modern tort of false-light invasion of privacy, see Prosser and Keeton §117, at 863.

In line with these holdings, it has long been assumed that the First Amendment is not offended by prominent criminal statutes with no close common-law analog. The most well known of these is probably 18 U. S. C. §1001, which makes it a crime to "knowingly and willfully" make any "materially false, fictitious, or fraudulent statement or representation" in "any matter within the jurisdiction of the executive, legislative, or judicial branch of the Government of the United States." Unlike perjury, §1001 is not limited to statements made under oath or before an official government tribunal. Nor does it require any showing of "pecuniary or property loss to the government." *United States* v. *Gilliland*, 312 U. S. 86, 93 (1941). Instead, the statute is based on the need to protect "agencies from the perversion which *might* result from the deceptive practices described." *Ibid.* (emphasis added).

Still other statutes make it a crime to falsely represent that one is speaking on behalf of, or with the approval of, the Federal Government. See, *e.g.*, 18 U. S. C. §912 (making it a crime to falsely impersonate a federal officer); §709 (making it a crime to knowingly use, without authorization, the names of enumerated federal agencies, such as "Federal Bureau of Investigation," in a manner reasonably calculated to convey the impression that a communication is approved or authorized by the agency). We have recognized that §912, like §1001, does not require a showing of pecuniary or property loss and that its purpose is to " 'maintain the general good repute and dignity' " of Government service. *United States* v. *Lepowitch*, 318 U. S. 702, 704 (1943) (quoting *United States* v. *Barnow*, 239 U. S. 74, 80 (1915)). All told, there are more than 100 federal criminal statutes that punish false statements made in connection with areas of federal agency concern. See *United States* v. *Wells*, 519 U. S. 482, 505–507, and nn. 8–10 (1997) (Stevens, J., dissenting) (citing "at least 100 federal false statement statutes" in the United States Code).

These examples amply demonstrate that false statements of fact merit no First Amendment protection in their own right.14 It is true, as Justice

Breyer notes, that many in our society either approve or condone certain discrete categories of false statements, including false statements made to prevent harm to innocent victims and so-called "white lies." See *ante*, at 4. But respondent's false claim to have received the Medal of Honor did not fall into any of these categories. His lie did not "prevent embarrassment, protect privacy, shield a person from prejudice, provide the sick with comfort, or preserve a child's innocence." *Ibid*. Nor did his lie "stop a panic or otherwise preserve calm in the face of danger" or further philosophical or scientific debate. *Ibid.* Respondent's claim, like all those covered by the Stolen Valor Act, served no valid purpose.

Respondent and others who join him in attacking the Stolen Valor Act take a different view. Respondent's brief features a veritable paean to lying. According to respondent, his lie about the Medal of Honor was nothing out of the ordinary for 21st-century Americans. "Everyone lies," he says. Brief for Respondent 10. "We lie all the time." *Ibid.* "[H]uman beings are constantly forced to choose the persona we present to the world, and our choices nearly always involve intentional omissions and misrepresentations, if not outright deception." *Id.,* at 39. An academic *amicus* tells us that the First Amendment protects the right to construct "self-aggrandizing fabrications such as having been awarded a military decoration." Brief for Jonathan D. Varat as *Amicus Curiae* 5.

This radical interpretation of the First Amendment is not supported by any precedent of this Court. The lies covered by the Stolen Valor Act have no intrinsic value and thus merit no First Amendment protection unless their prohibition would chill other expression that falls within the Amendment's scope. I now turn to that question.

B

While we have repeatedly endorsed the principle that false statements of fact do not merit First Amendment protection for their own sake, we have recognized that it is sometimes necessary to "exten[d] a measure of strategic protection" to these statements in order to ensure sufficient " 'breathing space' " for protected speech. *Gertz*, 418 U. S., at 342 (quoting

NAACP v. *Button*, 371 U. S. 415, 433 (1963)). Thus, in order to prevent the chilling of truthful speech on matters of public concern, we have held that liability for the defamation of a public official or figure requires proof that defamatory statements were made with knowledge or reckless disregard of their falsity. See *New York Times Co.* v. *Sullivan*, 376 U. S. 254, 279–280 (1964) (civil liability); *Garrison*, 379 U. S., at 74–75 (criminal liability). This same requirement applies when public officials and figures seek to recover for the tort of intentional infliction of emotional distress. See *Falwell*, 485 U. S., at 55–56. And we have imposed "[e]xacting proof requirements" in other contexts as well when necessary to ensure that truthful speech is not chilled. *Madigan*, 538 U. S., at 620 (complainant in a fraud action must show that the defendant made a knowingly false statement of material fact with the intent to mislead the listener and that he succeeded in doing so); see also *BE&K Constr.*, 536 U. S., at 531 (regulation of baseless lawsuits limited to those that are both "objectively baseless *and* subjectively motivated by an unlawful purpose"); *Hartlage*, 456 U. S., at 61 (sustaining as-applied First Amendment challenge to law prohibiting certain "factual misstatements in the course of political debate" where there had been no showing that the disputed statement was made "other than in good faith and without knowledge of its falsity, or . . . with reckless disregard as to whether it was false or not"). All of these proof requirements inevitably have the effect of bringing some false factual statements within the protection of the First Amendment, but this is justified in order to prevent the chilling of other, valuable speech.

These examples by no means exhaust the circumstances in which false factual statements enjoy a degree of instrumental constitutional protection. On the contrary, there are broad areas in which any attempt by the state to penalize purportedly false speech would present a grave and unacceptable danger of suppressing truthful speech. Laws restricting false statements about philosophy, religion, history, the social sciences, the arts, and other matters of public concern would present such a threat. The point is not that there is no such thing as truth or falsity in these areas or that the truth is always impossible to ascertain, but rather that it is perilous to permit the state to be the arbiter of truth. **Or the arbiter of what speech has a "valid purpose"?**

Even where there is a wide scholarly consensus concerning a particular matter, the truth is served by allowing that consensus to be challenged without fear of reprisal. Today's accepted wisdom sometimes turns out to be mistaken. And in these contexts, "[e]ven a false statement may be deemed to make a valuable contribution to public debate, since it brings about 'the clearer perception and livelier impression of truth, produced by its collision with error.' " *Sullivan, supra*, at 279, n. 19 (quoting J. Mill, On Liberty 15 (R. McCallum ed. 1947)).

Allowing the state to proscribe false statements in these areas also opens the door for the state to use its power for political ends. Statements about history illustrate this point. If some false statements about historical events may be banned, how certain must it be that a statement is false before the ban may be upheld? And who should make that calculation? While our cases prohibiting viewpoint discrimination would fetter the state's power to some degree, see *R. A. V.* v. *St. Paul*, 505 U. S. 377, 384–390 (1992) (explaining that the First Amendment does not permit the government to engage in viewpoint discrimination under the guise of regulating unprotected speech), the potential for abuse of power in these areas is simply too great.

In stark contrast to hypothetical laws prohibiting false statements about history, science, and similar matters, the Stolen Valor Act presents no risk at all that valuable speech will be suppressed. **"Valuable," according to whom?** The speech punished by the Act is not only verifiably false and entirely lacking in intrinsic value, but it also fails to serve any instrumental purpose that the First Amendment might protect. Tellingly, when asked at oral argument what truthful speech the Stolen Valor Act might chill, even respondent's counsel conceded that the answer is none. Tr. of Oral Arg. 36.

C

Neither of the two opinions endorsed by Justices in the majority claims that the false statements covered by the Stolen Valor Act possess either intrinsic or instrumental value. Instead, those opinions appear to be based on the distinct concern that the Act suffers from overbreadth. See *ante*, at

10 (plurality opinion) (the Act applies to "personal, whispered conversations within a home"); *ante,* at 8 (Breyer, J., concurring in judgment) (the Act "applies in family, social, or other private contexts" and in "political contexts"). But to strike down a statute on the basis that it is overbroad, it is necessary to show that the statute's "overbreadth [is] *substantial*, not only in an absolute sense, but also relative to [its] plainly legitimate sweep." *United States* v. *Williams*, 553 U. S. 285, 292 (2008); see also *ibid.* (noting that this requirement has been "vigorously enforced"). The plurality and the concurrence do not even attempt to make this showing.

The plurality additionally worries that a decision sustaining the Stolen Valor Act might prompt Congress and the state legislatures to enact laws criminalizing lies about "an endless list of subjects." *Ante,* at 11. The plurality apparently fears that we will see laws making it a crime to lie about civilian awards such as college degrees or certificates of achievement in the arts and sports.

This concern is likely unfounded. With very good reason, military honors have traditionally been regarded as quite different from civilian awards. Nearly a century ago, Congress made it a crime to wear a military medal without authorization; we have no comparable tradition regarding such things as Super Bowl rings, Oscars, or Phi Beta Kappa keys.

In any event, if the plurality's concern is not entirely fanciful, it falls outside the purview of the First Amendment. The problem that the plurality foresees—that legislative bodies will enact unnecessary and overly intrusive criminal laws—applies regardless of whether the laws in question involve speech or non-expressive conduct. If there is a problem with, let us say, a law making it a criminal offense to falsely claim to have been a high school valedictorian, the problem is not the suppression of speech but the misuse of the criminal law, which should be reserved for conduct that inflicts or threatens truly serious societal harm. The objection to this hypothetical law would be the same as the objection to a law making it a crime to eat potato chips during the graduation ceremony at which the high school valedictorian is recognized. The safeguard against such laws is democracy, not the First Amendment. Not every foolish law is unconstitutional.

The Stolen Valor Act represents the judgment of the people's elected representatives that false statements about military awards are very different from false statements about civilian awards. Certainly this is true with respect to the high honor that respondent misappropriated. Respondent claimed that he was awarded the Medal of Honor in 1987 for bravery during the Iran hostage crisis. This singular award, however, is bestowed only on those members of the Armed Forces who "distinguis[h] [themselves] conspicuously by gallantry and intrepidity at the risk of [their lives] above and beyond the call of duty." 10 U. S. C. §3741; see also §§6241, 8741. More than half of the heroic individuals to have been awarded the Medal of Honor after World War I received it posthumously.[15] Congress was entitled to conclude that falsely claiming to have won the Medal of Honor is qualitatively different from even the most prestigious civilian awards and that the misappropriation of that honor warrants criminal sanction.

* * *

The Stolen Valor Act is a narrow law enacted to address an important problem, and it presents no threat to freedom of expression. **It only suppresses pure speech, and subject to strict scrutiny fails both prongs of that test: compelling interest, and narrowly tailored.**I would sustain the constitutionality of the Act, and I therefore respectfully dissent.

Footnotes

1

Although the Act does not use the term "knowing" or "knowingly," we have explained that criminal statutes must be construed "in light of the background rules of the common law . . . in which the requirement of some *mens rea* **intent** for a crime is firmly embedded." *Staples* v. *United States*, 511 U. S. 600, 605 (1994). The Act's use of the phrase "falsely represents," moreover, connotes **but statutorily does not denote** a knowledge requirement. See Black's Law Dictionary 1022 (8th ed. 2004) (defining a "misrepresentation" or "false representation" to mean "[t]he act of making a false or misleading assertion about something, usu. with the *intent to deceive*" (emphasis added)).

2
See Black's Law Dictionary, *supra*, at 1327 (defining "representation" to mean a "presentation of fact"); see also *Milkovich* v. *Lorain Journal Co.*, 497 U. S. 1, 20 (1990) (explaining that the Court has protected "statements that cannot 'reasonably [be] interpreted as stating actual facts' about an individual" so that "public debate will not suffer for lack of 'imaginative expression' or the 'rhetorical hyperbole' which has traditionally added much to the discourse of our Nation" (quoting *Hustler Magazine, Inc.* v. *Falwell*, 485 U. S. 46, 50 (1988); alteration in original)).

3
Colimore, Pinning Crime on Fake Heroes: N. J. Agent Helps Expose and Convict Those with Bogus U. S. Medals, Philadelphia Inquirer, Feb. 11, 2004, http://articles.philly.com/2004-02-11/news/25374213_1_medals-military-imposters-distinguished-flying-cross (all Internet materials as visited June 25, 2012, and available in Clerk of Court's case file).
4

Crewdson, Claims of Medals Amount to Stolen Valor, Chicago Tribune, Oct. 26, 2008, (www.chicagotribune.com/news/local/chi-valor-oct25,0,4301227.story?page=1).

5
Half of MOH Entries in Oral History Project Are Incorrect, Marine Corps Times, Oct. 1, 2007, 2007 WLNR 27917486.

6
Ibid.

7

Young, His Honor Didn't Get Medal of Honor, Chicago Tribune, Oct. 21, 1994, http://articles.chicagotribune.com/1994-10-21/news/9410210318_1_congressional-medal-highest-fritz.

8

Rutenberg, At Fox News, the Colonel Who Wasn't, N. Y. Times, Apr. 29, 2002, (www.nytimes.com/2002/04/29/business/at-fox-news-the-colonel-who-wasn-t.html?pagewanted=all&src=pm).

9

B. Burkett & G. Whitley, Stolen Valor: How the Vietnam Generation Was Robbed of Its Heroes and Its History 179 (1998).

10

Indeed, the first person to be prosecuted under the Stolen Valor Act apparently "parlayed his medals into lucrative security consulting contracts." Zambito, War Crime: FBI Targets Fake Heroes, New York Daily News, May 6, 2007, (www.nydailynews.com/news/crime/war-crime-fbi-targets-fake-heroes-article-1.249168).

11

Dept. of Justice, Northwest Crackdown on Fake Veterans in "Operation Stolen Valor," Sept. 21, 2007, (www.justice.gov/usao/waw/ press/2007/sep/operationstolenvalor.html).

12

Cato, High Court Tussles With False Heroics: Free Speech or Felony? Pittsburg TribuneReview,Feb.23,2012,(*http://triblive.com/usworld/nation/1034434-85/court-military-law-false-medals-supreme-valor-act-federal-free).*

13

In addition, since the Department may not disclose the Social Security numbers or birthdates of recipients, this database would be of limited use in ascertaining the veracity of a claim involving a person with a common name. Office of Undersecretary of Defense, Report, at 3–4.

14

The plurality rejects this rule. Although we have made clear that "[u]ntruthful speech . . . has never been protected for its own sake," *Virginia Bd. of Pharmacy* v. *Virginia Citizens Consumer Council, Inc.*, 425 U. S. 748, 771 (1976), the most the plurality is willing to concede is that "the falsity of speech bears upon whether it is protected," *ante,* at 9. This represents a dramatic—and entirely unjustified—departure from the sound approach taken in past cases.

Respondent and his supporting *amici* attempt to limit this rule to certain subsets of false statements, see, *e.g.,* Brief for Respondent 53 (asserting that, at most, only falsity that is proved to cause specific harm is stripped of its First Amendment protection), but the examples described above belie that attempt. These examples show that the rule at least applies to (1) specific types of false statements that were neither illegal nor tortious in 1791 (the torts of intentional infliction of emotional distress and false-light invasion of privacy did not exist when the First Amendment was adopted); (2) false speech that does not cause pecuniary harm (the harm remedied by the torts of defamation, intentional infliction of emotional distress, and false-light invasion of privacy is often non-pecuniary in nature, as is the harm inflicted by statements that are illegal under §§912 and 1001); (3) false speech that does not cause detrimental reliance (neither perjury laws nor many of the federal false statement statutes require that anyone actually rely on the false statement); (4) particular false statements that are not shown in court to have caused specific harm (damages can be presumed in defamation actions involving knowing or reckless falsehoods, and no showing of specific harm is required in prosecutions under many of the federal false statement statutes); and (5) false speech that does not cause harm to a specific individual (the purpose of many of the federal false statement statutes is to protect government processes).

15 See U. S. Army Center of Military History, Medal of Honor Statistics, (www.history.army.mil/html/moh/mohstats.html).

CHAPTER 9

What is the Fake Warrior Act of 2012, and why is it indispensable?

The Stolen Valor Act [2006] infringes upon
speech protected by the First Amendment.
—Associate Justice Anthony Kennedy, *United States* v. *Alvarez*

If Fake Warriors will lie to Congress, to whom won't they lie?

In the Introduction to the First Edition of *Fake Warriors: Identifying, Exposing, and Punishing Those Who Falsify Their Military Service, in 2003*, we wrote that:

> Unknown to most Americans, there is a virtual epidemic of imposters in this country — countless thousands of men who, since the Vietnam War, have been either inventing a non-existent military service, or inflating their war records.
>
> Veterans' benefits amounting to hundreds of millions of dollars are being stolen. Military decorations are being falsely claimed, and often worn, by men never authorized to receive them — the kind of medals earned the hard way by genuine war heroes.

The next year, presidential candidate John Kerry's campaign website claimed that he had been awarded not only three Purple Hearts and a Silver Star (all undeserved), but the Silver Star was adorned with a Combat 'V'. That combination (Silver Star *and* "Combat 'V') has never in all history been issued by the United States Navy because the 'V' (for valor) is redundant to the Silver Star (for valor).

During the 2010 election, it was revealed that the successful Democratic Party candidate for a Connecticut seat in the United States Senate, Richard Blumenthal —former United States Attorney for the District of Connecticut and State Attorney General — lied for years about serving in Vietnam. (If every veteran and their families and friends in Connecticut had voted against the Fake Warrior, perhaps the election's outcome would have been different.)

In the first edition of *Fake Warriors*, we wrote that "[u]nless something is done about . . . Fake Warriors, their shameless, self-aggrandizing, and costly conduct will not only continue unabated, it will grow."

Whatever the influence — Burkett and Whitley's *Stolen Valor*, our *Fake Warriors I*, or something else — several years before the Blumenthal fiasco, a dedicated group of patriots formulated an anti-Fake Warrior federal statute, lobbied fiercely for it, and succeeded in having it enacted by Congress and signed into law on December 20, 2006 by President George W. Bush. It was called the Stolen Valor Act of 2005 (SVA), and is discussed at length in Chapter 7 and by the Supreme Court of the United States in Chapter 8.

The Act amended 18 U.S.C 704 (a), which for years had criminalized the *wearing*, *manufacture*, or *sale* of unauthorized military decorations, medals, and awards. Note the italicized words. They all constitute acts, not *pure speech*.

In support of the SVA, Congress made a finding that Section 704(a) had previously inadequately protected "the reputation and meaning of military decorations and medals." (Put aside the question of whether "military decorations and medals" can themselves, rather than individuals, have a *reputation*).

Accordingly, the SVA amended, and broadened, Section 704, to read as follows:

> (b) Whoever falsely represents himself or herself, *verbally* or in *writing*, to have been awarded any decoration or medal authorized by Congress for the Armed Forces of the United States, any of the service medals or badges awarded to the members of such forces, the ribbon, button, or rosette of any such badge, decoration or medal, or any colorable imitation of such item shall be fined under this title, imprisoned not more than six months, or both.

Note the two words I have italicized, which describe not *acts*—such as wearing, manufacturing or selling—but *pure speech*.

Under this amendment, if the Fake Warrior claims to have been awarded the Medal of Honor, Distinguished Service Cross, Navy Cross, Air Force Cross, Silver Star, or Purple Heart, punishment for the crime is enhanced to not more than one year in prison, or both.

Throughout the drafting of the SVA and the legislative process leading to its enactment — and, for that matter, later while the Act was in force and prosecutions were occurring — Professor Holzer repeatedly told the Act's partisans and others that as admirable as the law's intention was, because it punished pure speech it violated the First Amendment and was thus unconstitutional.

As an Army veteran who served in Korea in the mid-1950s, and co-author of this book who considers "Fake Warrior-ism" reprehensible, Professor Holzer much preferred to have reached the opposite conclusion.

But as a constitutional lawyer for over fifty years, it was clear to him that Section 704(b) of the SVA was a content-based suppression of pure speech that could not be justified by the kind of requisite narrowly tailored, 'compelling' federal interest the Court has found in a very few other Free Speech cases — such as punishing defamation, "fighting words," and hard-core pornography, and protecting the psychological and physical well-being of children. Indeed, the Supreme Court has more than once said that a "compelling government interest is an 'interest of the highest order.'"

Professor Holzer's legal conclusion was vindicated on June 28, 2012, by the 6-3 decision of the Supreme Court in the *Alvarez* case, holding Section 704(b) unconstitutional.

We have corrected the problem of unconstitutionally punishing pure speech in our **FAKE WARRIOR ACT OF 2012**. It follows:

An Act

To punish false and fraudulent claims to having received military decorations, medals and other awards authorized by the Congress and Armed Forces of the United States.

Be it enacted by the Senate and House of Representatives of the United States of America in Congress assembled,

SECTION 1. SHORT TITLE. This Act may be cited as the "Fake Warrior Act of 2012."

SECTION 2. FINDINGS. Congress makes the following findings:

(1) Citizens of the United States are justifiably grateful to members who currently serve, and have served, honourably in the Armed Forces of the United States, and hold them in high esteem.

(2) Members of the Armed Forces of the United States who have been recipients of military decorations, medals and other awards are held in even higher esteem by citizens of the United States.

(3) Gratitude to members of the Armed Forces of the United States generally, and to those who have received military decorations, medals and other awards in particular, makes citizens of the United States susceptible to fraudulent claims by persons falsely purporting to have received such decorations, medals, and awards.

(4) That susceptibility can and does result in citizens of

the United States being fraudulently induced by persons who falsify their receipt of military decorations, medals and other awards to part with something of tangible or other actual value to which the fraudsters are not entitled and with which the victims would not otherwise have parted.

(5) Fraudulent claims of the receipt of military decorations, medals and awards results in serious harm to the citizens of the United States, including but not limited to unauthorized access to classified and other sensitive information and installations, undeserved receipt of veteran and related benefits, unwarranted leniency at sentencing for crimes, and by the unfair treatment of abuse victims by those claiming to have suffered trauma in military service.

(6) Legislative action by Congress is necessary to punish the false and fraudulent claims by persons purporting to have received military decorations, medals, and awards.

SECTION 3. ESTABLISHMENT OF CRIMINAL OFFENSE RELATING TO FALSE AND FRAUDULENT CLAIMS ABOUT RECEIPT OF MILITARY MEDALS AND AWARDS.

(1) FALSE AND FRAUDULENT CLAIMS ABOUT RECEIPT OF MILITARY DECORATIONS, MEDALS, AND AWARDS.

Whoever knowingly and falsely, with the intent to obtain something of tangible or other actual value to which he or she is not entitled, represents himself or herself, verbally or in writing, under circumstances where such representation may reasonably be expected to be believed, to have been awarded any military decoration, medal or award authorized by Congress for the Armed Forces of the United States, any of the service medals or badges awarded to the member of such forces, the ribbon, button, or rosette of any such badge, decoration, medal, award, or any colorable imitation of such item, and who as a result of such representation obtains something of tangible or other actual value to which he or she is not entitled, shall be fined $5,000, imprisoned not more than six months, or both.

(2) ENHANCED PENALTY FOR OFFENSES INVOLVING CERTAIN OTHER MEDALS.

If a military decoration, medal, or award involved in an offense described in Section 3 (1) is a Medal of Honor, Distinguished Service Cross, Navy Cross, Air Force Cross, Silver Star, POW Medal, or Purple Heart, in lieu of the punishment provided in such section the offender shall be fined $10,000, imprisoned not less than nine months nor more than twelve months, or both.

You'll note that the **FAKE WARRIOR ACT OF 2012** differs from the Stolen Valor Act of 2005 in at least two significant ways.

First, we have grounded the government's interest not in punishing pure speech because, as the *Alvarez* Court demonstrated, in the Fake Warrior context there is no narrowly tailored compelling government interest that will justify doing so. Instead, we have rested that interest on criminalizing a traditional type of fraud, one that has been a common law and statutory crime for centuries.

And we have supported the government's interest with "Findings" that emphasize the statute's *anti-fraud* intention, instead of resting it on the suppression of pure speech (as Section 704(b) of the SVA regrettably and unconstitutionally did). These Findings will provide a reviewing court with an unambiguous understanding of the legislation's sole anti-fraud purpose.

A word of warning, however.

On May 5, 2011, while litigation was occurring in the federal courts over Section 704(b) of the Stolen Valor Act of 2005, and its constitutional infirmity was becoming more apparent, Representative Joe Heck (R-NV-3) introduced the Stolen Valor Act of 2011 (H.R. 1775). On October 18, 2011, Senator Scott Brown introduced the identical bill in the Senate (S. 1728). Heck's bill was referred to the House Committee on the Judiciary, and Brown's to the Senate Committee on the Judiciary.

While we respect and applaud their desire to rectify the constitutional problem of the Stolen Valor Act of 2005 with their new bill, regrettably, the proposed legislation is woefully inadequate to deal with Fake Warrior claims and, like the SVA of 2005, is on shaky ground constitutionally.

The core of the Heck-Brown bill is this: *"Whoever, with intent to obtain anything of value, knowingly makes a misrepresentation regarding his or her military service. . . ."*

The proposed law then limits the "misrepresentations" to individuals who "served in a combat zone, served in a special operations force, or was awarded the Congressional Medal of Honor."

There are many problems with their bill, among them that:

- Our Fake Warrior Act's requirement of *falsity*, has been replaced with mere *misrepresentation* — a milder word which has a different legal meaning.
- The word *value* in the proposed SVA of 2011 is too vague, compared to our Fake Warrior Act's use of *tangible or other actual value.*
- Since one could intentionally misrepresent to obtain something of value to which he *was* entitled, our Fake Warrior Act's requirement of *not entitled* is crucial.
- The Heck-Brown bill does not specify whether the misrepresentation must or can be written or oral. Our Fake Warrior Act does.
- The proposed SVA of 2011 acknowledges no reliance factor by the recipient of the misrepresentation, compared to our Fake Warrior Act of 2012 which requires that the claimant have a reasonable expectation that he will be believed and that reliance occurs.
- Under our Fake Warrior Act, the false statement must succeed, and the claimant actually receive something of *tangible or other actual value*. Not so under the Heck-Brown bill.
- In the Heck-Brown bill, the misrepresentation must be about *military service*, which is defined, among other ways, as "receipt of any decoration or medal authorized by Congress for the Armed Forces of the United States." Presumably, this includes

the Good Conduct Medal, a trivial award in the company of those our Fake Warrior Act (and their bill) criminalizes: Medal of Honor, Distinguished Service Cross, Navy Cross, Air Force Cross, Silver Star, POW Medal or Purple Heart.

- For *misrepresentations* about the POW Medal, our Fake Warrior Act has a penalty enhancement. The Heck-Brown bill does not.

We stress these differences not to nit-pick either the laudable intention of the Heck-Brown bill but because, as the Congressman and Senator themselves realize, the Fake Warrior scandal must be dealt with through Congressional legislation that will successfully get the job done. For that to happen, a statute must be comprehensive and constitutional. Unfortunately, the Heck-Brown bill is neither. (Their bill should be either withdrawn or buried in committees.)

Soon after the Supreme Court decision in *United States* v. *Alvarez* similar curative bills were introduced in the Senate and House of Representatives. On July 11, 2012, with the ink hardly dry on the *Alvarez* decision, Senator Jim Webb introduced S. 3372, an amendment to 18 United States Code, adding a new Section 704(b):

> Whoever, with the [1] *intent* of securing a [2] *tangible benefit or personal gain*, [3] *knowingly*, [4] *falsely*, and [5] *materially* represents himself or herself through any written or oral [6] communication (including a resume) to have [7] served in the Armed Forces of the United States or to have been [8] *awarded any decoration, medal, ribbon, or other device* authorized by Congress or pursuant to federal law for the Armed Forces of the United States, shall be [9] *fined* under this title, [10] imprisoned for not more than [11] *6 months*, or [12] *both*.

We have inserted in brackets and then italicized the necessary elements contained in Webb's bill. In essence, it punishes knowing, false and material statements that one has been in the military or has received an award—if there was an intent to obtain, per new Section 704 (b)(2), "(A) a benefit relating to a military service provided by the Federal Government or a State or Local Government; (B) employment or professional advancement; (C) financial remuneration; (D) an effect on the outcome of a criminal or civil court proceeding; and (E) an impact on one's personal credibility in a political campaign."

There is so much wrong with this bill that it's difficult to know where to begin.

At the top of the list is its absence of findings, which in the Fake Warrior Act of 2012 establish the context for the core concept on which the bill is predicated: *fraud.*

Webb's bill in Section 704(b)(2) contains a severely restricted kind of benefits/gains (A through E above) and is not nearly as broad in its coverage as the "actual value" benefits/gain provision of the Fake Warrior Act of 2012.

In applying to "*any decoration, medal, ribbon, or other device* authorized by Congress or pursuant to federal law for the Armed Forces of the United States," Webb's bill scoops up into its coverage even the most minor awards, like the Good Conduct Medal and the National Defence Service Medal — and, it would appear, awards to entire units, such as the Republic of Vietnam Civil Actions Unit Citation.

Even more lacking in Webb's bill are the requirements found in the Fake Warrior Act of 2012 that the thing of value obtained by the speaker be something to which he is not entitled, that he has reason to believe his words will be relied on, and that he actually obtain what he is seeking.

Last, and crucial, unlike the Fake Warrior Act of 2012, the Webb bill has no penalty enhancements recognizing that there is a incalculable difference between lying about a Good Conduct Medal and the Medal of Honor.

In place of these bills, and similar ones which doubtless will soon appear, the **FAKE WARRIOR ACT OF 2012** should promptly be introduced, enacted, and become law.

Then, and only then, will federal prosecutors have the weapon they need to identify, expose, and punish those who falsify their military service.

CONCLUSION

"Great is truth, and mighty above all things."[457]

The revelations in this book are unsettling. They paint a picture of dysfunction, immorality, deception, venality, callousness, and more. They necessitate comparisons between the concocted stories of the Fake Warriors and the actual experiences of those who lived the reality of being wounded, held captive, losing limbs — comparisons between imposture and honor.

Yet, there is a glimmer of hope in the revelations. Some Fake Warriors, to their credit, have confessed their lies, and for the correct reasons. If these men have the courage — not just to go public and admit their wrongdoing, but to explain *why* they did what they did — there is, perhaps, reason for optimism that others will either desist or even own up to their deplorable conduct.[458]

Harry Granger,[459] was a twenty-five year Army veteran who retired as a Lt. Colonel. Not a corporal, or even a captain. But a Lt. Colonel. He had been a Ranger/Aviator, ending his distinguished career after Operation Desert Storm in the early 1990s. Along the way, he had been awarded the Distinguished Flying Cross, Purple Heart, Bronze Star, and Legion of Merit — certainly, a record of which anyone could be proud.

But in October 2002, Granger sent a series of unsolicited emails to a Phony Buster:

> I have a self-confession which is heavy on my heart and I am ashamed of — I know it and it is "killing me inside." I have falsely claimed to have been a POW — a claim that I have been carrying around
> with a great amount of shame and [which] degrades my past accomplishments. I am so sorry for my actions and hope that POW
> veterans and families can forgive me.
>
> I have told my story to friends — why I just don't know — but maybe to fill a void. For so long we Viet Nam veterans were not looked upon as being anything other than "baby killers"[[460]] and so long we have fought that image — and in my sick mind I was building myself up to be something I wasn't. It is confusing, but I recently have come to realize, as my wife tells me, that I must accept who I am and be satisfied with that image — I have been a "good soldier," a good father, a good man and never intended to hurt anyone — just to boost my image — what I was really doing was breaking down my image.
>
> I can honestly tell you that I never told this lie to gain money; promotions; or job enhancements. My self admission is the first part of my healing and I will NEVER DO THIS AGAIN — I do respect the POW as a great soldier who [has] done his duty for God and Country — I would appreciate it if you would print this apology [on your website] for everyone concerned. Please pass this on . . . .[461]

Even Richard Davis[462] — whose imposture embraced at least three cities, two decades, the chartering of three chapters of the Military Order of the Purple Heart, falsification of his DD-214, membership in several veterans organizations, criminal conduct to obtain POW license plates, and more —

finally came to terms with the lie he had been living and chose to confess his wrongdoing. It is clear from the following account that Davis' conscience was finally catching up with him and that, quite apart from the harm he'd done to others, he had hurt himself and his loved ones even more.

> I realized in the past year or so that I had been living the life of a phony for so long that I was beginning to believe the lies I told. I became very paranoid. I was constantly in fear of being found out. I began drinking again after 2 years of sobriety, I was abusing prescription drugs. I became a loner.
>
> One day about 3 weeks ago I looked up "phony pow" on my computer. That was the first time I had known that I had been found out! I had first been reported in Ky. and the second time was Dec. of 2001. I felt sick, almost suicidal. My god. What would my family and friends say or think if they found out??? * * * I would have paid for the POW tag's if there had been a charge. I used the military b.s. to be someone that I wanted to be.
>
> Since coming clean with family and some of my friends I wake up in the morning happy. The dark cloud has been lifted. I was so excited about having real tags on my car that the day I turned in the POW tags I put the real tags on at the DMV. I didn't even wait to get home. Soooo." How long did it last[?]" from [19]81 until Jan. of 2001. 20 loooong years. Hard for even me to believe!! Perhaps I have given you more than you asked for. There is a lot of the story left out. Not of my hero charade but of the many things before and during. Rather moot of course but would I have done it if I knew that it would have caused the pain to myself as well as to many others? Yes. I was a pretty sick cookie. I attempted suicide 3 times in those 20 years. I was in and out of alcohol and drug treatment centers. I made and lost many friends due to my actions. I can now say I am traveling down my own road of recovery. I have a very supportive wife and 2 wonderful sons. To say I am "sorry" for what I had done sounds so hollow. *I didn't make bad mistakes. I made very bad decisions.* I DECIDED to fabricate

> my military past or lack thereof.[463]

Davis's identification about how he made, not "bad mistakes," but "bad decisions," is very insightful — and very true. To his credit, he does not fall back on some variation of "The Devil made me do it." On the contrary, implicitly acknowledging the fact that he — like all Fake Warriors — has free will, he takes full responsibility for his actions. This attitude, in our judgment, goes a long way towards earning him the forgiveness he so desperately seeks.

It is also gratifying to observe how Davis has set about trying to set matters right:

> I want to thank you [POW Network] for your web site. If not for the site I would have continued my life of lies. I notified MOPH [Military Order of the Purple Heart] today and asked them to remove me from their membership list as I have never been awarded the PH [Purple Heart]. I will return the POW tags on my car . . . and get real tags. I have removed all stickers from my car that implied I was a Nam vet, a PH recipient or a POW. I have told my wife all. She suspected that I was not honest concerning my military records. I will talk with both of my sons this weekend. By the way, they both served proudly in the U.S.A.F. If asked by anyone that notices that I no longer have a POW tag, I will tell them "I never was a POW nor did I serve in Viet Nam." Again, I wish to thank you and the persons that reported my lies.[464]

Along with reformed Fake Warriors — men like Harry Granger and Richard Davis — who help strengthen our resolve to turn a spotlight on the Fake Warrior phenomenon to slow and hopefully end much of it, there are young people who give us pause. The following email to a Phony Buster was from someone who didn't even include his last name. He didn't have to. To us, Ron B. is a symbol of hope:

> Hi, my name is Ron and I am a college student in Colorado. I was just browsing the web checking out various Navy Seal sites when I

> came across the "phony veterans" web page. * * * All of my uncles served in Vietnam . . . . * * * Looking at this site about these phony veterans makes me very appalled . . . [at] the audacity to manifest these foolish tales of heroism and bravery. . . . * * * It is a total insult to me as an American and I haven't even served my country in the military. * * * I'm sure all of the men and women who have served this country, alive and dead, would be and are very proud of you all. * * * KEEP UP THE GREAT WORK. Ron B.[465]

This young college student is representative of millions of young Americans who never served in the military, but who share with our veterans and their families, a sense of patriotism and love of country.

In the nine years since publication of the first edition of *Fake Warriors: Identifying, Exposing, and Punishing Those Who Falsify Their Military Service*, and even in recent months while we have been preparing *Fake Warriors II*, we've often been asked *why* we've devoted so much of our time to this subject.

We touched on a brief explanation of our motive in the Introduction where we wrote that "the Fake Warrior phenomenon is a national disgrace which harms our nation and many of our citizens in cruel and insidious ways." That's true enough, but the obvious has to be emphasized: *Fake Warriors clothe themselves in unearned heroism.*

Warrior heroes fight, are wounded, endure captivity, and often die — while Fake Warriors indulge their fantasies to satisfy unhealthy psychological and material needs. For twenty-one months United States Army Sergeant First Class Isaac Comacho is shackled to a tree by the Viet Cong while being starved, worked nearly to death, and stuffed into a lightless hole for the slightest infraction — while a 'Colonel' Connolly struts around on a sunny Independence Day in Colorado, phony from his head to toe, basking in the adoration of credulous Americans.

The imposture of Fake Warriors is many things: unfair, dishonest, cruel, unpatriotic, fraudulent, deceitful, corrupt, lying, and more.

Worst of all, *Fake Warrior imposture is morally wrong.* That is why we wrote this book originally, and why we've now updated it for this second edition: to heighten public awareness of this moral wrong, and to provide a way for those who deplore Fake Warriors to identify, expose, and punish them.

That's the least we, who've never been called upon to act heroically, can do for those who have.

Fake Warriors must be identified, exposed, and punished......

...... In the name of all of us who served honorably.

Especially those who never returned.

(ENDNOTES)

1 **NOTES**

A series of three asterisks (* * *) indicates that for editorial reasons the authors have removed at least one sentence. Elipses (. . .) indicate that less than one sentence has been omitted.

2 Henceforth, *Stolen Valor* will be cited as "Burkett and Whitley." Emphasis supplied.

3 Our emphasis throughout.

4 A Paramount feature film based on *Eye for an Eye*, starring Sally Field and Kiefer Sutherland, was directed by John Schlesinger.

5 Former Marine Corps helicopter pilot. E-mail in possession of authors.

6 Captain McGrath was a prisoner of war in North Vietnam for nearly six years, and is recent past-president of NAM-POW, the fraternal organization of those held captive during the war.

7 See Chapter 6.

8 McGrath had already visited the academy's Athletic Director's office to confirm that Connolly actually was the coach of the judo club, and that he was seen often on the academy grounds in the uniform of a United States Air Force Colonel.

9 Through an examination of Jane Fonda's activities in Hanoi (which consisted of more than radio broadcasts), and an analysis of the American law of treason (including the five World War II broadcast cases), *"Aid and Comfort"* proved conclusively that there was sufficient evidence to indict and convict Fonda for treason. In addition, *"Aid and Comfort"* revealed why the Nixon Department of Justice failed to prosecute Hanoi Jane. *"Aid and Comfort"* contains transcripts of all of Fonda's radio broadcasts from Communist North Vietnam. For further information, see (www.henrymarkholzer.com).

10 Among the leaders of this group have been Mary and her late husband Chuck Schantag of P.O.W. Network, a 501(c) (3) tax-exempt educational organization (see www.pownetwork.org). P.O.W. Network has for many years been dedicated to the exposure of military impostors. Founded on Veterans Day in 1989, P.O.W. Network has spent 23 years archiving information about American POWs and MIAs in Southeast Asia. From that activity, the POW Network became the central non-governmental source for debunking claims of POW status and exposing other military phonies.

11 See (www.henrymarkholzer.com, www.henrymarkholzer.blogspot.com and www.erikaholzer.com).

12 For example, in mid-2002, a respected friend of the authors — a former Vietnam Special Forces officer and later FBI agent — sent them this e-mail: "One of my best friends for the past 35 years" has died. Attached to our friend's e-mail was an obituary extolling the deceased's military accomplishments and his heroism as a highly decorated SEAL in Vietnam. The deceased was quoted as having said in an earlier interview that "he was most proud of the time he and six other men liberated 26 prisoners of war from a camp on October 6, 1968."

Our alarm bells went off. We knew that no 26 American POWs had ever been liberated anywhere in either South or North Vietnam on that date, or at any other time. We were between the proverbial rock and a hard place. We respected our friend, who had vouched for the deceased. Yet we knew the POW-liberation story could not be true. Accordingly, we began to question the deceased's veracity and our friend's judgment.

Inquiries were made, and the truth came out. Understandably, anyone reading the obituary would have thought that the SEALs had liberated *American* prisoners of war, which never happened. But the story, to our great relief, turned out to be true after all.

The POWs in question had been *South Vietnamese*.

The point we're making with this anecdote is that because we and the Phony Busters whom we consulted about the deceased SEAL had become so suspicious of heroic claims, when we heard (and still hear) heroism stories that sound the least bit dubious, our first reaction, unfortunately, is skepticism. It is impossible to know how many legitimate heroes have suffered, wrongly, from reactions such as our initial one.

13 The phenomenon of Fake Warriors has existed throughout history and in all cultures. However, in this book we are concerned only with the United States. Temporally, we have zeroed in on Fake Warriors only from the Vietnam War era to today because, given the aging of World War II veterans and even those from the Korean War, the problem that exists today is almost entirely attributable to men — and a few women! — dating from the Vietnam period to the present.

This is not to say that other conflicts have not produced their share of Fake Warriors. For example, in 2000, three Associated Press reporters were awarded a Pulitzer Prize for exposing in 1999 a supposed massacre of South Korean civilian refugees early in the Korean War, at a place called No Gun Ri. A principal source for the story was one Edward Daily. It turned out, however, that contrary to his claims Daily had not been an officer, had not been a POW, and had not been awarded our nation's second-highest medal for valor. Indeed, *he had not even been at No Gun Ri when the incident was supposed to have occurred.* Worse even than having been a Fake Warrior responsible for making grievously damaging allegations against the United States Army, Daily had obtained undeserved medical care and other benefits from the Veterans Administration for some *fifteen years*. When he pleaded guilty to federal charges of defrauding the government of over $400,000, Daily admitted that he had not participated at a massacre at No Gun Ri. (See Michael Taylor ,"A War of Words on a Prize-Winning Story/No Gun Ri authors cross pens on First Amendment battlefield," *San Francisco Chronicle,* April 7, 2002.)

As we shall see later in this book, the Afghanistan campaign, too, has produced (and will continue to produce) its share of Fake Warriors. For example, a bomb-loader on the USS Kitty Hawk falsely claimed he had been a SEAL. Home on leave, he claimed to have been wounded and wore a military jacket with a SEAL patch. A story in his local newspaper set off alarms in the SEAL community and the impostor was exposed — much to the embarrassment of his family which had considered him a hero, the Navy whose laws he had broken, and his local newspaper which had swallowed the young man's tale whole without checking. (See Don Bosley, "Navy discredits sailor's story of being a SEAL in Afghanistan," *Sacramento Bee,* February 7, 2002.)

Not surprisingly, the Iraq campaign has also produced (and will continue to produce) its share of Fake Warriors — even before any hostilities began: "I have new orders, back to Qatar. * * * I'm in Norfolk VA. I leave Jan. 3rd. The war is to start Jan. 26th. I'm SOQ, commander, of the Colo. Rangers mag-11, Special [F]orces, USMC. We're assigned to the KURDS, in the north, close air support, and troop cover. A lot of lives depend on me, and my leadership, and combat experience." This letter was from a fake Marine Corps major to his girlfriend. E-mail in possession of authors.

At about the same time the "Major" was off to Iraq, an international Fake Warrior scandal hit the newspapers. A British subject who had served with the United States Army in Vietnam published his memoir — for which he had received hundreds of thousands of dollars and substantial media coverage in the United States and Great Britain — claiming he been a highly decorated POW who escaped from captivity. The details of his story tracked almost exactly certain episodes of the Hollywood movie *The Deer Hunter*, and the Fake Warrior was soon exposed on, among other places, MSNBC.

14 Preeminent among the books that have treated the subject of military impostors — albeit on a larger scale — is B. G. Burkett and Glenna Whitley's *Stolen Valor, How the Vietnam Generation was Robbed of its Heroes and its History*, from which we have drawn many of the examples of Fake Warrior conduct contained in Chapter 2. A monument to prodigious research and righteous anger, Burkett and Whitley's book is a veritable encyclopedic catalogue of the wrongs suffered by Vietnam veterans, and *Stolen Valor* is must reading for anyone seeking information and insights on that subject.

15 We will use the word *imposture* frequently throughout this book. *Webster's New World Dictionary of the American Language* defines the term as "the act or practice of an impostor."

16 Because some of the seven Appendices are lengthy —Appendix D alone contains hundreds of names — we have provided links to (www.fakewarriors.org) where all of them are located. That site is a project of P.O.W. Network, the leading force in the United States addressing the Fake Warrior phenomenon.

17 James Thurber, *The Secret Life of Walter Mitty.*

18 *Webster's New World Dictionary of the American Language*. Synonyms for impostor are common: hoaxer, cheat, thief, confidence man (or woman). However, in this book we have used the term "impostor" to embrace those who may be any or all of these things, but who also engage in an ongoing masquerade.

19 While not all liars are impostors (because they may not pretend to be someone or something that they are not), all impostors are liars (because

the very concept of impostor implies a lie).

20 Charles V. Ford, *Lies! Lies! Lies!*, 101.

21 See generally Gerald Sparrow, *The Great Imposters*; Charles V. Ford, *Lies! Lies! Lies!: The Psychology of Deceit*; George Sullivan, *Great Imposters*; Egon Larsen, *The Deceivers: The Lives of the Great Imposters*; J.A. Barnes, *A Pack of Lies: Towards a Sociology of Lying;* Diane M. Komp, *Anatomy of a Lie*; David Nyberg, *The Varnished Truth;* Burkett and Whitley, *Stolen Valor*.

22 Interview by authors.

In Chapter 4 we related the story of a Vietnam veteran with a phony SEAL brother-in-law who passed the buck to P.O.W. Network to *do something* about "the farce." It turned out that the vet later corresponded with another Phony Buster, continuing his tirade about the military marker on his brother-in-law's grave. During the course of his rambling, he made the following revealing statement about his *own* motivation:

> When my brother-in-law was given a fund-raiser spaghetti dinner last year, a female reporter . . . did a nice piece on him. She took it as fact that he had served in Vietnam as a Navy SEAL. Once he saw it in print he bought tons of papers and gave them to his friends and family members. It was sort of a confirmation that he had pulled off the hoax . . . . My wife knew my feelings about her older brother's lie so she put me in the far corner of the room during the fund-raiser dinner. I was talking with some friends about why I was sitting where I was when a guy with long hair and lots of tattoos took the microphone and declared, "I never knew when I got drafted that I would become a Navy SEAL!" Since the Navy didn't draft anybody during the Vietnam conflict [and since no one has ever been drafted into the SEALs], chances are that he was one of the wannabes too. (*I said as much to my friends at my table*). It is my belief that once we are aware of the attempted "stolen valor" we are *somewhat* responsible to help correct the situation . . . . Our emphasis. E-mail in possession of authors.

The enabler, apart from lacking the courage of his convictions, reveals a seeming need to see *himself* as a Phony Buster — to, in effect, ride on the backs of their achievements without really sticking his neck out. He sanctions the very hoax he purports to abhor by attending the fund-raiser dinner for the phony SEAL, and all he does is grumble to his tablemates while another probable phony takes the microphone.

What this suggests to us is that the enabler derives some pseudo self-esteem from having a Fake Warrior in his own family. It allows him to feel superior, and to see *his* identity as a would-be Phony Buster, if only with his friends.

23 See Chapter 4.

24 Our emphasis.

25 Email in possession of authors.

26 Email in possession of authors.

27 McFarland & Co., Jefferson, N.C. Available in print and eBook editions at (www.amazon.com).

28 171 F.2d at 942. Our emphasis.

29 171 F. 2d at 943.

30 171 F.2d at 94. Our emphasis.

31 171 F.2d at 944. Our emphasis. Material quoted from *"Aid and Comfort": Jane Fonda in North Vietnam* is from pages 118 to 120, inclusive.

32 Geoffrey Chaucer, *The Canterbury Tales.*

33 We will not address in this book the sub-phenomenon of impostors who, in order to obtain veterans' benefits to which they are not entitled,

falsely claim they suffer from Post Traumatic Stress Disorder or other service-connected disabilities. That subject is covered thoroughly in Burkett and Whitley's *Stolen Valor*.

34 *Exotic* may be an understatement. At a national cemetery dedication of a Veterans Memorial, a known Fake Warrior participated while wearing "a non-standard uniform." Claiming to be a Navy Commodore who had served in four wars, he spoke of having been a POW three times, of having shot down "five Japanese aircraft in one day," of being "interred [*sic*] in Japan" and having escaped "aided by two Japanese frogwomen who were his former neighbors in Hawaii," after which he "swam out 2.5 miles and was picked up by the USS Thunderchief, a submarine he trained on in Groton, CT." He also claimed to have been a Navy Seal who "got a special exemption from two Admirals to join the Navy at age 16, his wife (?) was by his side holding the POW/MIA flag" and he "wore the Silver Star, Bronze Star, Purple Heart and others and on and on." E-mail in possession of authors. Regarding delusional, one impostor said that he had made a deal "with the devil to give up his first born to the Prince of Darkness in return for safe deliverance from his Communist captors." (*Baltimore Morning* Sun, March 31, 1997). Another claimed that he "had to kill 7 American soldiers because he could not get them out." E-mail in possession of authors.

The Fake Warrior phenomenon is not limited to the United States. On April 27, 2002, *The New York Times* reported that "a former Russian Army officer who said last month that he had fled the battlefield in Chechnya in 1999 to escape pressure from fascist cadets to execute civilians during Russia's assault, was not serving in the army at that time . . . ." The imposture apparently was in aid of Mr. Samorodov's application for political asylum in the United States — which was granted!

35 *The New York Times,* August 10, 2001.

36 Burkett and Whitley, *Stolen Valor,* 430. Burkett and Whitley substantiate this Fake Warrior example, as the others they cite, with copious supporting references.

37 Burkett and Whitley, *Stolen Valor,* 436-37.

38 This Fake Warrior was actually a convicted felon and a likely parole violator. E-mail in possession of authors.

39 *The New York Times,* August 10, 2001.

40 *The New York Times,* August 10, 2001.

41 This Fake Warrior was a convicted felon and parole violator. E-mail in possession of authors.

42 *The New York Times*, April 29, 2002.

43 *The New York Times,* August 10, 2001.

44 Burkett and Whitley, 360-61.

45 Burkett and Whitley, 179.

46 Burkett and Whitley, 516.

47 *Victoria Advocate*, March 3, 2000.

48 *The New York Times*, August 10, 2001.

49 E-mail in possession of authors.

50 E-mail in possession of authors.

51 E-mail in possession of authors.

52 E-mail in possession of authors.

53 E-mail in possession of authors.

54 *The New York Times*, August 10, 2001.

55 Burkett and Whitley, xii.

56 E-mail in possession of authors.

57 *Newsday New York*, April 8, 2001.

58 Burkett and Whitley, 178.

59 Burkett and Whitley, 199-200.

60 Burkett and Whitley, 180.

61 Burkett and Whitley, 181.

62 Burkett and Whitley, 194-95.

63 Burkett and Whitley, 370.

64 Burkett and Whitley, 513.

65 Burkett and Whitley, 136-37.

66 Burkett and Whitley, 191.

67 Burkett and Whitley, 204.

68 Burkett and Whitley, 503.

69 E-mail in possession of authors.

70 Burkett and Whitley, 573.

71 Burkett and Whitley, 391-92.

72 Burkett and Whitley, 476.

73 The organization was not NAM-POW, which has no chapters.

74 Burkett and Whitley, 503.

75 Burkett and Whitley, 189.

76 E-mail in possession of authors.

77 E-mail in possession of authors.

78 E-mail in possession of authors.

79 E-mail in possession of authors.

80 *Maui Time*, August 29, 2000.

81 Burkett and Whitley, 164.

82 E-mail in possession of authors.

83 *The Record*, Bergen County, New Jersey, February 9, 2001.

84 E-mail in possession of authors.

85 E-mail in possession of authors.

86 Burkett and Whitley, 381.

87 Burkett and Whitley, 288.

88 Burkett and Whitley, 478.

89 E-mail in possession of authors.

90 E-mail in possession of authors.

91 Burkett and Whitley, 399.

92 Burkett and Whitley, 404.

93 Burkett and Whitley, 385.

94 E-mail in possession of authors.

95 Burkett and Whitley, 487.

96 E-mail in possession of authors.

97 E-mail in possession of authors.

98 Burkett and Whitley, 360.

99 Burkett and Whitley, 362.

100 Burkett and Whitley, 196.

101 Burkett and Whitley, 203.

102 Charles V. Ford, *Lies! Lies! Lies!,* 100.

103 Burkett and Whitley, 182.

104 *The New York Times,* August 10, 2001, A1.

105 Burkett and Whitley, 173.

106 Burkett and Whitley, 182.

107 Burkett and Whitley, 184-85.

108 Burkett and Whitley, 425-26.

109 Burkett and Whitley, 184.

110 E-mail in possession of authors.

111 Burkett and Whitley, 382.

112 Burkett and Whitley, 190.

113 Burkett and Whitley, 186.

114 Burkett and Whitley, 187-88.

115 E-mail in possession of authors.

116 *Winona Daily News*, June 14, 2002. The reporter who wrote this story later retracted, admitting that, "I interviewed a man in a wheelchair (*like myself*) and trusted what he said was true." Our emphasis. Email in possession of authors.

117 As we shall see in the next chapter, four major categories of lies predominate in the tales of Fake Warriors. One category is the convenient fabrication that the impostor was "a member of an elite unit, engaged in covert operations" — activities so secret that the Fake Warrior cannot, even now, divulge them. The second category is that the impostor's records no longer exist — supposedly because they were destroyed in a fire at the St. Louis records center. Another is that the impostor had been captured, became a prisoner of war, and then escaped — often killing his captors along the way. The fourth is that the impostor had been awarded countless combat medals and unit citations —among them the Medal of Honor, Distinguished Service Cross, Navy Cross, Air Force Cross, POW Medal, Combat Infantry Badge, Combat Action Ribbon, Silver Star, Bronze Star with a Combat V, Purple Heart, Ranger Tab, Special Forces Tab, Combat Medic Badge, Air Force Pararescue Badge, Navy/Marine Parachute Badge, Navy SEAL Trident, Parachute Badge. Even, believe it or not, the occasional French

Croix de Guerre.

118 E-mail to Captain John Michael McGrath, in possession of authors.

119 Burkett and Whitley, 590, 591.

120 Burkett and Whitley, 481.

121 Burkett and Whitley, 442.

122 A pilot frequently claimed he was a NASA astronaut, a CIA agent, and a Medal of Honor winner. And he had the paper credentials to prove it. Using them, he infiltrated the Houston space agency's highest security areas. There, he obtained "access to a Navy flight simulater, [*sic*] at the console of Mission Control at the Marshall Space Flight Center and receive[d] non-public technical material about the space shuttle." The pilot was an impostor, and his papers were fraudulent. (*San Antonio Express-News*, June 3, 1998.) Another pilot — with only four years' experience, who had never been in the service — claimed he flew jet fighters. This was bad enough, but he used this phony story to stunt-fly at air shows, doing low level high speed passes in front of unsuspecting onlookers whose lives he puts in jeopardy. Email in possession of authors.

123 Burkett and Whitley, 377. See the Aviation Security Act of 2001, which gives preferences to military retirees for jobs in airport security. Secretary of Veterans Affairs Anthony J. Principi has been quoted as saying: "With the men and women of the armed forces now in harm's way in the war on terrorism, it's entirely appropriate that the legislation born of the September 11 attack acknowledges the value our veterans bring to the workforce. . . . We recognize the importance of security in our public transportation. Men and women who wore their nation's uniform can be depended upon to help provide that security. The skills and experience of those retired veterans will allow them to make a major contribution to our national security. This not only extends their service in an important effort, but allows the country to benefit from the investment already made in their training. . . ." (If they aren't Fake Warriors, that is). (*Vets News*, National

Veterans Organization, December 12, 2001.)

124 The stories of Fake Warriors ripping off the VA are well known in the Phony Buster community. One man, for example, claiming to have been a POW, received some $485,000 in VA care and benefits. Not bad for someone who had never served a single day in military service. Email in possession of authors.

> In May 2002 Christopher Newton of the Associated Press reported that "a crackdown on fraudulent veterans' benefits claims in the Philippines has halted nearly $20 million in illegal payouts and brought down a large-scale crime syndicate. . . ." Despite the "crackdown," the VA has no idea how much in benefits was stolen by the ring, which took advantage of the fact that some Filipinos are entitled to benefits from the VA in the United States. Press Release, Associated Press, May 18, 2002, in possession of authors.

125 Burkett and Whitley, 451.

126 Burkett and Whitley, 180.

127 P.O.W. Network received a letter from the wife of a supposed POW, seeking information about "how and where we can apply [for a] POW award for my husband. * * * My husband served in Da Nang as a . . . Seabee in '68-'69. He was captured in the jungle and held for about 6-8 hours after they killed his buddies on an ambush in the brush while on patrol. * * * He is a 100% service connected disabled vet from the VA with 40% from PTSD . . . . My husband was a POW and the injury he received and has lived with is honorable and should be recognized. My husband . . . becomes panicked and upset just to remember what happened. . . . He was badly beaten with a long pole all over his body for hours. They tied him with ropes like a dog and dragged him naked through the jungle for hours. They repeatedly raped him like an animal." E-mail in possession of authors.

Even when this poor deluded wife was disabused of her husband's story by Phony Buster Mike McGrath, she stubbornly refused to believe the truth. The following lengthy quotation captures in one e-mail various aspects of the Fake Warrior phenomenon: credulity, rationalization, enabling, dysfunction, anger, hostility, specialness, incoherence.

Dear Mister Mike McGrath, I will respond to your letter in the order it was written. My husband is not on any "official" list by the government because his experience was not reported the way it should have been. He was actually rescued not escaped.

The military, especially in Vietnam, failed to report many incidents that they thought were embarrassing or trying to keep within the "acceptable" standards for their combat soldiers. The fact he is not on the list only proves it was not reported. This does not mean it did not occur. The only idea we have to produce any type of proof of his sufferings may be any medical records of his active service in combat. Records of why he was in the MASH unit and why he was being treated and what injuries.

My husband ... received two purple hearts. One was for shrapnel he received in a firefight where he was also awarded the silver star. The second one was for the injuries he received for his capture and treatment by the Viet Cong. The second he had bruises and scrapes all over his body and the pads of his feet all cut and torn from walking in the jungle and being dragged by ropes. At the MASH unit they treated him in a matter of minutes by a medical corpsman not a doctor. A few weeks later they gave him the purple heart for these injuries. This he is sure of because he did not get any other wounds in combat. My understanding is they had to report why he was given the purple heart and some circumstances to explain how it was from combat not just exercises or training. Where are these records? What do they say of his purple heart and why? This we must locate first.

We have requested his active duty records for his tour several times in many places. The answer has been this. "We have no records that he served in the Navy or We have only medical records from time of his medical discharge date. "We have only one record and this is his DD214," which was not correct or accurate either. WHERE ARE THE RECORDS!!!!!!!! This could be a starting point for us to find the records and read them ourselves if none will take the time to do this for us.

The topic of escapes. There were only 30 escapes and a few rescues this we are aware of. This is because there were few "survivors" to live to tell what happened to them. The dead do not tell stories or the MIAs they became later when not found. How can they get statistics from the MIAs or the POWs who died? They know nothing of what they did endure or the circumstances of their captivity.

They found them tortured, mutilated, covered with dirt and blood and ripe with the humidity. If they were sexually mutilated this was obvious even on the dead but raped? They were raped first then mutilated. They found them naked and hung up. I do not think they were looking for "rape." This was probably not the cause of death. I do not think they examined them that well. And so few that survived to tell any tales. My husband says that the rapes were common among all the classes of people, local villagers or military captured, done mostly by the Viet Cong. The guys in his unit knew this would happen to them also if captured. They all said they would rather die than survive being raped by the enemy. It went unreported like many other issues in Vietnam that made the American combat soldier appear weak and helpless. My husband was not the only combat personnel in Vietnam to be sexually assaulted. Here in Sacramento at the local vet center where he goes to counseling on a regular basis, he is with a special unit of several professional who specialize in "sexual assault." When I called there they identified their unit as "specializing in sexual assault." Maybe I do not get it right? Do they mean sexual assault of military personnel by women after they came back to the states? Can you explain this to me any other way? Because there may not be any actual statistics on sexual assault of combat soldiers in Vietnam has nothing to do if it was actually happening or the frequency of the victims. My husband may be the only statistic that lives and breaths [*sic*]still alive. He suffered terrible humiliation and pain, terror and torment that he lives with now.

My husband is a POW and needs to be recognized by this nation, they owe him this much. E-mails in possession of authors.

The wife's barely coherent response after being told the truth about her husband's bizarre tale of capture, abuse, and rescue, is not uncommon. Obviously, whatever rational judgment she might otherwise possess had gone out the window, leaving her to defend her husband's pathetic imposture—a masquerade in which she was heavily invested.

128 "**Utah lawmaker duped into giving medals to undeserving vet.**"

01/19/2012 — By MATT CANHAM, Salt Lake Tribune
SALT LAKE CITY - A Utah congressman has turned over to federal prosecutors a binder full of evidence that he was duped into presenting medals to a Korean War veteran that the Pentagon says he didn't earn, which may lead to a criminal probe.
Rep. Jason Chaffetz, R-Utah, also plans to call a congressional hearing on "stolen valor" cases and the difficulty in verifying military honors since the Pentagon keeps no official list.
"Others have been burned by this. I have too, but I want to solve the problem," he said.
Chaffetz's actions come more than a month after The Salt Lake Tribune first reported on Myron Brown, an 86-year-old Provo, Utah, resident who presented fraudulent documents awarding him the Distinguished Service Cross, Silver Star and Purple Heart.
One of the letters says the citations, which include the Air Force's second- and third-highest-ranking honors, had been misfiled for the past 60 years.
Brown asked Chaffetz to publicly present him with the medals and the congressman did so at a town meeting in June.
Activists who track such medals first raised questions about the authenticity of the documents, noting typos, odd formatting and emblems that appeared to be lifted from other documents.

Then, in late November, The Tribune asked Air Force archivists at Maxwell Air Force Base in Alabama to check the citations Brown presented to Chaffetz against the official records from the 1950s. They didn't match.

Chaffetz said at that time that he wanted a letter from the Pentagon definitively stating that Brown's documents were fakes before he would denounce the medals and take action.

"Otherwise it would be unfair to tarnish a veteran's career," he said.

Brown on Wednesday said he did not want to comment on any potential investigation, but he did reiterate what he told The Tribune in November, that he deserves the medals and didn't falsify documents. Brown said he received them in the mail after he asked the Air Force to review his file.

"I didn't do them. That is all I know," he said. "I have not the slightest idea what these people are talking about."

But in a letter to Chaffetz sent Dec. 28, the Pentagon unequivocally states that the documents are not official, Brown never received the medals and, in fact, he has made attempts to claim these honors before.

The letter largely relied on the same citation discrepancy cited by The Tribune in November. But it also discloses that Brown previously claimed in 2000 and again in 2007 that he had received documentation saying the Air Force had discovered the same lost honors, none of which actually came from the Air Force. A Pentagon review of Brown's military service found medals he did earn, but they were not the Distinguished Service Cross, the Silver Star or a Purple Heart.

"The documentation provided by Mr. Brown does not appear to be official," the letter reads.

That was enough for Chaffetz to request a meeting with prosecutors at the U.S. Attorney's Office in Utah. Faking military honors is a misdemeanor crime under the 2006 Stolen Valor Act. One judicial circuit has found this law to be unconstitutional, but it remains in effect in the district that includes Utah.

"No matter his age, I believe there is enough evidence now that he is lying," Chaffetz said. "It is embarrassing and it is wrong. I want

> to make sure these people get prosecuted."
>
> The congressman said he plans to hold a congressional hearing that will question why the Pentagon doesn't have a simple way to verify military honors.
>
> "There is no one-stop shop for members of Congress or employers to confirm that someone has earned the medals they represent that they have," he said. "The record keeping at the Pentagon is atrocious."
>
> That hearing will involve Brown's case and other instances of falsified medals.

129 The "Captain" of whom the vet spoke was probably John Michael McGrath (USN Ret.).

130 Email in possession of authors.

131 As most lawyers know, this statement by the defense attorney — though well within the bounds of his ethical responsibility not to divulge anything about his client — was a clear signal to all parties at the proceeding, especially the judge, that his client had lied to the lawyer, the prosecution, and the court, and that the claim of his client's fraud had merit.

132 This case's facts and the quotations can be found in the *Milwaukee Journal Sentinel*, April 3, 10, 19, 2001, and May 1, 2001.

> In a similar case, the wheelman in a liquor store holdup-killing was convicted of first-degree murder and sentenced to life. After serving twenty-three years, in support of his request for a sentence commutation he told TV's *60 Minutes* that his crime had been sparked by a heroin addiction he'd acquired to kill the nightmares arising from his experiences in Vietnam. Veterans groups, including Vietnam Veterans Against the War, CBS newsman Mike Wallace, two Boston newspapers, the state Parole Board, and the governor's counsel, all weighed in on the murderer's side — though none of them, including Wallace, had bothered to check the facts. When the Massachusetts governor,

a former United States Attorney, approved the killer's release, the governor observed that the prisoner had gone "to serve his country in Vietnam. He returned a scarred man and he has served a lengthy prison sentence."

Touching. But a lie. Exposed by *Stolen Valor's* B.G. Burkett, the facts showed that the murderer, though a veteran, had never set foot in Vietnam. Eventually, the convict admitted the falsehood and apologized to the parole board and the then-acting governor, who observed: "It appears there was a massive fraud perpetrated on a lot of people." ("Lie May Land Killer Back In Jail," "Lie prompts arrest of freed murderer," Associated Press, August 26, 29,1998.) The convict, Joseph Yandle, was returned to prison. Email from B.G. Burkett in possession of authors.

In yet another case, a man was charged with aggravated assault for fondling his girlfriend's 8-year-old daughter. To show his good character, and because it was his word against the child's, the defendant claimed to be a decorated Vietnam War hero with two Purple Hearts for wounds suffered, and two Bronze Stars for valor. The lie backfired by ruining his credibility when he was exposed by B.G.Burkett, co-author of *Stolen Valor*. The child molester was sentenced to twenty years in prison. Email in possession of authors.

One criminal bragged that he had received a lesser sentence for bank robbery because his lawyer told the jury he was unable to obtain a bank loan when he returned from Vietnam, although others (including Vietnamese) could. (We're skeptical of this story because it's not the jury who sentences, but the judge. If the braggart was telling the truth, however, he was admitting that the loan story caused the jury to convict him on a lesser charge which, in turn, resulted in a lesser sentence).

133 Often, after serving a certain number of years, the sitting judge must then run either in a contested political election, or in a non-partisan

retention election.

134 The impostor's degree was not from the law school he claimed to have attended, but from a woefully undistinguished institution. Indeed, the judge had failed the bar examination five times.

135 His Honor had no Master's degree, had never been in the Army—let alone in Vietnam—had never worked for the CIA, and he had never been employed by the prestigious law firm.

136 The judge's lawyer admitted — as an additional defense! — that the judge was a compulsive liar suffering from a curable mental disease called "pseudologia fantastica," a fancy term for lying.

137 This case's facts and the quotations can be found at "L.A. Judge Charged With Lying About His Past," *San Francisco Chronicle*, July 7, 2000; 'Pseudologia Fantastica' Won't Fly," *The Recorder*, May 18, 2001; "Commission Removes L.A. Judge," Associated Press, August 8, 2001.

138 Remember the shrapnel-dodging Marine judge advocate? The judge who had the temerity to lay claim to *two* Medals of Honor? The candidate for County Commissioner Court — an alleged SEAL — who had been engaged in "classified" operations? See the text accompanying notes 43, 44, 45 and 46 in Chapter 2.

139 Press release, "Georgia Man Sentenced for Impersonating Veteran," Inspector General, Department of Veterans Affairs, March 24, 1999, in possession of authors. In another case, a man pretending to be a SEAL was interviewed at the Vietnam Veterans Memorial Wall by *Good Morning America*. He pointed to the names of supposedly fallen comrades. In actuality, to support his false claim of having won the Navy Cross, he was using a real SEAL's Medal of Honor citation. *Pittsburgh Post-Gazette,* June 20, 1999.

> Identity theft by Fake Warriors can have even worse consequences. A retired general officer and former POW has for nearly three decades been plagued by an impostor with the same name, whose impersonation has cost his victims enormous sums of money.

Despite the intervention of Senator John McCain, the Federal Bureau of Investigation has done nothing to provide the authentic general any relief, nor has the FBI done anything to prosecute the impostor despite the harm he has done and the outrageousness of his tales.

Said the authentic general: " My friends and I were approached by this Fake on July 26, 2002 at the Hilton Hotel on singer Island, Riviera Beach, FL. He wore a bright red USMC baseball cap and said he was a retired USMC LTGen. The only reason he did [not] get his fourth star was because he pissed off Powell and Swatrtzkoff [sic] during the Gulf war. (Right). He stated he and others had Saadam Huissin [*sic*] in their midst and were ready to kill him but was told not to because the Arab Allies did not want it done and did not want the U.S. in possession of an oil country with the provisional government that would be set up. He showed us membership (president) to the St. Andrews Golf Club. He stated he was the former owner of the Hilton we were at. He stated he was a POW and the only "jewish" General in the USMC next to Haime [sic] Rickenbacker [*sic*] (USN).

He was running for the senate in Florida in the next election. He owns a G-3 jet. He has a 90' yacht in FT Lauderdale. His family owns the Fairmont Hotel in San Fransisco. He owns the Philadelphia Eagles. He used to own a baseball team. He is 69 years old and does one handed push-ups daily. He did not know Lt. Alvarez the Navy POW (that bothered me). He stated his two sons are in Calif and are associated with the film industry. States he is currently not married. His daughter was 9/11 victim." Email in possession of authors.

140 This case's facts and the quotations can be found at "... VFW official steps down from post," "... post reports unauthorized credit purchases," *The Sun News*, January, 19, 2002. The January 19th article reported also that the post commander "said there is also an outstanding [bank] loan ... taken without permission of post members for $30,000 that cannot be repaid. A five-year lease on a building formerly occupied by the VFW is also in default. He said post members have voted not to repay the lease or the loan, since it was taken out without their permission."

141 Our emphasis.

142 E-mails in possession of authors.

143 Both quotations from e-mail in possession of authors.

144 "He'd go to veterans' clubs. . . . I met him at our local Vets club. He

claimed to be an ex-POW. . . . He claimed to be retired from the Navy after 32 years. He showed a picture and a letter that said he was a prisoner of war for three years, four months and 11 days. The letter said he won a purple heart and silver stars. . . ." Far from being a former POW, Bobby Joe, whose pickup truck was adorned with VFW stickers, was a con man with at least eight aliases who specialized in bigamy and larceny, leaving a trail of swindled wives in perhaps as many as ten states. "When I tried to check him out and couldn't," said one of his ex-wives, "he said it was because he'd been in special forces." How did Bobby Joe get away with his scams? "They admired him," explained a detective who pursued the bigamist/thief. *Detroit News*, Metro Section, March 3, 2000; APBnews.com, March 6, 2000.

Another classic case of a bigamist Fake Warrior, this one masquerading as a retired four-star general, can be found in a series of three articles by Laura Ayo in the Knoxville, Tennessee, *News-Sentinel*, October 21, 22, 23, 2001. "My so called husband was supposedly dying of leukemia. He claimed to be a POW * * * He ended up being a con man with 12-24 different names. * * * He has been in prison for bigamy and fraud. * * * He cons women and others out of money. He has ruined me financially and reputation wise. He even conned the Shriners and the Masonic order." E-mail in possession of authors. A Fake Warrior posing as a former SEAL and Medal of Honor winner forced a new widow into bankruptcy. E-mail in possession of authors.

Women, of course, are not the only financial victims of Fake Warriors. A man claiming he had rescued American prisoners of war during covert missions in Vietnam was convicted of bilking investors in at least four states out of hundreds of thousands of dollars; he even lied when seeking mercy from the judge. "Letters from victims reveal betrayal by con man," *Pittsburgh Tribune-Review*, March 22, 1998; "Man convicted of fraud lists accomplishments to judge at sentencing," *Pittsburgh Tribune-Review*, March 29, 1998.

145 145 It is worth noting that while instances of female Fake Warriors are very few, they do exist. For example, the president of a group of military women who served in Vietnam — not nurses — made the following inquiry of a Phony Buster: "I've been contacted by two women (one former marine and the other WAC [Women's Army Corps]) who claim to have been POWs. I've talked with several of the top WAC brass . . . and although we know how much the government were hiding things back then, we agree that [it] is quite unlikely that the US military had women POWs. One of these women I've talked to quite extensively, and have found holes in her story. Though I've asked to see her DD-214, I've yet to receive it." Email in possession of

authors.

Here's another example, from a letter to a Phony Buster. "I once worked for a woman . . . [who] claimed that she was a POW and had been tortured for several months before escaping. She ran until she couldn't run anymore, then she walked until she couldn't walk anymore. She also told us of how she shot one of the men holding her captive. She said she shot him in the face with a .45. * * * Most of the people that I worked with thought she was full of it, as did I. * * * She is a disgrace to all veterans, service men and women as well as the armed forces as a whole." Both e-mails in possession of authors. See also *Stolen Valor*, 475-81 for several other stories of female Fake Warriors from the Vietnam era. The post-Vietnam War Era has seen some female Fake Warriors, most of whom were imposters for money or other material gain.

For the record, however, there were no female American military prisoners of war in Vietnam. Not one.

146 There were also suspicions of theft at the previous school.

147 E-mail in possession of authors. Two related dangers arise when Fake Warriors come in contact with youngsters. An apparently highly decorated soldier, sailor, marine or airman will appear at a school, church, or similar place, and regale his audience with typical impostor stories: heroism, decorations, and the like. If the impressionable kids buy the tall tales, they receive a largely distorted view of military service. If they don't, or later learn that they've been lied to, their disillusionment necessarily takes a psychological toll.

148 E-mail in possession of authors.

149 A husband told his wife incredible stories: he had been a sniper, he was captured in Hanoi but escaped within 7-10 days, several of his fellow escapees were killed or captured, only a few men survived, three of whom went crazy. "Bruce used to have flashbacks — terrible flashbacks — of when he was captured. I would stay by his side for hours trying to talk him back,

keep him safe. . . . I awoke one time with his hands around my throat. During the last 10-15 years of our marriage, he used to tell me he knew 101 ways to kill a person. * * * We were married for 29 ½ years. This shouldn't matter at this point, but there are some things that need closure. My grown children ask if he really was in Vietnam . . . . It has been my rule of thumb not to speak badly about their father . . . . But in the same turn, I don't want to perpetuate a lie."

A Phony Buster answered: "Bruce needs to tell his children the truth. Sadly, we have seen this situation at its worst — the veteran's death! The military honors denied for the funeral. The FBI knocking [at the door] after the funeral, removing and confiscating POW license plates and Medal of Honor plates. Claimed in life, found not true in death. Not only must his family face the loss of him, but must also deal with the humiliation of finding out he lived a lie and they are paying the price." E-mail in possession of authors.

150 AUTHENTISEAL ceased operations about seven years ago.

151 E-mail in possession of authors. The man's identity has been omitted.

152 The deceased's identity has been changed to spare his survivors any further embarrassment.

153 E-mail in possession of authors. Our emphasis.

154 E-mail in possession of authors.

Here's another example — a letter received by P.O.W. network:

To Whom It May Concern: We read with interest, an obituary that appeared in the Burlington, Iowa Hawkeye Paper online on April 12, 2002 regarding a Gene Autry Leazer. He was from our hometown area. The obituary, enclosed, listed this man as a Medal of Honor Recipient and a POW/MIA. We went to your website, and as we suspected, he was not listed. In a small town, you KNOW who was a POW and you would KNOW who was awarded the Medal of Honor. While he very well may have served in the Air Force, we don't know for certain, we are quite certain, after checking your website, that he is a phony in his other claims. Even though he is no longer living, we feel this record should be set straight. Do the VFW and American Legion not check into the validity of a member's claims?

Following is the obit as it appeared in the Burlington paper, website:

Gene Leazer

> Gene Autry Leazer, 64, of Franklin, died Tuesday, April 9, 2002, at VA Medical Center in Iowa City.
>
> * * * Mr. Leazer was a U.S. Air Force veteran, serving from 1956 to 1974, with the rank of captain. He received the Medal of Honor and was a Vietnam POW MIA. He was a member of Salem Congregational Church, the American Legion, Veterans of Foreign Wars and Am Vets. * * * Burial will be in Oakland Cemetery in Fort Madison, with military rites. A memorial has been established.

The Phony Busters expressed their thanks to P.O.W. Network for "providing the records and services to check the validity of these dishonest people." E-mail in possession of authors.

155 E-mail in possession of authors.

156 E-mail in possession of authors. The deceased was, of course, a phony. Whether or not he ever served in the military is irrelevant. What matters is that he was not a "Medal of Honor recipient." What matters is that he had never been a POW — let alone "a POW MIA," whatever that is supposed to mean. What matters is that either the obituary writer was duped, or was a willing accomplice in the deceased's imposture. What matters is that his surviving wife, two sons, brother, three grandchildren, two stepsons, two stepdaughters, ten step-grandchildren, thirteen great great grandchildren, four step great great grandchildren, and assorted nieces and nephews, probably believe that the deceased was a hero when,

at best, he was a pathetic impostor and, at worst, a conniving Fake Warrior.

157 E-mail in possession of authors. In another case, an Iowa obituary had reported that the deceased was "a U.S. Air Force veteran, serving from 1956 to 1974, with the rank of captain. He received the Medal of Honor and was a Vietnam POW MIA.[!]" This was more than a neighbor could swallow, so she wrote to a Phony Buster: "Even though he is no longer living, we feel this record should be set straight." It was. Email in possession of authors. See (www.thehawkeye.com), April 12, 2002, Burlington, Iowa.

158 The "agonizing experiences," in addition to being a prisoner of war, were more-or-less the usual: constant torture, deprivation of food and water, incarceration in bamboo cages, being forced to play Russian Roulette, killing captors in order to escape. "My dear friend . . . [and fellow escapee was] shot in the back and killed about 5 feet behind me. I had all of about 5 seconds to pick up his head and say . . . 'I love you, pal, but I've got to go.'" If this impostor's "ordeal" sounds familiar, see such movies as *The Deer Hunter* and *Rambo I*.

159 Emphasis added. For this quotation and the two that precede it, and for other details of this story, see "Still a Captive of Vietnam," *Newsday New York*, April 8, 2001 and untitled, *Newsday New York*, April 11, 2001.

160 This is not the only example of reporters having to eat crow because they allowed themselves to be taken in by Fake Warriors. A story entitled "Mistreated Boy, Medal of Honor Man" was about an alleged highly decorated Vietnam veteran who told tales about parachuting into Cambodia to save an American general, and how the "hero" then carried the general on a stretcher for nine miles. The newspaper's editor later found himself in the unenviable position of having to acknowledge a grievous error. In a letter to a Phony Buster the journalist wrote: "Thank you for your letter and for your service to our great nation. We too have confirmed and retracted the story about the gentleman in question. We are in the process of considering legal action." *Searcy Daily Citizen*, June 18, 2000.

Here's a tall tale that a credulous reporter for the *Maui Time* swallowed whole.

A true humanitarian is a person who can suffer from pain and injustice, then filter his experience to help others. The actions taken by Glenn Mabson, President of The Epileptic Foundation of Maui, prove that he is one. During the Vietnam War, American men had the choice of joining the service or attending college. Mabson decided to get his education. So while the war raged on, Mabson graduated and was hired by CBS as a Production Sound Engineer. Fighting overseas was the major focus of the news, and before long, Mabson was offered an opportunity to fly into the heat of the battle to tape live footage for CBS. After he was promised $4,000 for two week's worth of work, he went.

Once the news team hit the ground, pure hell broke loose. Mabson was walking in front of the camera man, when a mortar shell exploded behind them and tore the camera man's body in half. Both of them were blown into a hole, where Mabson could only wait and listen while chaos continued on the outside. He remembers, "For four days I laid in a hole with a dead man staring at me -— until the Viet Cong came and pulled me out." Mabson was taken to "The Duck Bill," an area of land shaped like its name, where prisoners were taken to be tortured or traded. During the year and a half that he was kept there, Mabson underwent severe physical trauma, which progressed from daily beatings to severe forms of torment that his captors created for him.

Since he was a civilian, rather than a soldier, the Viet Cong thought Mabson was a spy and punished him accordingly. They made him dig a hole that was as deep as he was tall, and line it with bamboo shoots. He was forced to stand in the hole while it was filled with dirt so that he was trapped up to his neck, with only his head above ground. He was then left in that position for days, on the side of a walkway. The Viet Cong soldiers would walk by and kick him in the face, knocking out all of his top teeth. If it were not for . . . [his] bare feet, the blows would have killed him.

> The prisoners were usually fed a bowl of rice and a handful of vegetables per day, but most of their nutrition came from the cockroaches. Mabson says, 'Those huge cockroaches that fly around here in Hawaii are the same as the ones we had to eat in Vietnam. Most people don't know that they are 100% protein. They taste horrible, but they keep you alive.' Mabson's overseas experience came to an end after he was burned so severely with a Hibachi that he went into a coma. With the grill, his captors burned a deep ring around his leg and then repeated the procedure every day until he had lost all consciousness. When he woke up, he had been traded and was being treated at a hospital in California." *Maui Times*, August 29, 2000. Email in possession of authors.

While another reporter had to retract her story about a Fake Warrior — an alleged covert operative incarcerated in China and Hanoi who ate a raw rat, and then escaped — the best her editor would do was to write a "We should have checked"/"Who really knows?" piece. ("Home, brew and Jesus helped Vietnam POW escape," "Salitpa man's name added to list of 'phony' Vietnam vets," "Taking someone's word is not always the best thing to do," "Vet's claims unsubstantiated . . . What can we say? We made a mistake and regret having made it." *The South Alabamian*, May 25, June 8, 2000)

See also *Stolen Valor*, 196, for another incident of media retraction of a Fake Warrior story.

A sub-category of false information finding its way into the media is that of the many books purportedly about Vietnam and the Americans who served there. The fact is that the amount of erroneous information, misinformation, disinformation, and plain self-serving lies in many of these books beggars the imagination. Sadly, most editors of such books were either indifferent to the truth, grossly negligent concerning verification, or naïve in the extreme. See Chapter 17 of *Stolen Valor.*

On the other hand, some reporters are scrupulous about their research and sourcing: "I'm a reporter with *The Arkansas Democrat-Gazette*. I was going to do a story on an annual veterans' gathering and know several area vets. They suggested that I speak with a man . . . whom they said was a POW for several months during a tour with the Special Forces. I found he's not on the military's list of POWs." Email in possession of authors.

161 "Taking someone's word is not always the best thing to do." *The South Alabamian*, June 8, 2000.

162 The writer's identity has been changed to protect her privacy.

163 Not his real name.

164 Our emphasis.

165 This case's facts and the quotations are in a series of e-mails in possession of authors. Our emphasis.

166 Not infrequently, parents, especially fathers, worry about men their daughters have become involved with. One dad wrote to a Phony Buster: "He is in the Marines and is trying to bullshit my daughter with all kinds of crap. He said that he was . . . captured for three months and also a unit was sent in to rescue him and a few others. This is just one more thing that I might be able to keep my daughter here at home where she belongs." Email in possession of authors. Another father wrote: " My daughter has met this guy on the internet that claims to be a POW of the Vietnam War. * * * We are under the conclusion that he is lying about this. Naturally we are very concerned about our daughter's safety here. * * * He claims to be retired from the Florida Highway
Patrol. . . ." Email in possession of authors. In each case, the men were impostors.

A more recent example of the price paid by the loved ones of Fake Warriors is the story of David Stump.

When he died in 2010, some of his personal papers reflected that the Illinois man had been awarded a Bronze Star and three Purple Hearts.

So that's what was chiseled into his federal cemetery granite headstone.

According to a December 28, 2011 article by Steve Mills, a Chicago Tribune newspaper reporter, an authentic "Vietnam veteran read Stump's obituary and grew suspicious. The obituary said Stump was a paratrooper and Ranger who had made some 50 jumps behind enemy lines, had been awarded three Purple Hearts for being wounded and even received a Bronze Star. (Apparently, there was no room on his tombstone for all that.) The veteran's suspicious were correct. Stump was a Fake Warrior.

His tombstone was removed and replaced.

There was more. Another one of the deceased's documents said that he had been only "one of three survivors of the 'Bien Hoe Massacre' and the first American to receive the Cross of Gallantry Medal."

Pathetic—and not only embarrassing for Stump's widow and other survivors, but more reason to wonder about anyone claiming heroic military conduct.

167 "Richard Davis." E-mail in possession of authors.

168 See Chapter 1.

169 See Chapter 2.

170 See Chapter 3.

171 E-mail in possession of authors.

172 His name has been changed to protect his privacy.

173 The roots of this lie apparently lay in Davis having been assigned to medic training during his short-lived Air Force enlistment some years earlier.

174 The technique Davis used to doctor his DD-214 will be described later in this chapter.

175 Davis purchased the Purple Heart and Bronze Star medals at a gun show in Northern Florida. In answer to the authors' query about why he'd added the medals to his doctored DD-214, Davis replied, "Looking back, if I

was going to be a nam vet I might as well be one with medals."

At least Davis, to his credit, never purchased or used military uniforms. "I never even considered a uniform." But had he, any flea market, thrift shop, or Army-Navy store — let alone countless mail-order catalogues — could easily have satisfied his needs.

176 Davis wanted the POW automobile license plates because they "would validate to others that I had been a former POW."

177 "P.J." refers to Para-Jumper. Davis had "promoted" himself from being "merely" a medic to a member of Air Rescue, an elite group trained not only in medical skills but also in rescue techniques. "I was no longer satisfied with being just a medic," he has told the authors.

178 Davis' membership in American Ex-POWs was eventually revoked though the efforts of two Phony Busters.

179 Davis's sons joined the Air Force, he told the authors, not because of their father's imposture, but rather because, for them, it was a logical step following their Boy Scout experiences and having been in Air Force ROTC in high school. Davis reports that he "never made a big deal about [his] military past" to his family.

180 Davis' story and the quotations are sourced by a series of e-mails between him and the authors.

181 See Appendices B, C and D.

182 In the fall of 1997, Phony Buster Mike McGrath wrote to Air Force officials and others: "I have in my hand a copy of a letter dated July 15, 1993 with a Department of the Air Force letterhead. It appears to be an official letter. . . . It purports that one [Richard Davis] 'Para-rescueman,' was a Prisoner of War and is entitled to all benefits thereof. There are numerous inconsistencies in the letter which do not ring true. Mr. [Davis] has joined or tried to join various POW organizations based on the strength of this letter.

I have conferred with . . . the Defense Prisoner of War/Missing Personnel Office and we concur that this is a fraudulent claim. . . . * * * Would you be so kind as to check your letter files to ascertain that this letter was or was not originated in your office?" E-mail in possession of authors.

Not surprisingly, Captain McGrath never received an answer because Davis had forged the letter that purportedly had been sent to him by the Air Force.

This letter is worth describing. It is on Department of the Air Force letterhead, Washington, DC, 20030-1000. Flanking that, on each side is an impressive-looking official seal. Then there appear various capital letters and numbers, an address to Randolph Air Force Base, and the name and service number of the impostor, together with what seems to be his Air Force Specialty Code, and the word "Para-rescueman." The text reads: "While serving on active duty SSgt. [Davis] was forcibly detained on 4-21-69 and held as a prisoner of war by the enemy of the U.S. Govt./Republic of N. Vietnam. SSgt. [Davis] was captured while on a joint rescue mission to recover a U.S. Navy pilot that had been downed in a classified area in S.E. Asia. He was later repatriated to the U.S. Govt. SSgt. [Davis] meets all qualifications to receive all benefits awarded by the U.S. Govt. to former military prisoners of war." The letter was supposedly signed by an Air Force Colonel with the title "Chief, Military Personnel Division" at Randolph Air Force Base. A copy was sent to Davis, the Department of Veterans Affairs, and others. Davis, of course, already had a copy, having written the letter himself.

183 Apparently, it is not difficult to obtain a charter for a chapter of the Military Order of the Purple Heart. In another case, at least one Fake Warrior, a former VFW post commander, obtained a MOPH charter for a post in Nevada. The organizer claimed, modestly, that he had served seven tours in Southeast Asia, was wounded three times, and then was taken prisoner. He was an impostor. See "Purple Heart veterans start LV chapter of national organization," *Las Vegas Sun*, December 19, 1997.

184 "When he showed up at the VFW he announced to all that he had been a Navy SEAL. He was very boisterous. I took an immediate dislike to him. I think it was the second time he came into the VFW. I was with a

few friends and we all agreed the guy was a fake. I called him on his SEAL claim and told him he was full of shit. If he had been a SEAL he wouldn't brag about being one. He attempted to intimidate me by physical threats. I asked him why he was so defensive. If he were a SEAL he would have proof. He told me to 'fuck off' and left, never to return." E-mail in possession of authors.

185 Often, along with the medal, the purchaser receives a blank citation form to be filled in with whatever "facts" he wishes. See Burkett and Whitley, 358.

186 For the going prices about 20 years ago, see Burkett and Whitley, 358.

187 H.L.I. Lordship Industries, the largest manufacturer of military medals for the government, was the only company allowed to manufacture the Medal of Honor. The Federal Bureau of Investigation eventually ascertained that Lordship was making additional Medals of Honor and selling them to a friend of the company's owner, who would then resell them on the black market, which, of course, is illegal. Eventually, Lordship was caught, admitted the sale of some *three-hundred* illicit Medals of Honor, pleaded guilty to a misdemeanor — and was allowed to get away with paying a miniscule fine. The only meaningful punishment that was imposed is that Lordship can no longer receive government contracts. See (www.fbi.gov/fbinbrief/tour/medalhonor/medal2.htm); "Firm Plans Guilty Plea in Illegal Medal of Honor Sales, *The New York Times* News Service, October 19, 1996; Burkett and Whitley, 358.

188 In New Mexico, for example, a DD-214 gets the veteran a special license plate and a tag saying either: Army, Navy, Marine Corps, Air Force, Coast Guard, DSC, NC, AFC, SS, BS, Combat Wounded, Bataan Survivor, Navajo Code Talker, Atomic Veteran, WW I, WW II, Korea, Vietnam, Granada, Panama, Desert Storm, Afghanistan and Iraq.

189 In some states, the same proof that suffices to obtain military plates also allows reduced real estate taxes, special parking privileges, and free

hunting and fishing licenses. See Burkett and Whitley, 352.

190 Forged DD-214s not only aid Fake Warriors in their imposture. These documents also facilitate financial and other types of fraud. Historically, veterans groups have encouraged their members to file their original DD-214s with their local county clerks; this way, there would always be an accessible record of their military service. But doing so can be disadvantageous, even dangerous: "I had a retired Master Chief come by my office this morning with a scary story. His identification was stolen . . . . He received a call from a lady at American Express because someone had established credit with them (in his name) and was trying to cash a $9,000 check in his name. . . . The lady flagged the check because apparently she had a different address on file for the Master Chief than showed on the check. * * * Last night, the Master Chief received a call from an investigator telling him that they finally tracked down the fellow who stole his identification. *The guy is a lawyer and had a laptop computer with several thousand military names, SSNs and other information.* Each military person was a separated or retiree and *their common link was that they had their DD-214s filed with a county clerk.*

The Master Chief was told that this lawyer had accessed the DD-214 information through the public court computer system. I called our Camden County courthouse this morning and asked about their procedures for DD-214s. The clerk there told me that although DD-214s were not put on their computers, they were public record. In fact, with the exception of adoption papers, anything filed through the courthouse was public record. A check with the county clerk in Brunswick revealed the same information. In fact, when asked directly if someone could obtain a certified copy of a DD-214, the answer was 'yes.' The clerk did say that they would verify the SSN (which of course you could look up in the public record first!)." Our emphasis. Email in possession of authors.

191 "White Out" and similar products seem to work just as well.

192 To create the forged Air Force letter, Davis took the letterhead from a document he had once received from the Air Force dealing with

an entirely different subject and "took a blank sheet of paper and pasted it under the letterhead, [typed what I wanted], and again photo copied." Email in possession of authors.

Had Davis not wanted to do the work himself, he could have utilized the services of individuals or even document mills that churn out forged DD-214s and other military documents. One magazine advertised: "Combat Veterans. You can receive monthly VA money and benefits for combat stress (PTSD) by submitting one letter. *Expert personal help.*" Our emphasis. Advertisement in possession of authors.

Another ad said: "Lost Documents Replaced. Military Medals. . . . *Special projects welcome.*" Our emphasis. Advertisement in possession of authors.

On the Internet auction site eBay, one can find virtually every military document imaginable.

193 The documents relating to this case are in possession of authors.

194 Email in possession of authors.

195 There are a host of *other* phony documents, illegally obtained, which Fake Warriors use, including active duty ID cards and military base automobile stickers.

196 Email in possession of authors.

197 Happily, there are exceptions. American Ex-POWs expelled Davis when the group learned he was an impostor. The helicopter pilots' organization works hard to remove Fake Warriors, as does Cyberseals and NAM-POW. The current Chapter Adjutant and past State Commander for the Military Order of the Purple Heart in one eastern state wrote to a Phony Buster that he had in his chapter "an individual who claims to have been a POW. In my gut I think he's a phony. * * * I would sure appreciate it if you can help me. If he's legitimate, I will apologize. On the other hand, if he's a 'wannabe' I will take great pleasure in exposing him." E-mail in possession of

authors.

As compared with the Veterans of Foreign Wars—whose membership criteria include having served overseas — the impostor problem does not arise nearly as often in the American Legion, whose membership is open to veterans who have not served outside the United States. If a non-overseas veteran desires to join an organization like the VFW that *does* require overseas service, he must necessarily resort to lying.

Many have. The organization American Ex-Prisoners of War is very careful about membership applications: "ONE OR MORE OF THE FOLLOWING ITEMS OF PRIMARY PROOF MUST BE SUBMITTED WITH THIS APPLICATION.

> 1. Copies of the communications from your branch of service or other government agency or employer to your next-of-kin informing them of your status as a prisoner of war or civilian internee or other such communications concerning your status.
>
> 2. A copy, or copies, of documentation in your military records (OTHER THAN FORM DD-214) confirming that you were a prisoner of war. Said copies may be procured from the Military Records Center in St. Louis, Missouri. For detailed instructions, the Army may be reached at (314) 538-4122, Navy and Marine Corps at (314) 538-4200 and the Air Force at (314) 538-4218.
>
> 3. Copies of your unit's Morning or Muster reports for the date/dates of your status change to missing in action or captured. These records for the U.S. Army, U.S. Army Air Force and U.S. Air Force are located at the St. Louis Center and may be obtained as indicated in #3 above. (None of these records were destroyed in the fire.) The records for the Navy and Marine Corps may be obtained by writing: Archives II Textual Reference Branch 8601 Adelphi Road College Park, MD 20740-6100
>
> 4. A copy of the first and other applicable pages of the USAAF Missing Air Crew Report (MACR) can be used to verify the fate of

flyers downed during WW II. A copy may be obtained by writing the Archives II address in #3 above. Requests must include a minimum of name and WW II serial number. The date and, if available, the aircraft tail number may help speed up the request. Enclosing a money order for $6.00 will avoid further correspondence and delay.

5. Copies of the War Claims Commission letter will be accepted as proof from civilian internees only.

6. Other items of record may be accepted as documentation by the organization, i.e. a copy of your German capture card; a copy of a Kriegsgefangenenpost letter or post card you sent from captivity; a copy of an International Committee of the Red Cross form listing you as a POW; or copies of newspaper articles from your capture/recovery time frame concerning your captivity. Do not send any documentation as proof of captivity if obtaining it required an item of basic proof listed in numbers 1 through 5, above. For example, the following do not constitute proof: VA patient data card; a letter or form from the VA concerning your inclusion in their POW program; a letter or form from the Defense Finance Service; the Foreign Claims Settlement Commission or the War Claims Commission regarding pay for unused leave or compensation for poor diet or treatment unless you are a civilian internee; an auto registration form granting a POW license plate; correspondence indicating the award of the POW medal; or a newspaper article or other type of report of a talk you gave on your experiences."

198 E-mail in possession of authors. When writing the first edition of this book, the authors were recently forwarded the following email: " I'm glad to find your web site, it's a good thing. I'm a VFW member here in Alabama and I've cancelled my membership because of the way that things are being done in Alabama. *** I have sent letters to the state and National Hqs to complain to no avail. The VFW posts here in South Alabama are all filled with phony membership and phony members, how can I get someone

to investigate the membership of these posts? The numbers are so inflated with deceased, eligible people and constitutes fraud and is a betrayal of the honorable personnel that served in the military, and no one seems to care. *It's all a numbers game for the VFW to maintain their political power and to receive Federal Funds.* Do you have any suggestions on what I should do? Your help will be greatly appreciated." Our emphasis. E-mail in possession of authors.

Another e-mail, concerning a well-known Fake Warrior, was received just as we finished writing the first edition: "My name is Jim . . . . . I am the club manager of VFW Post . . . . Sometime in the summer or early fall, a representative from a POW/MIA organization came into [the] post . . . and asked me if [name omitted] was a member . . . . I informed him that he was. The person then informed me that [he] was a lying bastard, that he had never been a POW, earned the Navy Cross, and never had a Purple Heart. He said [he] was a big phony and what was I going to do about it. To make a long story short, I took the appropriate actions and [the impostor] admitted he was a fraud and gave his life membership card to our judge advocate and said he would never step foot in [the Post] again. Well, on August 9, 2002, Mr. [Fake Warrior] walked into [the Post] again and stopped right by the post POW/MIA memorial display. What happened next made me so sick I thought I was going to vomit. [The Post] Sr. Vice Commander, Jr. Vice Commander, Post Chaplain, Past All American [Post] Commander, and all the rest of the VFW Post and Ladies Aux members present gave [the impostor] a hero's welcome. They hugged him, shook his hand, they even rang the ship's bell, which is supposed to be reserved for dignitaries. You would have thought it was VJ Day. I was so upset I had to leave right away. I promptly went to the Fleet Reserve and informed them of the disgrace that [the Post] just committed. Well, in conclusion Mr. [Fake Warrior] has no remorse for what he has done and is now a daily patron at [the Post]. I am going to ask you or anybody that will listen — what are we going to do about this damn phony? He is back in action and you know it is just a matter of time until he starts lying again."

This frustrated veteran was advised to tell his story to a local reporter.

199 They are now available as Appendices B, C and D to this book.

200 In fairness, some Post commanders do try to be conscientious. One — a Vietnam veteran — recently wrote to P.O.W. network inquiring about a proposed transferee into the commander's Post: "As Commander I have an obligation to confirm the eligibility of any person attempting to join our organization. Despite the fact that [the potential transferee] holds a membership card for [his former Post] I am reluctant to accept his transfer without proof that he really [is who he says he is] and actually did serve in Vietnam." E-mail in possession of authors.

201 Interview by authors with Phony Buster.

202 The quotations in this paragraph are from Burkett and Whitley, 203-04.

203 Most organizations do not — as they should — require the applicant to sign a Form 180 waiver (See Appendix A) so that his DD-214 can be obtained directly from the National Personnel Records Center in St. Louis.

204 The survey appeared on a CD provided to VFW members. Printout in possession of authors.

205 The existence of Fake Warriors on the membership rolls of the VFW, VVA, and other federally chartered veterans organizations, is a ticking time bomb. It's a requirement, not an option, that every member be at least a veteran. Yet some impostors have never even been in the military. Since this is an unquestionable violation of any such federally granted charters, the organization could be at substantial legal and financial risk.

206 Here's another unsettling possibility. National organizations like the VFW, the VVA, and the American Legion, are usually in the forefront of lobbying state and federal legislatures and administrative agencies for veterans' benefits, financial and otherwise. Quite apart from the hypocrisy of engaging in lobbying on behalf of members whom the VFW and the other

organizations *know* to be impostors, a more sinister motive may be at work. The more members on the post's roster, the more benefits the lobbyist is likely to receive.

And just as authentic veterans are hurt when — thanks to the machinations of a Fake Warrior — people cast suspicion on the valor of these legitimate vets, so, too, are the merely careless veterans' organizations tarred with the same brush as the post that may be engaged in lobbying for fraudulent purposes. For this reason alone, the VFW and VVA, are long overdue in cleaning house.

207 Burkett and Whitley, 203.

208 Our emphasis. E-mail in possession of authors.

209 See Chapter Six.

210 One Phony Buster called the VA Inspector General "worthless." E-mail in possession of authors.

211 *Webster's New World Dictionary of the American Language*, Second Edition. Emphasis in original.

212 Email in possession of authors. Occasionally, a relative is more honest. A "younger brother and a Viet era vet" wrote to P.O.W. Network about his sibling: I just found your web page [and his brother listed there as a phony] and words cannot explain the [disgust]. * * * On behalf of our family, I am very sorry" E-mail in possession of authors.

A not uncommon twist to the enabling phenomenon is "killing the messenger." For example, one enabler attacked P.O.W. Network website:

> What a crappy website. * * * I am writing in reference to the section on Steve . . . . He IS all of those things that he claims to be and is more than happy to show proof to those with the balls to come up and ask him. PLEASE remove the information on the website

> pertaining to him and his dedication to our country . . . and do some research before you start posting crap like that. As far as I knew, we in America are innocent until proven guilty. Where is the proof he is NOT what he claims to be? E-mail in possession of authors.

Putting aside that Steve wasn't being charged in a court of law (which is where the presumption of innocence applies), and putting aside that Steve had the burden of proving his claims—to the Silver Star, Purple Heart, Combat Infantryman Badge, and to having been a SEAL and Green Beret, among other things—P.O.W. Network took up the challenge. Their letter to Steve's defender is a classic response to a Fake Warrior's enabler:

> First, might suggest you go to the Moc Hoa veterans website and see if you can find Steve on the roster and just contact their webmaster. Then take a look at the photo on [our] website of Steve in Vietnam (the black and white one) and enlarge it. You can see the M.A.R.S. pocket patch on his jungle fatigues with 'Steve' embroided on it and on his sleeve is the 1st Signal Brigade patch, and of course no CIB or parachute badge. Then you can go to military.com website and look up Steve on the Find a Buddy icon. He comes up as an E-4, O5c, Teletype Operator. If that doesn't do it you can call Mike Karr, President of the 5th SFG association in Bothell, WA (he will give you the straight scoop).
>
> As far as the innocence until proven guilty remark goes, he WAS found guilty and that is why he was discharged from the Guard after the Inspector General's report. If all else fails, take a look at Steve's driver license. The birth date is 1951. That would put him in high school until 1969, a full 2 years after the claims to have been in Vietnam. If you do the math you would know Steve could not have gotten in country until 1970 at the earliest and in fact was there in 1971. * * * Nice try. E-mail in possession of authors.
> Predictably, nothing more was heard from Steve's enabler.

213 Our emphasis. E-mail in possession of authors.

214 Anonymous. E-mail in possession of authors.

215 With that serial number or social security number, it is possible to make a search (discussed below) for the claimant's military records.

216 The questions are gender-neutral, applying equally to males and females.

217 Depending on the circumstances, it may be possible, and sometimes even necessary, to create a record by asking these questions in writing. Prospective employers certainly should.

218 If you're dealing with an impostor, merely asking pointed questions, which shows that you know what you're doing, will often cause the impostor to cut and run— in which case, you won't have to evaluate his answers because there won't be any.

219 Contrary to what some Fake Warriors claim, *there is no time limit on how long one had to have been a captive in order to qualify for POW status.* Some Americans were held captive for only a few hours or days before escaping. Often, an impostor will claim he is not officially listed as a prisoner of war because he was not held at least 30 days. This is a red herring and a dead giveaway. The 30-day requirement relates to VA benefits and has never been a precondition to POW status or recognition.

220 50 App. United States Code, Section 2005(f)(1)(B). Interestingly, the sentence quoted in the text continues: ". . . except any such member who, at any time, voluntarily, knowingly, and without duress, gave aid to or collaborated with, or in any manner served, such hostile force." The significance of this exception to the statutory definition of Vietnam War POWs is that any American held captive by either the Viet Cong or the North Vietnamese who "in any manner served" those enemies legitimately can be denied the honorable designation of "prisoner of war."

Unfortunately, there were such men in both South and North Vietnam.

But except for one notable watered-down court-martial conviction in the Marine Corps for collaboration with the Viet Cong — the collaborator was Private Robert Garwood — no other American captive who returned from Vietnam has ever been charged with serving the enemy or has been denied the right to be called a "prisoner of war." Several should have been, however. Garwood is no longer listed as a "returnee," but rather as "AR": "AWOL/ Deserter/Collaborator – returned."

Over a decade ago, the Pentagon realized "that the status designation for a number of individuals did not actually fit their circumstances. * * * We established a category to handle people who were deserters or AWOL or collaborators, and who had returned. Since Garwood wasn't a POW, and was convicted by the USMC of collaboration, he fell within this category." E-mail from Larry Greer, Pentagon, in possession of authors.

The DPMO data base carries twenty-two military personnel in the "AA" category: "AWOL/Deserter." These men have never returned.

221 There were a total of 30 American military escapees from captivity during the Vietnam War, two from Laos and 28 from within South Vietnam. All 30 successfully returned to United States control. No American escaped from North Vietnam and successfully returned to United States control. See Appendices B, C, and D.

Included in the 30 American military "escapees" are three who, technically speaking, did not escape but who were rescued. Larry Aiken was rescued from his camp after the Viet Cong abandoned it. Shot by the Communists, he died fifteen days later in Bethesda Naval Hospital. Roger Anderson was rescued by a helicopter from a sampan taking him to Cambodia. William Taylor was rescued when Army Cobra gunships attacked his POW encampment.

During the Vietnam War, numerous attempts were made to rescue American prisoners. Between 1966 and 1970, some 91 rescue missions were launched against known POW installations, but Larry Aiken, an Army enlisted man, was the only prisoner actually liberated as the result of a deliberate rescue attempt.

222 At Appendix D — U.S. prisoners of war who returned alive from the Vietnam War —it is possible to ascertain which prisoners were released before all remaining POWs were repatriated in the early 1973 Operation Homecoming simply by referring to the date of release. Operation Homecoming began February 12th and ended April 1st when the last American who would be released was repatriated.

223 See Appendix D.

224 John M. McGrath. *Prisoner Of War: Six Years in Hanoi,* ix. Emphasis in original.

225 Essay, *Mac's Facts, No. 22*, December 29, 1999, by John M. McGrath (USN, Ret.). Our emphasis. Mr. Greer, responded to telephone, fax, email, and snail mail inquiries concerning American prisoners of war repatriated from Southeast Asia.

226 Essay, *Mac's Facts, No. 22*, December 29, 1999, by John M. McGrath (USN, Ret.). Our emphasis. As to PTSD, such diagnoses are no longer "rare" because of the conflicts in Afghanistan and Iraq. Recently, claims for that condition have skyrocketed, and many are fraudulent.

227 In the experience of those who have exposed countless Fake Warriors, not one impostor has ever proved the Department of Defense list wrong. Over the years, spelling errors, duplicate names, erroneous names, and the like, have been purged from the list and today it is unassailably accurate.

228 Our thanks to Mike McGrath for providing us with most of these questions, which he has used for years to identify and expose impostors.

More questions — these posed by a POW from the Korean War who asks would-be prisoners from that period: When were they captured, what was their unit, what camp were they in, when were they released, and who were some of the men in their squad in the camp? "If I get too many, 'I can't remember,' I am immediately suspicious." The Korea POW adds: "I try to get his service number and then I contact people I know at the Pentagon within the service he states he was a member of. Other good contacts are men in the local recruiting office."

As to the Vietnam era, he continues: "I am suspicious when I see an individual at the VFW or [American] Legion Post dressed in cammies [camouflage], looking like he just came in off a 30-day search and destroy mission. Most of the answers are, 'I can't discuss that; it's still classified,' or 'I was SOG [Studies and Observation Group, a clandestine unit] or SF' [Special Forces]. At this time I say 'yeah' and walk off." E-mail in possession of authors.

229 On occasion, a Fake Warrior pretending to be a former prisoner of war may have become so knowledgeable about his imposture — from books, movies, and other sources — that he's able to answer some, if not all, such questions with seeming assurance. But no matter how accurate his answers seem to be, they won't hold up when they're checked for accuracy.

230 Mr. Robinson's book is no longer being printed. However, copies can be purchased through his website, (www.moosecreekforge.com), until remaining supplies are exhausted.

231 By law, only males can be SEALs.

232 During the Vietnam Era, every man who successfully completed Basic Underwater Demolition/SEAL (BUD/S) Training was obligated to spend two years serving in Naval Special Warfare before he could "un-volunteer" and return to regular Navy duties. This contractual obligation was created to ensure the Navy would receive fair value for the time and money spent in training a man for duties in the UDT and SEAL Teams. Over the decades, the length of the contractual obligation has increased because of the increasingly complex and extensive technical training given to SEAL candidates. In 2012, that contractual obligation is 52 months. Anyone claiming — as some have — that he was "drafted" into becoming a SEAL, is a liar.

233 E-mail in possession of authors.

234 To complicate matters further, some men did not attend parachute training at Fort Benning, but were sent instead to jump school at Lakehurst Naval Air Station in New Jersey. On the West Coast some SEALs were sent to the Navy's Experimental Parachute Testing Facility for parachute training at times when courses were not available at Ft. Benning on a timely basis.

235 Until the later years of the Vietnam conflict there was a standing requirement for any BUD/S candidate to have served a minimum of one full year in the regular Navy fleet before being accepted for UDT/SEAL Training. This requirement was altered, removing the one-year minimum service, due to increased demands for SEALS to be sent to Vietnam.

236 For an excellent and thorough description of SEAL training, see the recently published non-fiction book by Eric Blehm entitled *Fearless.*

237 None of the following questions relate to SEALs as prisoners of war because no SEAL in Vietnam ever became a POW. Moreover, no entire SEAL unit of any size was ever wiped out in Vietnam, and no SEAL unit in Vietnam ever suffered such severe casualties so that only one member survived.

238 Phony Buster Larry Bailey reports: "I only ask class number, team, first commanding officer. I've never seen one [impostor] get past those three. A couple [of phonies]who had started training and knew a class number made me hiccup for a couple of seconds, but a quick check of the database put the lie to their claims." E-mail in possession of authors.

239 It has to be emphasized that absent a compelling reason, and as a matter of strict Navy policy, the Naval Special Warfare Command (NSWC) will not identify any serving SEAL. The reason should be obvious. The Command is greatly concerned about our enemies learning a SEAL's identity, thus posing a serious threat to his family. The serving SEAL and his effectiveness would be severely compromised.

Active duty SEALs, and SEAL reservists who are still serving, are specifically directed to maintain a very low public profile due to the requirements of operational and personal security and Personal Security. The Navy is very serious about this. A SEAL who violates this directive — for example, by posting information on an online social network, appearing in the media, or even sounding off in a saloon, will have his SEAL status revoked and quickly be removed from his SEAL Team.

In light of this swift and decisive Navy reaction, it's a safe bet that anyone openly bragging about being a SEAL is not an active duty or reservist SEAL. They know better than to court publicity or shoot their mouths off.

240 Steve Robinson, for example, takes the delicacy of his task very seriously. He reports that when responding to a potential Fake Warrior inquiry he provides the following qualification:

> The SEAL Database which I use for confirming SEAL credentials is HISTORICAL in nature, created by the Naval Special Warfare Archives [see the next Note] and derived from official military records. It is the database used by unofficial, fraternal and historical UDT/SEAL organizations for verifying successful graduates of the Naval Special Warfare (NSW) training course, and it contains only the names and very (VERY!) abbreviated information regarding successful graduates of NSW training.
>
> The NAVAL SPECIAL WARFARE COMMAND maintains an official master TRAINING database which not only includes the names and detailed information about every successful graduate, but also all of the names and data for all those who started the training program but did not successfully complete the course. While there is a complete overlap of graduates' names between the HISTORICAL database I use and the official master TRAINING database maintained by NSWC, the amount of data appearing in the official NSWC Database is far more detailed and comprehensive."

That said, it must be clearly understood, as Steve Robinson reminds us, that neither he nor any other SEAL verifiers "have access to the official NSWC master database. The NSWC database is very closely held, has very (VERY) limited authorized access, and is not available to anyone other than the officers and men designated for that tasking by the US Navy. The NSWC Chain of Command is very sensitive about this matter." As it should be.

241 See, for example, (http://www.navyfrogmen.com), the Naval Special Warfare Archives — *not the NSWC database* — a not-for-profit founded and run by former Navy SEAL, R.D. Russell and his wife Pam. "The Russells created the original 'BUD/S' or 'SEAL' database using military records they obtained by requesting them from the Navy. That database was finally completed and then presented to the Navy in 1999 (although the Russells retain ownership of their original document). The Navy immediately set about expanding that document by including all training records for every man who ever attended the course, including data related to some 4,000 WWII members, detailed information about each man's unit assignments, and much, much more. The Russells have worked with several individuals and with the POW NETWORK over the years in support of the efforts to answer inquiries about men making SEAL claims. . . . Every UDT/SEAL database in existence, including the one used by the Navy and all those used by non-governmental personnel, is either a copy or a subset of the original UDT/SEAL database created by the Russells.

The authors have been assured that the database listing all men who successfully trained and served as SEALs, or as members of precursor units (S&R, NCDU, UDT), from 1943 to the present day is accurate and complete (except for the occasional misspelling or legal name change). There are other sites on the Internet devoted to the subject of Fake Warriors, although they do not make that claim. Among them are:

http://www.specialoperations.com/Phonies/;
http://www.midcoast.com/~waterman/fakevets.html;
http://home.att.net/~Lzzzbolt/BEWARE.htm#Spotting;
http://www.marinescoutsniper.com/wannabes.html;
http://www.geocities.com/Pentagon/Camp/7287/prove_me_wrong.htm;

http://www.homeofheroes.com/a_homepage/community/imposters/;
http://www.freerepublic.com/forum/a381304e439db.htm;
http://www.nightscribe.com/Military/seals/seal_id_card.htm;
http://www.nightscribe.com/Military/seals/fake_seal_challenge_coin.htm;
http://www.geocities.com/recon_bubba/;
http://www.glanmore.org/wannabes.html.

Some of these sites refer and link to others, not listed above.

242 E-mail in possession of authors. Capitalizations are as they appear in the original. Our emphasis.

243 Capitalizations are as they appear in the original.

244 E-mail in possession of authors.

245 Steve Robinson notes that many imposters are tripped up by claiming that they were SEALs at a time and/or location before any SEAL Teams existed, or by claiming membership in a specific SEAL Team at a time when that specific SEAL Team didn't exist. E-mail in possession of authors.

Until 1983 there were only two SEAL Teams (ST-1 on the West Coast and ST-2 on the East Coast). Steve Robinson reports that he has "lost count of the number of times I've learned of imposters claiming to have served with "SEAL Team THREE" or "SEAL Team SIX" in Vietnam. Knowing when each Team came into existence, and where they were deployed is a primary means of isolating the liars from the truthful SEAL claimants." E-mail in possession of authors.

According to Robinson,

> [t]he tasking for the UDTs was maritime in nature, and their *primary* area of responsibility was described as ranging 'from the high water mark or shore, to the twenty-one fathom mark at sea.' The UDTs, however, were trained and capable of operating inland as needed. The SEAL Teams were created in January 1962 with

> men drawn from the ranks of the UDTs. The tasking for the SEAL Teams was exactly the opposite of the UDTs. The SEAL's *primary* area of responsibility began at the high water mark and moved inland, with a *secondary* area of responsibility in the maritime environment from the high water mark to seaward. By the early 1980s it became apparent that men within the Naval Special Warfare community were rotating through both UDTs and SEAL Teams, that training and supply were virtually identical, and that both units were performing identical tasking. The duality of command and supply lines was deemed unnecessary and overly burdensome, and in the first quarter of 1983 all of the existing UDTs were decommissioned, and subsequently re-commissioned as SEAL Teams. E-mail in possession of authors.

He continues:

> There are currently ten SEAL Teams. Odd numbered Teams are based on the West Coast and even numbered Teams are based on the East Coast. SEAL Teams ONE, THREE, FIVE, and SEVEN are based out of Coronado, California. SEAL Teams TWO, FOUR, EIGHT, and TEN are based out of Little Creek, Virginia. A special counter-terrorism SEAL Team designated as the NAVAL SPECIAL WARFARE DEVELOPMENT GROUP or "DevGru" (formerly SEAL Team SIX) is based on the East Coast in Dam Neck, Virginia. SEAL DELIVERY TEAM ONE, specializing in the use of small submersibles called SEAL Delivery Vehicles or "SDVs," is based in Hawaii. Each SEAL Team is designated for tasking in a specific region of the globe, with supplemental training and specialization keyed to their assigned region, but all SEAL Teams are capable of functioning in any environment and supporting other SEAL Teams as necessity dictates. E-mail in possession of authors.

246 Long Range Recognizance Patrol/Long Range Patrol.

247 Shelby L. Stanton, *Rangers at War, LRRPs in Vietnam*, 13. The authors' reliance on the writings of Mr. Stanton is limited to only the material

specifically referenced.

248 Michael Lee Lanning, *Inside The LRRPS, Rangers in Vietnam*, 38.

249 Ranger training, however, continued. As Lanning has noted: "The Ranger course of instruction has . . . remained fairly constant over the years. Basic conditioning, patrolling, and operations are taught at Fort Benning. Mountain training is conducted in Northern Georgia near Dahlonega, and amphibious and jungle training in the Florida panhandle at Eglin Air Force Base. In more recent times, a desert training phase has been added at Dugway Proving Grounds, Utah." Lanning, *Inside the LURRPS, Rangers in Vietnam*, 41.

250 According to Stanton, neither company had a numerical designation, one being known as the "Victory Lerps," the other as the "Jayhaw Lerps"—Lerp being "a contraction of long-range reconnaissance patrol or LRRP (later Lerp became indifferently spelled as Lurp, by approximating the pronunciation." Stanton, *Rangers at War, LRRPs in Vietnam*, 15. We have been informed that use of the word "Lerp" or "Lurp" is disfavored, and so we will try not to use them." The creation of the two ranger companies in Europe was an obvious counterweight to our government's perception of a land threat from the Soviet Union.

251 Stanton, *Rangers at War, LRRPs in Vietnam*, 15. As we shall see below when examining the "Studies and Observation Group" impostors, this distinction between Rangers as *overt* operatives and SOG troops as *covert* operatives is an important one.

252 There has been an ongoing dispute in the United States Army, and among many of its veterans, about who should be entitled to wear the Ranger tab. As we shall see below, when on February 1, 1969, all LRRP/LRP units in Vietnam were amalgamated into one unit designated the "75th Rangers," the same men continued to perform the same duties-— traditional Ranger work — so there are many who believe the latter are entitled to wear the Ranger tab even though they had not attended Ranger school at Fort Benning. A discussion of that dispute — let alone its history and quasi-

resolution — is beyond the scope of this book. As one former Ranger put it, "[t]his whole LRP/Ranger thing is so screwed up, but fortunately we have a member base that has rarely let us down in trying to establish phonies from the Vietnam War. . . ." E-mail in possession of authors.

253 "MACV" was the acronym for "Military Assistance Command Vietnam," which was supposedly "assisting" the South Vietnamese in defending themselves against the Viet Cong and their North Vietnamese sponsors.

254 We emphasize the word "reconnaissance" because an important task of the LRRPs was observation of the enemy.

255 Lanning, *Inside the LRRPS, Rangers in Vietnam*, 47. Our emphasis.

256 Lanning, *Inside the* LRRPS, *Rangers in Vietnam*, 52. We will discuss below the role of Special Forces in Vietnam.

257 General Westmoreland's directive to organize long-range reconnaissance capabilities had fallen on the shoulders of then-Major Charlie Beckwith. His Project DELTA, later to include other Greek alphabet-named teams, was the predecessor of the LRRP/LRPs.

258 For an account of Lurp training at Recondo, see Larry Chambers, *Recondo, LRRPS in the 101st Airborne.*

259 See Don C. Hall and Annette Hall, *I Served*, 155. For example, Company F, 51st Long Range *Reconnaissance* Patrol (Airborne) Infantry became Company F. Long Range Patrol (Airborne) Infantry.

260 The only exception was F/51st LRP which, during all its time in Vietnam, was separate and autonomous on a Field Force level, not operating under a division, brigade, or any other unit. F/51st LRP operated for *multiple* divisions and brigades, reporting to Lt. General Fred C. Weyand, commander of II Field Force.

261 Lanning, *Inside the LRRPS, Rangers in Vietnam*, 71.

262 After the LRRP/LRP units in Vietnam were disbanded, their members were reassigned to various newly-formed 75th Ranger Regiment companies, with the designations from A to P. For example, when F/51st was disbanded, its members were reassigned to Ranger Companies D, O, and P.

263 Lanning, *Inside the LRRPS, Rangers in Vietnam*, 73.

264 But see previous note.

265 This does not apply to a abbed Ranger graduate of the Ranger School in Fort Benning.

266 On occasion, a Fake Warrior pretending to be LRRP/LRP or Ranger may have become so knowledgeable about his imposture — from books, movies, and other sources of information — that he is able to answer some, if not all, of the questions with seeming assurance. But his answers — no matter how smooth — will not hold up when checked for accuracy.

267 For excellent books about the United States Special Forces, see Anna Simons, *The Company They Keep, Life Inside The U.S. Army Special Forces* and Charles M. Simpson III, *Inside The Green Berets, The First Thirty Years*.

268 It is important to emphasize that the mandate of United States Special Forces has always included a non-military role. Public perception of Special Forces, however, is that of wild-eyed Rambos. In reality Special Forces have trained — and assisted — indigenous peoples in public works, medical care, education, and virtually every other type of non-military activity. However, since no Fake Warrior is going to claim his SF duties in Vietnam consisted of digging a well (rather than killing the enemy), our focus in this book is necessarily on the military role of United States Special Forces.

269 The Vietnamese Special Forces were called the LLDB: Luc Luong Dac Biet.

270 Simpson, *Inside the Green Berets, The First Thirty Years*, 94-96.

271 At (www.sfahq.com) you will find a search engine listing a large number of Special Forces websites, and links to many others of interest, among them Airborne, Special Operations, United States Air Force Air Commandos, Army Rangers, United States Marine Force Recon, and Navy SEALs. There are many others in this vast, useful resource.

272 For a while, the O in SOG stood for "Operations."

273 SOG insertions into Communist controlled North Vietnam had a 100% failure rate. All personnel were captured or killed in action. E-mail in possession of authors. SOG was officially deactivated as of April 30, 1972.

274 Without minimizing to the slightest degree the heroic contributions of the other special units discussed in this book, it is only fair to note that:

> The Vietnam War's most highly decorated unit, with five Medals of Honor, was SOG's under strength, sixty-man recon company at Kontum. Surely no unit that size had been so decorated since the Civil War. And in that final perilous year when SOG fought alone, Danang-based CCN [Command and Control North, the SOG base at Danang], with only about seventy combat operatives, earned two Medals of Honor and three Distinguished Service Crosses. Among SOG's recon units, Purple Hearts were earned at a pace unparalleled in American wars of this century. . . ." John L. Plaster, *SOG*, 354.

It should also be noted that due to the nature and scope of SOG's activities and the resultant classification of much that its guerrilla forces accomplished, neither the Americans who served in that unit nor their indigenous comrades ever fully received the credit or thanks that they richly deserve. Despite what some Fake Warriors may claim, no awards to SOG members were classified. Although the language used might be opaque — e.g. "deep penetration" being a euphemism for Laos or Cambodia — the award did exist and could be given to a deceased SOG member's next of kin.

275 In addition to the SOGs killed in action in Indochina, only one of the nearly sixty men missing in action in Laos and Cambodia ever returned to United States control. In June 1967, Sergeant First Class Charles Wilklow had been captured, but managed to escape during a bombing raid aimed at killing a high value North Vietnamese target, General Giap. Wilklow moved to high ground, was spotted by an American aircraft, and snatched up by a helicopter.

276 As the result of an outpouring of books and articles about the Vietnam War in general and clandestine operations in particular, much is now known about even such a secret operation as SOG. Accordingly, as is the case with impostor SEALs, Rangers, and others discussed above, it is not difficult for a SOG impostor to "talk the talk, and walk the walk" until challenged with pointed questions and checked against available personnel lists. Among the informative books about SOG activities in Vietnam are John L. Plaster's, *SOG, A Photo History of the Secret Wars.* There are also a number of other books with a more limited scope.

277 *Wikipedia Encyclopedia*, citing sources.

278 "Sting Ray operations were the exact opposite of Key Hole missions with goals more closely in line of offensive strikes, the . . . operators were heavily armed and used artillery and/or naval gunfire support, if available. However, what began as a 'key hole' patrol could become a 'sting ray' patrol with little warning. The versatility of [the Marines] is demonstrated when missions quickly turn, planned or not, from a deep reconnaissance patrol to a direct action engagement." *Wikipedia Encyclopedia.*

279 This quotation is from *Wikipedia Encyclopedia*, citing sources.

280 Orr Kelly, *From A Dark Sky*, 130-31.

281 At about the same time, also in response to President Kennedy's direction, Army Special Forces began to expand its roster and increase its

capabilities — and the Navy SEALs were born.

282 Five Air Commandos were awarded the Medal of Honor for heroism in the Vietnam War.

283 E-mail in possession of authors.

284 On the subject of impostors, a former Air Commando had this to say: "While there is less of a 'wanabee' queue saying they were Air Commandos, I have run across a few, and those were detected by asking the normal questions of places and people. They made themselves obvious by noting 'I can't tell you.' Ooops." E-mail in possession of authors.

285 Because so much is now known about the activities of Air Commandos in Vietnam, much of it through books and the Air Commando's own website, an impostor is better equipped to answer some of these questions with some degree of plausibility.

286 *Wikipedia Encyclopedia.*

287 See "That Others May Live," by John L. Frisbee, *Air Force Magazine*, October 1983 and Wright-Patterson Air Force Base press release, 8 December, 2000 in possession of authors.

288 John Cassidy, *PJ History*, (http://www.specialtactics.com/history.shtml).

289 *Wikipedia Encyclopedia.*

290 Some military personnel were "detailed" to the CIA, and were responsible for infiltrating enemy areas. They were usually on temporary duty from their home Special Forces units.

291 There are plentiful examples of former CIA agents having to obtain Agency permission before publishing books about their service. Most recently, the government in its prosecution of "Taliban John" Walker Lindh

fought successfully to keep secret the identity of "CS 1," the agent code-named "Dave" who was present at the Afghanistan prison uprising where CIA agent Mike Spann was killed.

292 *Wikipedia Encyclopedia.*

293 Title 10, United States Code, Section 8741. Exactly the same language is used for the naval service (Title 10, United States Code, Section 6241) and the Army (Title 10, United States Code, Section 3741), except that the latter statute uses instead of the word "distinguishes" the word "distinguished." Our emphasis.

294 Medal of Honor citation.

Then-Navy Commander James B. Stockdale (Vice Admiral, retired), long-term POW in North Vietnam, is a Medal of Honor recipient. "Ready to die or at least 'make them think that I was ready to die' rather than divulge the details of the note-drop scheme [by which the POWs communicated], that night Stockdale managed to break a window and with the glass shards chopped his wrists . . . ." Stuart I. Rochester and Fred Kiley, *Honor Bound*, 488. [This quotation opens Chapter 3 in the authors' book *"Aid and Comfort": Jane Fonda in North Vietnam.* The chapter is entitled "Captive Audience: The American POWs."]

Of the 239 Medals of Honor awarded for service during the Vietnam War (see Appendix "F"), more than half (150) were posthumous.

295 Title 10, United States Code, Section 8742. Exactly the same language is used for the Navy/Marine Corps (Title 10, United States Code, Section 6242), and the Army (Title 10, United States Code, Section 3742). Our emphasis.

296 The quotations which follow are the texts of the actual citations promulgated by each branch of the service in making the awards.

297 General Orders No. 91, 20 April 1970, in possession of the authors.

The other six infantrymen on that patrol were nominated for the Bronze Star with Combat V for valor.

If Captain Blunt's heroism is not enough to warrant contempt for, and condemnation of, Fake Warriors who claim the Distinguished Service Cross, perhaps the story of United States Army Captain Humbert "Rocky" Versace will suffice.

In *"Aid and Comfort": Jane Fonda in North Vietnam*, we wrote that she and then-husband Tom Hayden named their son Troi—now called "Troy" Garrity—"after Nguyen Van Troi, a Viet Cong terrorist who tried to assassinate Secretary of Defense Robert McNamara in 1964 but who was himself executed for the effort. * * * It is believed that in retaliation for Van Troi's execution, the Viet Cong executed American POW Rocky Versace."

Rocky Versace was a West Point graduate and an Army Ranger/Green Beret intelligence officer. In 1963 he, two other Americans, and several South Vietnamese were ambushed by Viet Cong. An eight-hour firefight ensued. Wounded and out of ammunition, the three Americans were captured.

For almost two years he suffered in a Viet Cong prison camp, adamantly refusing to accept his captors' vicious and inhumane attempts to make him sign propaganda statements and repeatedly trying to escape. Said retired U.S. Army Brigadier General John W. Nicholson:

> By spring of 1964 the farmers were talking about one U.S. prisoner in particular. They said he was treated very poorly, led through the area with a rope around his neck, hands tied, bare footed, head swollen and yellow in color (jaundice) and hair white. They stated that this prisoner not only resisted the Viet Cong attempts to get him to admit to war crimes and aggression, but would verbally counter their assertions convincingly and in a loud voice so the local villagers could hear. *During two long years of torture and maltreatment he resisted his communist captors before being executed in 1965.* The last thing fellow prisoners heard from him was the battered and emaciated Army officer defiantly

singing *God Bless America* in his cage the night before his murder. On September 26, 1965, North Vietnam's "Liberation Radio" announced the execution of Rocky Versace and another American POW ostensibly in retaliation for the deaths of 3 terrorists in Da Nang. *Newsletter*, Organization of Former Intelligence Officers, May 27, 2002, Section I. Our emphasis.

In a special ceremony in the East Room of the White House on July 8, 2002, President George W. Bush presented the Medal of Honor to Captain Versace — posthumously. See Dave Eberhart, "Hero to Receive Medal of Honor at White House," *NewsMax.com*, May 27, 2002.

298 The Navy Cross was awarded to RM2 Terrence J. Freund — posthumously. He was killed in action during the described engagement and his name appears on the Vietnam Memorial Wall at Panel 11E, Row 109. Documentation in possession of authors.

299 Richard Davis, who *pretended* to be a Parajumper medic, bears a heavy burden of shame for dishonoring dedicated heroes like William Pitsenbarger.

300 Other decorations often claimed by Fake Warriors are the Silver Star, Bronze Star with Combat V and Purple Heart. Here are the legal criteria for each:

Silver Star: "The President may award a silver star . . . to a person who, while serving in any capacity with the Air Force, is cited for gallantry in action that does not warrant a medal of honor or Air Force cross. . . ." (Title 10, United States Code, Section 8746.) Exactly the same language is used for the Navy/Marine Corps. (Title 10, United States Code, Section 6244). Title 10, United States Code, Section 3746, is the Army provision.

Bronze Star: Also a favorite of Fake Warriors, it can be awarded to any member of the Armed Forces or Coast Guard both for "heroic or meritorious achievement or service." This means that a Fake Warrior could legitimately have been awarded a Bronze Star for conduct having nothing to do with heroism, but he could claim that it did. A Combat V affixed to a Bronze Star denotes heroism.

Purple Heart: Title 10, United States Code, Section 1131, and Executive Order 11016, "Authorizing Award of the Purple Heart" (promulgated by President John F. Kennedy on April 25, 1962), authorized the medal for members of the Armed Forces "and any civilian national of the United States who, while serving under competent authority in any capacity with an armed force . . . has been, or may hereafter be wounded . . . ." Section 3 of the Executive Order provides that "A wound for which the award is made must have required treatment by a medical officer."

301 Obtaining a copy of the order making the award, and the citation accompanying it, is especially important regarding the Distinguished Service Cross, the Navy Cross, and the Air Force Cross. In *Stolen Valor*, co-author B.G. Burkett states: "I have always felt a public listing of the heroes of the Vietnam War would greatly diminish those claiming phony heroism. *The government, however, has no such list*. Through the efforts of Al Gleim, now deceased, the Distinguished Service Cross recipients are listed for the first time in an appendix to this book. The same is true of the Air Force Cross recipients. This list was compiled through years of research by Jeffrey Floyd. I am forever grateful for the work of these two truth seekers." Burkett and Whitley, xix; Our emphasis.

Unlike a Fake Warrior's claim to have been a POW or to have been awarded the Medal of Honor — which are readily verifiable from official lists — an impostor's claim to have been awarded one of the three Crosses is not so easily verified. Because the three lists appearing in the appendices to *Stolen Valor* are only presumptively comprehensive and by now considerably out of date, *it is essential to obtain the order making the award, and the citation accompanying it.*

302 A Marine "Mustang" (an enlisted man who becomes an officer) sums up the multiple awards point this way: "**An individual earning the awards mentioned [in the text] receives the** ***first*** **award in the form of**

the *actual medal*, **while subsequent awards of the same decoration are denoted with '***stars, bars and other devices***' as you denoted for each service. (In my own case, I received my** *first* **Navy and Marine Corps Commendation** *Medal* **with Combat 'V' for service in Korea (at that time called the '***Letter of Commendation***' but later changed to 'Navy and Marine Corps Commendation Medal'), and my second Navy and Marine Corps Commendation Medal with Combat V' in Vietnam, was in the form of a '***Certificate***' attesting to the second award, and NOT another Medal)."**

Section 5, Executive Order 11016. The policy of limiting the award of medals and decorations is not limited to those that honor heroic military service. For example, the Meritorious Service Medal (Executive Orders 11448 and 12312), the Defense Superior Service Medal (Executive Order 11904), the Vice Presidential Service Badge (Executive Order 11926), the Humanitarian Service Medal (Executive Order 11965), the Defense Meritorious Service Medal (Executive Order 12019), the Presidential Service Certificate and Presidential Service Badge (Executive Order 12793), Military Outstanding Volunteer Service Medal (Executive Order 12830), and the Armed Forces Service Medal (Executive Order 12985), are similarly limited and also contain the "additional award" provisions found in the statutes discussed above.

It's noteworthy that, from time to time, an imposter will claim service to the White House, and the award of a Presidential Service Badge. Each such award is, however, serialized and has an accompanying authenticating certificate. E-mail from recipient of Presidential Service Badge.

303 See Chapter 6.

304 Egon Larsen, *The Deceivers, Lives of the Great Impostors*, 93. The tale of "The Captain of Kopenick" is found in virtually every collection of stories about legendary impostors. Subsequent reference to Larsen's book will be to "Larsen."

305 Larsen, 97.

306 Larsen, 103.

307 Larsen, 104.

308 E-mail in possession of authors.

309 Our emphasis.

310 It is true, of course, that the erroneous promotion date could have been a typographical error. However, in virtually all instances where such an error appears, there are other erroneous entries as well. Cumulatively, its very rare that they're all typos.

311 Medal of Honor recipient George E. Day served in the Marine Corps during World War II, and in the Air Force during the Korean and Vietnam Wars.

312 The July 1, 1972, version of the DD-214 contains, in block 19, the number of days in Indochina. But nowhere on that form is there a place for a "POW" entry.

313 Only if a Vietnam POW had been discharged after the mid-1980s could he legitimately have the POW Medal shown on his DD-214. In this regard, it's worth remembering that the last American POWs were repatriated in early 1973 at Operation Homecoming.

314 DD-214 in possession of authors.

315 Regrettably, for the last decade it has become much easier — in ways which will not be revealed here — to obtain blank DD-214 forms, as well as scores of other government military-related blank forms.

Among them are: honorable discharge certificates; Army ID cards; CIA certificate of training as covert surveillance and reconnaissance expert; Republic of Vietnam Cross of Gallantry; graduation certificate, United States Army JFK Special Warfare Center, Ft. Bragg, 10th Special Forces Group (Airborne), *with signatures*; CIA Military Advisor Award.

The availability of these forms not only facilitates Fake Warrior impostures, but, even more, has serious implications for our national security. A sleeper terrorist, for example, could create a military record as a Special Forces

Vietnam combat veteran who had completed CIA training.

316 Perhaps it was the alleged shot to the head that triggered all those lies. This doctored DD-214 also contained all sorts of medals, a SEAL claim, and other heroic conduct. DD-214 in possession of authors.

317 There is reason to believe that some NPRC clerks were not as scrupulous as they should have been about access to the files, and were too accommodating about facilitating "corrections."

318 According to one of the authors' sources, "[i]t is a primary principle of Masonry and all concordant orders that members have no criminal background and never lie to a brother mason. If he [referring to an alleged Fake Warrior] has lied on this issue I intend to ask him to resign from masonry or lacking that I will file charges with the Grand Lodge of California and have him expelled from the Fraternity." E-mail in possession of authors.

319 E-mail in possession of authors.

320 E-mail in possession of authors.

321 There are countless examples of the print media, as well as television, running stories about military impostors. See for example Burkett and Whitley, 78-79.

322 E-mail in possession of authors. This publisher is a credit to his profession. His diligence shames the lazy, irresponsible or just plain indifferent attitude displayed by editors and reporters who publish unchecked stories and obituaries in their newspapers.

323 Even after confessing to imposture, Corley persisted in some of his lies: "I will admit to having stretched the truth about the time I was a captive and enhanced the escape story . . . . The records I do have will prove only a part of what I claim, but they will prove part of it."

Twelve minutes later Corley wrote to the Phony Busters: "I have always felt that I deserved formal POW status even though I was never officially given it. I will appear at no more presentations of the Wall except as a spectator and will make no more speeches."

Five hours later, however, in an inexplicable outpouring of apparent contrition, he wrote:

> I LIED. I was not a POW and cannot ever make that claim. . . . [T]he ribbons will be either donated to a museum or they will be destroyed . . . . I am moving from this city and it is no more than I deserve. My family has suffered enough shame because of me and I will cause neither them nor your organization more problems. I deserved to be shown up and I have been. For a few moments of attention, I have lost everything and it is no more than I deserve. I am leaving my business and my home and all that know me and that is hard, but I brought it upon myself and no one else is to blame. * * * Those of us who do this are little better than dirt and not worthy to even associate with those of you who were the real heroes. You will never see or hear from me in any way. I do not know why I did it and can make NO excuses. All I can do is apologize to the families of the REAL POWS and MIAS and to you and your group. Believe it or not I am a very patriotic person who does love this country. This one weekend has cost me my business and my friends and so much misery that I can hardly bear it, but that is entirely my fault. Once again.... you are doing the right thing. Goodbye sir. Emails in possession of authors.

324 George Saville, *Of Punishment.*

325 *Cohen* v. *California*, 403 U.S. 15 (1971).

326 "It cannot plausibly be maintained," Harlan noted, "that this vulgar allusion to the Selective Service System would conjure up such psychic stimulation in anyone likely to be confronted with Cohen's crudely defaced jacket." 403 U.S. at 20.

327 403 U.S. at 20.

328 Lucky for today's Fake Warriors, contemporary punishments for their *intentional* conduct is not nearly as severe as it once was.

> The law of England in the nineteenth century was still in spirit a feudal law aimed at preserving the property, in land and other possessions, of the governing class. Magna Carta was all very fine, but the penalties the law imposed on freemen who had stolen or cheated were the punishments of a feudal society. * * * Men and women were responsible for all their actions unless they were insane, and insanity meant raving lunacy or at least complete and obvious unhinging of the mental faculties. The impostors, some of whom were not normal by the medical standards of the day, benefited not at all by their mental instability. They were classified as cunning rogues—and that was that. Sometimes the punishment was ferocious, as in the case of Sara Wilson [who stole from the Queen of England]. No one appears to have realized the horrific aspect of sentencing her to death. True, the sentence was mitigated and converted into transportation to the American colonies for life, but this in itself was a fearful fate, for the American colonies were regarded as not much less barbarous than the Australian wilderness." Gerald Sparrow, *The Great Impostors*, 186.

329 This book does not address the court-martial charges that can be brought against military personnel on active duty. See, for example, *Uniform Code of Military Justice*, Title 10, *United States Code,* Sections 907, 921, 932 and 934.

330 For the purpose of this example, it doesn't matter how a Fake Warrior alters the document—although, from what we've seen, it is not difficult to imagine how he does it.

331 See Chapter 4.

332 This language is taken from the New Mexico "Application For Military Service Special Plate," Form MVD 10353, Rev. 09/94.

333 As illustrations, we'll use as examples the laws of the State of New York, which are typical of those existing in other states.

334 New York Penal Law, Section 170.10, forgery in the second degree. Our emphasis. Forgery in the third degree, a class A misdemeanor — "A person is guilty of forgery in the third degree when, with intent to defraud [or] . . . he falsely makes, completes or alters a written instrument" — omits most of the specificity found in forgery second degree. Our emphasis.

335 New York Penal Law, Section 170.20. Our emphasis.

336 New York Penal Law, Section 175.30. The first degree crime requires "the intent to defraud the state or any political subdivision, public authority or public benefit corporation of the state." Our emphasis.

337 New York Penal Law, Section 170.20.

338 This would be true even if (as in, say, New Mexico), the application itself was not sworn to or otherwise submitted under oath. The crime would be based not on the false "certification," but rather on the *use* of the forged DD-214 to support that certification. In certain jurisdictions, lying in a certification not under oath can also be criminal.

Under New York law, and the laws of many other jurisdictions, this type of lying is not considered perjury because the statement was not made under oath, or in a format which stated that untruths would be punishable. Indeed, in New York, the lesser crime of "Making a punishable false written statement" requires that the instrument contain "a legally authorized form notice to the effect that false statements made therein are punishable." New York Penal Law, Section 210.45.

339 New York Penal Law, Section 190.25.

340 176 F.2d 376.

341 Wight was sentenced to three years in prison and three years' probation.

342 A related federal statute, Title 10, *United States* Code, Section 771 — "Unauthorized wearing [of the uniform] prohibited — does not expressly contain a criminal penalty: "Except as otherwise provided by law, no person except a member of the Army, Navy, Air Force, or Marine Corps, as the case may be, may wear — (1) the uniform, or a distinctive part of the uniform, of the Army, Navy, Air Force, or Marine Corps; or (2) a uniform any part of which is similar to a distinctive part of the uniform of the Army, Navy, Air Force, or Marine Corps."

There is an exception: Title 10, *United States Code*, Section 772 — "When wearing [a uniform] by persons not on active duty authorized." This section's subsection (f) provided: "While portraying a member of the Army, Navy, Air Force, or Marine Corps, an actor in a theatrical or motion-picture production may wear the uniform of that armed force if the portrayal does not tend to discredit that armed force." In other words, Section 771 prohibits wearing the uniform, Section 772 (f) provides a "show business" exemption so long as there is no discrediting.

Together, these two statutes raise the question of what their relationship is to the criminal prohibition found in Section 702.

In the case of *Schacht* v. *United States*, 398 U.S. 58 (1970), the defendant was prosecuted under Title 18 *United States Code*, Section 702, for wearing a military uniform and cap as part of an anti-Vietnam War skit presented in front of a Texas induction center. Despite his defense under Title 10, *United States Code*, Section 772 (f), he was convicted, fined $250 and sentenced to six months in jail (the maximum fine and incarceration). The federal Court of Appeals affirmed the conviction, and the Supreme Court of the United States agreed to review it. There were two questions to be decided. The first was whether the skit was the kind of "theatrical production" contemplated by Section 772. If it was, Schacht's use of the uniform would be protected.

That question was easily answered. Schacht's skit *was* a protected "theatrical production."

But what of the statute's provision that even an otherwise protected theatrical production would be unprotected if it *tended to discredit* the armed force portrayed? Predictably — and correctly, in our view — the Supreme Court held that proviso unconstitutional: ". . . Congress has in effect made it a crime for an actor wearing a military uniform to say things critical of the conduct or policies of the Armed Forces. * * * The final clause of Section 772(f), which leaves Americans free to praise the war in Vietnam but can send persons like Schacht to prison for opposing it, cannot survive in a country which has the First Amendment. To preserve the constitutionality of Section 772 (f) that final clause must be stricken from the section." 398 U.S. at 62.

Reading Sections 771, 772 and 772 and the *Schacht* decision together, however, their meaning is clear: Fake Warriors' wearing of military uniforms is a federal crime to which there is no defense — except if the wearing is part of a "theatrical or motion-picture production."

343 The proper name for this unit award is "Vietnamese Gallantry Cross with Palm and Frame."

344 None of these awards are for personal heroism.

345 See Chapter 5 for descriptions of the requirements for some of these decorations.

346 An Assistant United States Attorney was present at this interview, during which Dinsmore showed scars from what he claimed were self-inflicted wounds, some connected with suicide attempts.

347 "Agreed Factual Basis" for plea of guilty, pursuant to Rule 11, *Federal Rules of Criminal Procedure*, prepared from information Dinsmore provided to the government and obtained by it during its investigation. The facts recited in Dinsmore's statement are not mere allegations. Dinsmore swore

to the truth of the entire content of this statement when he pleaded guilty.

348 Interview conducted by co-author.

349 It is noteworthy that, when the United States Attorney's office informed the Army Criminal Investigation Division agent who had referred the Dinsmore case to the FBI that the government was going to prosecute, the agent expressed surprise because, in his federal district, *prosecutors were not interested in bringing such cases.*

350 Probably, Dinsmore also could have been charged with impersonating a federal employee under Section 912. This is a discretionary call for the prosecutors, who weigh such factors as the defendant's mental condition, the amount of money involved, and the effect of multiple charges on the potential sentence. In addition, because Dinsmore's masquerade did not involve crimes against any VA programs, that agency played no part in his prosecution.

351 Dinsmore had purchased his uniform at a military Post Exchange while he was a member of the Tennessee Defense Force (a civil defense organization). However, when he joined the TDF, he had made false claims and, when he was unmasked, he was thrown out.

352 See Chapter 1. The Assistant United States Attorney was himself a veteran.

353 Dinsmore had a history of psychiatric problems. According to the government, at the time of his sentencing he was receiving mental health treatment at the VA Medical Center in Mountain Home, Tennessee. The sentencing judge added as a condition of Dinsmore's probation that he continue in treatment.

354 The Judge ordered Dinsmore to turn over his uniform and medals to "an appropriate organization" approved by his probation officer. Inman made it clear to Dinsmore that if he violated any of the probation conditions, he would go to jail.

355 For the source of these quotations, and for much of the description of Dinsmore's sentencing, see Cameron Judd, "Roger Dinsmore, Popular Inspirational Speaker, Admits He Misrepresented His Military Record," *The Greenville Sun*, March 3, 1999. Additional information was obtained through an interview of Mr. Judd conducted by a co-author.

There are those who believe that the underlying reason for Dinsmore's masquerade was an attempt to obtain some of the respect then being enjoyed by Vietnam combat veterans. Ironically, Dinsmore later became "chaplain" for a local VFW post—with the knowledge and approval of the court and the government—since he had actually served in Vietnam.

356 In an interview with a co-author, the United States Attorney who prosecuted Dinsmore was asked why he didn't also charge the defendant with impersonation. His answer was that although, arguably, he could have, he saw Dinsmore as a "mental case," the amount of money was minor, and no matter how many different charges were laid, Dinsmore's sentence would have been the same as the one he ultimately received.

357 Aucker was also commander of a local American Legion post.

358 The investigation was initiated and developed by the Inspector General of the National Archives.

359 Apparently, no one at the National Guard had bothered to check anything about Nicholson or his story, even though he didn't produce either an order awarding the Distinguished Service Cross, or a citation explaining it. It was believed that some of Nicholson's credibility derived from his position as a police chief. Through that position, he may have come to know the National Guard commander.

360 The scammed reporter never did admit her mistake — let alone apologize for being too lazy to check out the facts in advance. After all, Nicholson was deemed to have been credible because he was a retired local police chief.

361 Our emphasis. All things considered, the VA is the biggest sucker in the country. Its losses to Fake Warriors claiming medical and other benefits are incalculable. These losses do not include incalculable sums lost to other scams.

Recall the case of the non-veteran who assumed his dead twin brother's veteran identity. "For more than 5 years, continuing to use his brother's identity, Hinton devised several schemes to defraud VA. Following his brother's death, Hinton endorsed and cashed his brother's VA benefit checks. Hinton also admitted that he filed numerous false, fictitious, and fraudulent documents in order to obtain a home mortgage guaranteed by the VA."

Hinton's sentence? Twenty-four months in prison, thirty-six months' probation, and restitution of $40,000.

In an infamous Fake Warrior case, an impostor claimed American troops had slaughtered unarmed South Koreans at No Gun Ri — although he was nowhere near the place. The felon pleaded guilty to stealing hundreds of thousands of dollars from the VA in undeserved benefits. He was sentenced to only twenty-one months in prison and three years of supervised probation, and ordered to make restitution to the government of $412,839.00 which surely he did not have. Another non-veteran took the VA for nearly $500,000. The cases are legion, and little or nothing is done about most of them.

362 Our emphasis. There are exceptions, not relevant here, pertaining to judicial proceedings and legislative matters.

363 The *principal* federal perjury statute does require that some kind of an oath have been taken.

364 The closest case is that of an imposter who claimed he had been a SEAL. He had made false statements to FBI agents regarding bank loans and fraudulent invoices. He also had falsified his military papers and documents

— which would have triggered other sections of the federal criminal code, but not necessarily Section 1001.

365 The information and quotations concerning Toups/Crowder are taken from the affidavit of Federal Bureau of Investigation Special Agent Donald J. Albracht, which is in the possession of authors.

366 In writing about a Section 702 case in 1998, Burkett and Whitley reported: "The U.S. Justice Department found only two other instances of the medals fraud rule being enforced since 1990." Burkett and Whitley, *Stolen Valor*, 292.

367 The complaint is in the possession of authors.

368 The Section 1028 (a) (6) charge is a felony.

369 Sometimes, depending on the nature of the alleged crime and the demographics, a criminal investigation will be conducted by the state police.

370 Usually, the power to prosecute rests with the county district attorney. Sometimes, however, it is in the hands of the state Attorney General.

371 It's the FBI who acts — or declines to act — and not the investigating branches of the armed forces, because in virtually every Fake Warrior case a suspected impostor, at the time he's being investigated, is not then serving in the military. In the rare instance that he is, the investigation would be handled by agents from whatever branch of the service the suspect was attached to — say, the Army's Criminal Investigation Division. For example, a P.O.W. Network complaint to the Marine Corps about a Fake Warrior was handled by its Assistance and Investigations Division, Inspector General's office.

372 Unfortunately, for our purposes, governors also have the power to commute sentences and grant pardons.

373 In exposing and thus punishing a celebrity Fake Warrior, it is best to use a national newspaper or magazine. For example, if the subject is a movie actor, one could use *Variety* or *The Hollywood Reporter.*

374 One G.I. was captured in South Vietnam, but he escaped after only a few hours. His skeptical commanding officer didn't believe the soldier's story. Accordingly, he was never classified as a prisoner of war. His continued protestations never caused the Pentagon to change its mind. Many years later, however, as relations between Vietnam and the United States thawed, our government obtained access to Communist "after action" reports. Lo-and-behold, right there in the enemy's own documents were reports *that* the soldier had been captured, *where* he had been captured, and *when* he had been captured and later escaped. As a result, decades after he was entitled to be classified as a legitimate prisoner of war, the Pentagon finally corrected its records. When a Pentagon official telephoned the former enlisted man to inform him that his classification would be changed, in substance this conversation ensued:

> *Pentagon official*: We know that for many years you've been claiming to have been captured in Vietnam, and escaped after only a few hours.
>
> *G.I.:* That's right, but no one ever believed me.
>
> *Pentagon official*: Well, we believe you now. Enemy documents confirm your story. As of now, you're considered to have been a POW.

The soldier broke down and cried.

375 It is difficult for a celebrity to recover in a defamation lawsuit because he's a "public figure." Still, a wealthy celebrity may sue anyway, hoping to drown a Phony Buster, even one who has checked his facts and does speak the truth, in huge unrecoverable defense costs. So be forewarned: In the case of a suspected impostor who has the money and the will to fight it out

in the courts, even if you win, you lose. You will not be reimbursed for those defense costs.

In a *non-celebrity* defamation case, the threat of suit is usually not great — *if* the newspaper advertisement has its facts correct, and *if* the ad is cleared by an experienced lawyer. This is because, legally, truth is an absolute defense, and because, practically, non-celebrities usually lack the financial wherewithal to bring a defamation lawsuit.

Threats by Fake Warriors to sue for libel or slander are not uncommon: "I agree that lies should be exposed, however, publication of unsupported suspicions does constitute slander. And I resent your implication that I am not what I am. You keep on 'reporting' and impuning [*sic*] people's reputations 'with willful disregard' and the results might just surprise you."

Something like the following actual response from P.O.W. Network is usually sufficient to call the Fake Warrior's bluff:

> You made the unsupported claims. Should you have any evidence to support your claims, we would be the first to call the Pentagon, ask the lists be amended, apply for your POW Medal, arrange a public presentation, and announce to the world that we found the man the Pentagon did not acknowledge. By the way, we do go farther than requesting military records. We have been known to request after-action reports, morning rosters, commander's logs and journals, interview commanding officers, debriefers, and other members of the unit, in addition to speaking with real former POWs. Anyone held 50 days or 60 days would have been missed by CO, by family, by the paymaster, and reported as such. Anyone escaping with so many others would have been debriefed extensively. The files would be huge, and never lost. E-mail in possession of authors.

376 This chapter is taken in part from a paper written by Jackson Killion, St. Louis University School of Law, Class of 2013.

377 *Black's Law Dictionary*, Fifth Edition, 1979. The meaning of "valor," is simply "courage."

378 *What is the Purple Heart?*, Mil. Ord. of the Purple Heart, (www.purpleheart.org/PHTrail/Default.aspx) (last visited Feb. 9, 2012). This medal would later become the Purple Heart.

379 *See* General Orders of George Washington, Commander-in-Chief of the Army of the Revolution, Issued at Newburgh on the Hudson, 1782–1783, at 34–35 (Edward C. Boynton ed., 1909) (1883).

380 *Id.*

381 18 U.S.C. Section 704 Historical and Revision Notes (2006). Previous attempts to criminalize the unlawful wearing of certain military medals have existed since 1940 with no major constitutional decisions concerning them.

382 *Id.*

383 10 U.S.C. Section 1425 (1940). Our emphasis.

384 10 U.S.C. Section 1425 (1948).

385 18 U.S.C. Section 704 Historical and Revision Notes (2006).

386 18 U.S.C. Section 704 (1952).

387 *Id.* Our emphasis.

388 *See* 18 U.S.C. Section 704 (1958): 18 U.S.C. Section 704 (1964): 18 U.S.C. Section 704 (1970): 18 U.S.C. Section 704 (1976): 18 U.S.C. Section 704 (1988).

389 18 U.S.C. Section 704 (1994).

390 *Id.*

391 *Id.*

392 *Id.*

393 *The Medal of Honor*, Cong. Medal of Honor Soc'y, (www.cmohs.org) (last visited Feb. 9, 2012).

394 *Id.*

395 18 U.S.C. Section 704 (2000).

396 151 Cong. Rec. 5643 (2005).

397 *Id.*

398 *Id.*

399 *Id.*

400 He was also correct about how imposters dishonor themselves. He was not correct, however, about how imposters dishonor the actual recipients of valorous awards. There is no way to "steal" the courageous conduct of someone who has acted with valor. The deed belongs to the actor, no one else. It cannot be stolen, appropriated, robbed or otherwise taken from the individual who performed it. Despite the fine book *Stolen Valor*, and the "Stolen Valor" name attached to the 2005 Stolen Value Act and the recently proposed Stolen Valor Act of 2005, the authors have always believed that those titles were more connotatively emotional than literally correct.

401 *Id.*

402 *Id.*

403 *Id.*

404 H.R. 3352, 109th Cong. (2005).

405 *Id.* Section 2.

406 *Id.*

407 *Id.*

408 *Id.* Section 3.

409 *Id.*

410 *Id.*

411 *Compare* 18 U.S.C. Section 704 (1994), *with* H.R. 3352, 109th Cong. (2005).

412 H.R. 3352, 109th Cong. (2005).

413 *Id.* Section 3

414 *Id.*

415 *Id.* The bill created another section entitled "Other Medals" that allowed for increased punishment if the medal involved in the offense was a Distinguished Service Cross, Air Force Cross, Navy Cross, Silver Star, or Purple Heart.

416 *Id.*

417 S. 1998, 109th Cong. (2005).

418 *Compare* H.R. 3352, 109th Cong. (2005), *with* S. 1998, 109th Cong. (2005).

419 *Id.*

420 S. 1998, 109th Cong. (2005).

421 151 Cong. Rec. 9215 (2005).

422 152 Cong. Rec. 8819 (2006).

423 *See, e.g.*, United States v. McGuinn, No. 07 Cr. 471(KNF), 2007 WL 3050502, at *1 (S.D.N.Y. Oct. 18, 2007); United States v. Perelman, 737 F. Supp. 2d 1221 (D. Nev. 2010), *aff'd*, 658 F.3d 1134 (9th Cir. 2011); United States v. Robbins, 759 F. Supp. 2d 815 (W.D. Va. 2011).

424 18 U.SC. 704(b) (2006). Our emphasis.

425 746 F. Supp. 2d 1183 (D. Colo. 2010), *rev'd*, No. 10-1358, 2012 WL 247995, *1 (10th Cir. Jan 27, 2012).

426 *Id.*

427 *Id.*

428 *Id.* at 1192.

429 *Id.* at 1189–91.

430 *Strandlof*, 2012 WL 247995, at *1. The court noted that numerous other courts throughout the nation had analyzed whether or not the Stolen Valor Act was constitutional and had reached varying results. The court also discussed the earlier case of *United States* v. *Alvarez* (discussed below) and the strong dissents and critical concurrences associated with it. *Id.* at *2. Regarding some of those other cases, see, for example:

- United States v. Amster, 2011 U.S. App. LEXIS 26129 (11th Cir. Fla. Oct. 20, 2011): In a U.S. District Court in Florida, the defendant filed a post-trial motion claiming the SVA was unconstitutional. The court dismissed this claim in one sentence. Amster appealed, and the court suspended further proceedings until *Alvarez* was decided.

- United States v. Kepler, No. 11-2278 (8th Cir. docketed June 10, 2011): In a U.S. District Court in Iowa, the defendant was indicted for violation of subsection (b) and (d) of the SVA. He moved to dismiss on the ground of facially invalidity. The court granted the motion, and the government appealed. Pending the Supreme Court's decision in *Alvarez*, apparently nothing more happened.

- United States v. Lawless, No. 11-cr-475-PJM/11-mj-173-TMD (D. Md. Aug. 29, 2011): In a U.S. District Court in Maryland, the defendant moved to dismiss on the grounds that the SVA was unconstitutional. The court held the statute was not narrowly tailored to serve a compelling government interest. The government appealed. Further proceedings were delayed until *Alvarez* was decided by the Supreme Court. (Note: Fake Warrior Lawless had received gun manufacturer Glock's 2008 "Hero of the Year Award" based on his false claims.)

In other cases — despite the serious question about the SVA's constitutionality from Day One — several defendants pleaded guilty to Section 704(b) charges, among them:

ERIC GENE PIOTROWSKI (Eastern District of CA) - 2009
MICHAEL ALLAN FRASER (Eastern District of CA) - 2008
CHARLES T. WHITE (Middle District of FL) - 2009
THOMAS BARNHART (Eastern District of VA) - 2010
ANGEL MANUEL OCASIO-REYES (Middle District of FL) - 2010

431 *Strandlof*, 2012 WL 247995, at *1.

432 *Id.* *at 3.

433 *Id.* at *4.

434 *Id.*

435 *Id.* The court determined the "falsely represents" language in 18 U.S.C. Section 704(b) meant "to be guilty, a speaker must have had a specific intent to deceive." *Id.* Of course, that's not what Section 704(b) said.

436 *Id.* The court decided that because the Act required the intent to deceive, acting or satire, for example, could not be prosecuted. It could hardly be argued that an actor or author was trying to deceive his or her audience. *Id.*

437 *Id.* at *5.

438 *Id.* The court noted the First Amendment does not give blanket protection to all speech. *Id.* at *5–*8.

439 *Id.* at *7.

440 *Id.* at *9.

441 *Id.* at *10.

442 *Id.* at *13.

443 *Id.* at *17.

444 *Id.* at *18.

445 *Id.* There was also a lengthy dissent by Judge Holmes. He interpreted Supreme Court jurisprudence to mean that "injurious falsehood" was a specific historical category of constitutionally unprotected speech, but the Stolen Valor Act did not fit in that category. He argued that since the Act did not fall into an historical exception, it was required to satisfy a strict scrutiny analysis, which it failed. Consequently, Holmes thought the Act was an unconstitutional restriction on free speech. *Id.* at *43 (Holmes, J., dissenting).

446 Text appearing in brackets has been added by the authors.

447 The vote was 2-1. The government sought *en banc* review by all Ninth Circuit judges, which was denied over several dissents.

448 James Vicini, *Supreme Court Hears Military Medal Lying Case,* Reuters (Feb. 22, 2012), (www.reuters.com/article/2012/02/22/us-usa-military-medals-idUSTRE81L1VJ20120222).

449 *Id.*

450 *Id.*

451 Oral Argument at 22:06, United States v. Alvarez, Docket No. 11-210, *available at* (www.oyez.org/cases/2010-2019/2011/2011_11_210).

452 Vicini, *supra* note 73.

453 Tony Mauro, Justices May Uphold Stolen Valor Act, First Amendment Center (Feb. 23, 2012), (www.firstamendmentcenter.org) justices-may-uphold-stolen-valor-act.

454 Vicini, *supra* note 73.

455 Mauro, *supra* note 78.

Several years earlier, after Section 704(b) was ruled unconstitutional by the Ninth Circuit in the *Alvarez* case, there was a substantial movement to craft a statute that would survive constitutional scrutiny — some of that effort having been stimulated by Professor Holzer's preparation of the Fake Warrior Act. See Chapter 9.

Congressman Joe Heck introduced a new version of the Act, the Stolen Valor Act of 2011, to the House of Representatives (H.R. 1775, 112th Cong. (2011)). Subsequently, Senator Scott Brown introduced an identical version of the new Act in the Senate (S. 1728, 112th Cong. (2011)). The updated version of the Stolen Valor Act focused on making it illegal for people to *benefit* from false factual statements about their military service. The proposed version completely removed subsection (b) of Section 704 of the Stolen Valor Act of 2005, the section which contained the constitutionally troublesome language "whoever falsely represents himself or herself . . . to have been awarded any decoration or medal" that courts seemed to have the most issues with (*compare* H.R. 1775, 112th Cong (2011), *and* S. 1728, 112th Cong. (2011), *with* 18 U.S.C. Section 704 (2006)).

Textually, the Stolen Valor Act of 2011 seeks to criminalize only those individuals who make false statements about their military service *for their own benefit*. Specifically, the proposed Act seeks to punish "[w]hoever, with intent to obtain anything of value, knowingly makes a misrepresentation regarding his or her military service." This definition of an offense under the newly proposed version of the Act includes both a "knowingly" requirement and a requirement that the individual seek benefit from his or her lies, both elements having been noticeably absent from the Stolen Valor Act of 2005.

Another interesting change in the new version of the Act is that it specifically provides that an individual cannot be punished for misrepresenting he or she *did not* serve in the Armed Forces.

One of the more important safeguards included in the Act is an included defense. The proposed bills, in subsection (c), state, "[i]t is a defense to a prosecution under this section if the thing of value is *de minimis*." This section was likely included to make sure only cases where a false claim is made in order to gain a measurable benefit are prosecuted, so that petty violations do not clog the courts.

Congressman Heck's bill was referred to the House Committee on the Judiciary's Subcommittee on Crime, Terrorism and Homeland security on June 1, 2011. The Senate version was referred to the Senate Judiciary Committee on October 18, 2011. The bills have been languishing in the respective committees, apparently awaiting the Supreme Court decision in *Alvarez*.

456 This entire chapter consists of (1) the opinion of the Supreme

Court of the United States in *United States* v. *Alvarez*, and (2) the authors' commentary interspersed throughout in bold face.

457 *The Apocrypha*, 4:41.

458 There are, however, many examples of recidivism, where a Fake Warrior has repented, only to revert to his imposture. And there are a few examples of Fake Warriors repeating an ongoing process of imposture-repentance-imposture several times over. It is usually not possible to know whether a confession-apology is real and, if it is, whether it will last. For example, an outed Fake Warrior wrote to P.O.W. Network: "Sir, I meant no harm, I was in the Corps. I just did it to impress someone. Please. I have destroyed anything I had that I didn't rate. * * * Please. I beg you. I never knew that is was a crime to do this. Please sir. I have never been in trouble. I have lived a clean life. Please Sir. My sons all live close to me with their families. It would destroy my family." E-mail in possession of authors. Whether the remorseful writer will revert to his imposture is anyone's guess.

There are even examples of an outed Fake Warrior reacting drastically: "Things got so heated," a Phony Buster recounted, "that Rudy literally tried to throw himself out the second floor window. Brian and others were able to grab him halfway out; however, Rudy squirmed even more and fell two floors . . . ." E-mail in possession of authors.

459 It was the authors' decision to preserve Granger's privacy by using a pseudonym.

460 This characterization of our fighting men in Vietnam was popularized by anti-war activists such as Jane Fonda. See, for example, the Appendix to *"Aid and Comfort": Jane Fonda in North Vietnam*.

461 Capitalization in original. E-mail in possession of authors.

There are unambiguous apologies like this one, and then there are others that are equivocal.

One Fake Warrior maintained various websites on which he was represented as a larger-than-life hero: Operation Phoenix assassin, MACVSOG, 5th Special Forces, Rangers, service in Cambodia. Command Sergeant Major in Desert Storm, Sliver Star, Distinguished Service Cross, Soldiers Medal. When he was exposed, he wrote to P.O.W. Network:

> A friend of mine alerted me to this website some time ago. At first, I didn't know what to think. However, after intense thought, speaking with those who care for me, and vice-versa, I've decided to contact you about matters listed here, and hopefully make amends. How or why this came about is not the driving issue here. I just want to get this all straightened out, if I can. I have never been awarded the Distinguished Service Cross. I'm not that courageous or brave. My highest award is substantially less than that. I have never been awarded the Silver Star, for I'm not that courageous or brave. I have never been awarded the Soldier's Medal . . . . I have never been awarded the Purple Heart for wounds . . . . I know virtually nothing about Operation Phoenix and I have never killed anybody.
>
> I am not a Vietnam veteran; I am a Vietnam-era veteran. I was in the USAF, but was discharged with a General [discharge] under Honorable Conditions because I couldn't control myself with alcohol, racking up numerous debts and article 15s along the way. I did receive a Special Court Martial along the way, which preceded my being discharged for incompatibility. * * * I know nothing about Hamburger Hill, other than seeing the movie. The closest I ever came to the Rangers was completing the RIP phase of it. That's all. * * * The closest I ever came to Special Forces and the Q [training] Course was taking the SF PT test and failing it. I have great respect and admiration for those who wear both berets, and its clear to me why they are elite. * * *
>
> I don't know where this all started, and I don't want to know. This is a very painful portion of my life-self-inflicted by me and an addiction that I've been trying to put behind me. As stated before,

> I have great respect for the Rangers and Special Forces, based on my brief contact with them. I want to apologize for anything that has occurred concerning me that reflects adversely on them and the ones they have lost. * * * To any who have been offended, are angry with me, and to those I served with and those who serve today, all I can do is give you my support and apologize. I'm very sorry for this turn of events. It has caused me to re-examine some of the most painful moments of my life; so much so that I told my son the whole story about the end of my Army career, and that I was an alcoholic, would always be an alcoholic, and that he needed to know, since it is hereditary. He was too young to remember when all of this was going on. Thank you for this opportunity. E-mail in possession of authors.

Despite this apparent across-the-board confession and apology, the impostor did not address some of his more flagrant lies: service in Cambodia and assignment to
MACV-SOG.

462 See Chapter 4.

463 Capitalization in original. Our emphasis. E-mail in possession of authors.

464 E-mail in possession of authors.

465 This e-mail, in possession of authors, was sent to a Phony Buster who specializes in Fake Warriors claiming SEAL service.

APPENDICES

http://fakewarriors.org/FWAppendices.htm

A. National Personnel Records Center Form 180: How to use it to obtain military records.

B. Official list of United States civilian and military prisoners of war who escaped captivity during the Vietnam War.

C. Official list of all United States civilian and selected foreign

D. national prisoners of war who escaped during, who were

E. released during, and who were repatriated at the conclusion

F. of, the Vietnam War.

G. Combined list of all United States military prisoners of war who escaped during, who were released during, and who were repatriated at the conclusion of, the Vietnam War.

H. Official list of Vietnam War United States Prisoners of War

I. who died in captivity.

J. Official list of Vietnam War Medal of Honor recipients.

K. Official list of Post-Vietnam War Medal of Honor recipients.

ABOUT THE AUTHORS

HENRY MARK HOLZER

Henry Mark Holzer received his B.A. degree from New York University, where he studied Russian and political science.

After graduation in 1954 he served in Korea with United States Army intelligence, holding top secret security clearance as Chief Order of Battle Analyst (Chinese Communist Forces) at Eighth Army Headquarters in Seoul.

Following Holzer's military service, he earned his Juris Doctor degree at New York University School of Law. Since December 7, 1959, he has practiced constitutional and appellate law. (His clients have included owners of pre-legalized gold, veterans seeking medical benefits, Supreme Court litigants and the author Ayn Rand.)

In addition to Holzer's law practice, for over two decades (1972–1993) he was a full-time tenured professor of law at Brooklyn Law School, where he is now professor emeritus. Professor Holzer's courses included Constitutional Law, First Amendment and Appellate Advocacy.

Henry Mark Holzer is the author of approximately three hundred articles, essays, and reviews. He frequently publishes commentary on current legal and political issues in print and electronic media, and has often provided his commentary on, and been interviewed by, broadcast and cable media.

Several of Professor Holzer's out-of-print books — *The Gold Clause; Government's Money Monopoly; Sweet Land of Liberty? The Supreme Court and Individual Rights; The Layman's Guide to Tax Evasion; Speaking Freely: The Case Against Speech Codes*; and *Why* Not *Call It Treason? Korea, Vietnam, Afghanistan and Today* — are available from various Internet booksellers, including at (www.amazon.com).

With his wife, lawyer and novelist Erika Holzer, Professor Holzer is co-author of *"Aid and Comfort": Jane Fonda in North Vietnam*, a book that definitively answers the question of whether Fonda's trip to Hanoi during the Vietnam War, and her activities there, constituted constitutional treason. With Erika Holzer, Professor Holzer also co-authored the first edition of this book. Both books are available through (www.amazon.com).

Professor Holzer's *The Supreme Court Opinions of Justice Clarence Thomas, 1991–2006: A Conservative's Perspective,* was published in January 2007 by McFarland & Company, a noted publisher of scholarly, reference, and academic books. The second edition, covering the years 1991–2011, was published by McFarland in 2012 and is also available as an eBook.

Also published in 2012, as an eBook and in a print edition, was Henry Mark Holzer's *The American Constitution and Ayn Rand's "Inner Contradiction."*

At the same time, his *The Best Opinions of the Supreme Court of the United States, Vol. I (Race)* was published as an eBook. All three books are available through (www.amazon.com).

Professor Holzer's website is (www.henrymarkholzer.com), he blogs at (www.henrymarkholzer.blogspot.com), and he can be contacted at hank@ henrymarkholzer.com.

ERIKA HOLZER

Erika Holzer received her B.S. from Cornell University and her law degree from New York University.

For several years following her admission to the New York bar she practiced constitutional and appellate law with Henry Mark Holzer. Their clients included Soviet dissidents and defectors, and other lawyers for whom they prepared appellate briefs and Petitions for Certiorari for the Supreme Court of the United States.

One of the Holzer firm's clients (and later friend) was the novelist Ayn Rand, and because of her literary influence Erika Holzer switched careers from law to writing.

With Henry Mark Holzer, she co-authored *"Aid and Comfort: Jane Fonda in North Vietnam*, proving that Jane Fonda's trip to Hanoi during the Vietnam War, and her activities there, constituted constitutional treason.

Again with Henry Mark Holzer, Erika co-authored the first edition of this book. Her other non-fiction writing consists of essays, articles, reviews, political and legal commentary. In addition, she is author of the book *Ayn Rand: My Fiction-Writing Teacher: A novelist's mentor-protégé relationship with the author of Atlas Shrugged.*

Holzer's most recent short story, *Eyewitness*, appears in *Scout & Engineer*, available on Kindle and most other eBook readers and through (www.amazon.com).

Holzer's book-length fiction includes *Double Crossing*, a cold war thriller — a *Literary Guild* alternate that *Library Journal* dubbed "a spectacular twist on the old Iron Curtain escape tale" — soon to be available in an eBook and new print edition.

Author Nelson DeMille has said about Erika Holzer's novel *Eye for an Eye*, that it is "a serious and disturbing look at street gangs, urban violence, the criminal justice system, and vigilantism. Erika Holzer, an attorney, has created a plot from what could be any newspaper headline and carried it a step further. Her characters are vividly created, impassioned, and interestingly flawed so that we relate to them. Highly recommended. A sort of American *Clockwork Orange*." Holzer's *Eye for an Eye* became a Paramount Pictures feature film starring Sally Field and Kiefer Sutherland.

Erika Holzer can be contacted at (erika.holzer@erikaholzer.com) and through (www.erikaholzer.com).

AUTHORS' NOTE

Because of the ever-growing number of Fake Warrior cases, and this second edition of *Fake Warriors,* our colleagues at P.O.W. Network have recently created a new division within their organization: The Fake Warrior Project, A Division of P.O.W. Network.

Its website is (www.fakewarriors.org). The site will is *the* Internet resource for information about the Fake Warrior phenomenon. The Fake Warrior Project will regularly, via email, inform its supporters about current developments in the identification, exposure, and punishment of Fake Warriors. ***The only way to receive those notices is by sending an email to*** (signmeup@fakewarriors.org).

At www.fakewarriors.org and on www.YouTubecom, there is a video dramatizing the nature of the Fake Warrior problem and explaining why dealing with it is, among other reasons, a *moral* necessity.

Made in the USA
Monee, IL
06 November 2026

68085971R00204